Managing IT Skills Portfolios:

Planning, Acquisition and Performance Evaluation

Makoto Nakayama
DePaul University, USA

Norma Sutcliffe
DePaul University, USA

IDEA GROUP PUBLISHING
Hershey • London • Melbourne • Singapore

Acquisitions Editor:	Mehdi Khosrow-Pour
Senior Managing Editor:	Jan Travers
Managing Editor:	Amanda Appicello
Development Editor:	Michele Rossi
Copy Editor:	Maria Boyer
Typesetter:	Amanda Appicello
Cover Design:	Lisa Tosheff
Printed at:	Yurchak Printing Inc.

Published in the United States of America by
Idea Group Publishing (an imprint of Idea Group Inc.)
701 E. Chocolate Avenue, Suite 200
Hershey PA 17033 USA
Tel: 717-533-8845
Fax: 717-533-8661
E-mail: cust@idea-group.com
Web site: http://www.idea-group.com

and in the United Kingdom by
Idea Group Publishing (an imprint of Idea Group Inc.)
3 Henrietta Street
Covent Garden
London WC2E 8LU
Tel: 44 20 7240 0856
Fax: 44 20 7379 3313
Web site: http://www.eurospan.co.uk

Library of Congress Cataloging-in-Publication Data

Managing IT skills portfolios : planning, acquisition, and performance evaluation / Makoto Nakayama, editor, Norma Sutcliffe, editor.
p. cm.
Includes bibliographical references and index.
ISBN 1-59140-515-7 (hardcover) -- ISBN 1-59140-516-5 (pbk.) -- ISBN 1-59140-517-3 (ebook)
1. Information resources management. 2. Information technology--Management. I. Nakayama, Makoto. II. Sutcliffe, Norma.
T58.64.M357 2005
004'.068'3--dc22

2004003753

British Cataloguing in Publication Data
A Cataloguing in Publication record for this book is available from the British Library.

All work contributed to this book is new, previously-unpublished material. The views expressed in this book are those of the authors, but not necessarily of the publisher.

Managing IT Skills Portfolios:
Planning, Acquisition and Performance Evaluation

Table of Contents

Preface v

Chapter I
Skills, Management of Skills, and IT Skills Requirements 1
Makoto Nakayama, DePaul University, USA
Norma Sutcliffe, DePaul University, USA

Chapter II
An Approach for Managing an IT Skills Portfolio 26
Makoto Nakayama, DePaul University, USA
Norma Sutcliffe, DePaul University, USA

Chapter III
Challenges for Managing IT Skills Portfolio for E-Business 52
Abdulrahman A. Mirza, King Saud University, Saudi Arabia
Susy S. Chan, DePaul University, USA

Chapter IV
Skills and the Worker: Let's Get Real 81
Elizabeth Lahey, Elizabeth Lahey and Associates, USA

Chapter V
Optimizing IT Skills Management Initiatives 103
Ken Strauss, Bookman Testing Services, USA

Chapter VI
Government Involvement in Skills Issues 126
Elizabeth Lahey, Elizabeth Lahey and Associates, USA

Chapter VII
Japanese IT-Skill Dilemma 150
Yoko Takeda, Yokohama National University, Japan

Chapter VIII
Eliminating the Weakest Link: Leveraging Human Capital with Strategic Alliances in IT Outsourcing Supply Chains 176
Diana J. Wong-MingJi, Eastern Michigan University, USA

Chapter IX
An Exploration of the Value of Information Systems Certification: The Perspective of the Human Resource Professional 210
John E. Anderson, East Carolina University, USA
Kevin Barrett, Dixie State College, USA
Paul H. Schwager, East Carolina University, USA

Chapter X
Extreme Interviewing to Find Team Oriented Programmers 232
Clement James Goebel, III, Menlo Innovations LLC, USA
Richard Sheridan, Menlo Innovations LLC, USA
Thomas Meloche, Menlo Institute LLC, USA

About the Authors 251

Index 257

Preface

Today's economic and technological environments make IT skills ever more important for both firms and individual IT professionals. On the one hand, a study done by the benchmarking firm Hackett shows that the primary causes of firms' earning shortfalls and reduced productivity include: (a) the inability to leverage technology investments, and (b) the inability to access information causing slowing and deterioration in decision-making quality (PR Newswire, 2001). As the use of IT spreads across industries and large to small firms, it is critical that skilled IT professionals deliver efficiently well-designed and functioning information systems (IS) to firms and their IS users.

On the other hand, especially after 9-11, the economic downturn forced firms to downsize their workforce. According to the AeA (formerly known as American Electronics Association) study, the high-tech industry lost 540,000 jobs in 2002 (McGee, 2003). Of 540,000 lost jobs, more than 200,000 are IT jobs (King, 2002). In addition to workforce downsizing, firms started using global outsourcing to further contain IT costs. A recent IDC study indicates that offshore delivery of IT services may increase as much as 23% by 2007 (Claburn, 2003).

While the dependency of IT use increases at firms, the number of IT professionals who deliver IT skills is dwindling—at least in the U.S. We are probably at the critical juncture to consider what IT skills really are and what they mean to firms in the short and long term.

Despite the critical nature of IT skills, their planning and management are not necessarily easy for several reasons. First, IT skills are not easy to measure. The skill of typists can be measured by the number of letters and words they type per time period and the number of errors they make in those typed words. In comparison, the IT skills of systems analysts are not as simply defined as typists' skills, let alone to measure.

Second, different people have different notions of IT skills. Some regard IT skills as how one uses a PC, others think of IT skills as some kind of broad technological knowledge. In reality, IT professionals deal with a variety of technologies, tools, and work contexts. Some IT skills pertain to the design of particular systems. A "pure" programmer realizes that he cannot do his work effectively without having good communication skills to deal with his peers, analysts, and customers. In the past, we used such terms as "hard" skills (pure technology skills) and "soft" skills (non-technology skills). With the advancement of technologies and tools, it is not clear now where to draw a line between "hard" and "soft" skills because they have become so intertwined.

Third, the substance of IT work is becoming more sophisticated and complicated. Even smaller firms use a variety of computing hardware and software. In some cases, a "VB programmer" wears a hat of systems analyst to develop a system in a short time frame, interacting heavily with an end user.

Fourth, the line between IT professionals and IT end-users is becoming obscure if not extinct. Often, we see end users developing their own reports from information they extracted.

With those reflections, it is high time that we made ourselves aware of where we stand in our understanding, and lack of understanding, on what IT skills really are, what they mean to firms, how firms can plan and manage IT skills, and how government and individual IT professionals approach IT skills.

This book provides:

- taxonomy and management tools for IT skills,
- an example of strategic skills management using IS projects and skills portfolios,
- an example of strategic skills management for e-commerce,
- the view from the individual IT professionals on IT skills,
- the view from the government on planning and developing IT skills,
- an international perspective on IT skills management, and
- the view from the HR department on planning and acquiring IT skills.

With these different scopes, this book gives a baseline for further research and builds our knowledge on the management of IT skills.

Organization of the Book

This book is divided into five sections aimed at: IT management, IT professionals, IT testing, national issues, and finally human resource issues. The first section, covering Chapters I through III, looks at the IT managerial issues surrounding IT skills.

Chapter I focuses on the concept and nature of skills—skills in general and IT skills specifically. To begin, the chapter examines a broader overview on IT skills: What are recent statistics on IT skills, and what do they indicate to firms and individual IT professionals? Then, it pins down the definition, characteristics, assessment, and classification of skills, generally drawing the findings of past studies. Although not all of us are interested in the theoretical aspects of skills, it is important to take an inventory of taxonomy on skills so that we have "vocabulary" to describe and plan IT skills strategically later. The chapter then looks into what makes IT skills different from non-IT skills based on our skills taxonomy.

Based on the foundation from Chapter I, Chapter II provides an example of strategic IT skills management using the firm-level IS projects and IT skills portfolios. First, the chapter draws three key principles for managing IT skills strategically derived from past studies. They are: people-centered organization, multi-mission capability, and work-based learning. Using these principles as the foundation, the chapter presents a framework that uses the business-goal-driven, firm-level portfolio analyses. In these portfolio analyses, the three levels of firm-level IS/IT management—(i) IS projects, (ii) key IS project deliverables, and (iii) IT skills—are prioritized by using (a) time scopes (current vs. future) and (b) a criticality assessment (e.g., how crucial to objectives, how difficult to deliver, how risky against contingencies). In the end, the framework presents four types of sourcing options based on the analysis findings.

Unlike traditional backend application systems, the development and implementation of e-commerce IT applications face a unique set of challenges. These include rapidly advancing technologies, often complex requirements for business-to-business interorganizational operations, and rather tight time constraints from analysis and design to implementation and post-implementation requirements. In Chapter III, Mirza and Chan look into how strategic IT skills management can be done in such a challenging environment. They present a framework in which the process of IT skills management (skills acquisition, skills development, and skills maintenance) is outlined at five levels (strategy level, architecture level, systems level, project level, tools and technology level).

In Section II, covering Chapter IV, we look at the how IT skills are affecting the IT professional.

Chapter IV turns to the perspectives of individual IT professionals. Over her career as an IT professional, Lahey has seen the work environments of IT professionals shift from the employer-driven IT skill acquisition to the individual-driven IT skill acquisition without extensive, protective help from employers. Applying the Organization Man model (Whyte, 2002) and Adult Learning theory (Knowles, 1990), she portrays rich pictures of such a shift by drawing on her experience as an IT training expert at McDonald's Corporation and career challenges of three IT professionals. Lahey introduces the TechCareer Compass® (TCC) as a useful and reliable tool to assist in career decision making for individual IT professionals.

In Section III, covering Chapter V, attention turns to measuring IT skills through testing. One of the most challenging aspects of IT skills management is how to assess IT skills objectively. Leveraging his extensive experience as an IT skills assessment expert, Strauss discusses in Chapter V how to construct IT skills tests that can be readily used by managers for hiring and performance assessments. Using programming proficiency testing examples, he shows step-by-step how to present and use the testing results and their interpretations (feedback) for managing IT skills. Moreover, the chapter walks us through different IT skill assessment methods. It then informs us on which one(s) to use for a given objective. Among them, the details of adaptive testing (tests that adapt the proficiency of test-takers) are presented.

In the next section of the book, Chapters VI and VII, attention turns to the issues that IT skills present nations dealing with international competition.

A growing portion of the national economy is created and sustained by technology products. Furthermore, the days are long gone when access to computers was a privilege; now computer/computing literacy is a necessity down to frontline workers. Thus, governments are concerned about the IT skills of their constituents for maintaining and growing the nation's economic strength. A particular concern of the U.S. government is the increasing number of IT skill gaps found in the workforce. In Chapter VI, Lahey details how the U.S. government is coordinating state, national, and international projects for standardizing IT skills, as a first step.

In Chapter VII, Takeda examines the dilemma that Japan is facing with its IT skills. Japan has prided itself on using IT to meet the aims of greater efficiency.

Its firms have prided themselves on using in-house developed systems and on their IT staff's greater productivity. Unfortunately, Japanese firms find it very difficult to abandon their unique systems for the newer technologies that their international competitors have embraced enthusiastically. In response, the government has promoted policies to increase the number of engineers, develop more advanced technical expertise, and diversify the work experience. Takeda then goes on to examine how the Japanese IS vendors have responded to their clients' customization demands, further reducing the adoption of newer technologies. The chapter concludes with a number of recommendations for resolving the dilemma of introducing newer technologies while resolving their "not-made-for-us" syndrome.

In the last and fifth section of the book, covering Chapters VIII, IX, and X, we look at the human resource (HR) issues for IT skills.

In Chapter VIII, Wong-MingJi outlines a model for constructing human capital portfolios that will help firms strategically leverage their IT outsourcing. The model is based on two organizational capabilities (the rational and the connective) that provide integrating mechanisms for competencies in the HRIS (human resource information systems), the IS function, and supply chain management. While the rational organizational capabilities that deal with formulating strategies and the processes for attaining strategic goals are emphasized in many firms, the role of the connective organizational capabilities are also just as important. Thus organizational learning and improvisation, along with systems integration and relational contracting skills, play an important role in creating human capital portfolios for strategic IT outsourcing. This model assists firms in identifying and strengthening their portfolios using a multi-level and multi-disciplinary approach.

In Chapter IX, Anderson, Barrett, and Schwager present the results of their study that looked at the perceptions of HR professionals on IT certification, education, and work experience. In particular the study wanted to know how well did each substitute for another. The study found that they were imperfect substitutes for each other. HR professionals did associate certification holders with enhanced technical credibility, as well as having received valuable preparation for other positions. Also, the study looked at how well HR professionals perceive the candidate who has education, experience, and certification. The study found that such balanced candidates enjoyed a halo effect.

In Chapter X, the problem of improving the rate of successful hires by changing the hiring process is examined. Because the organization used the extreme programming method, where communication and teamwork skills arc critically important, Goebel, Sheridan, and Meloche argue that the traditional hiring practices were inadequate. Thus, they implemented a new hiring process where applicants can demonstrate their communication and teamwork skills as well as programming skills. The entire hiring process is discussed, including the interview process with its use of exercises and multiple interviewers.

From the expanding set of skills that the new technologies require to the issues surrounding offshore outsourcing, IT is asked to provide more and more. The aim of this book is to help IT practitioners and IT researchers address the problems involved in many aspects of managing IT skills at both the organizational and individual level.

References

Claburn, T. (2003). Study: Offshore outsourcing may not cause flood of lost jobs. *InformationWeek,* (November 20). Accessed December 6, 2003, from: http://www.informationweek.com/story/showArticle.jhtml?articleID=16400105.

King, J. (2002). Hard times: Tech workers trying to find jobs face a bleak future. *Computerworld,* (April 29). Accessed August 4, 2003, from: www.computerworld.com/careertopics/careers/recruiting/story/0,10801,70626,00.html.

Knowles, M. (1990). *The adult learner: A neglected species.* Houston, TX: Gulf Publishing.

McGee, M.K. (2003). High-tech jobs dwindle, but the worst may be over. *InformationWeek,* (November 19). Accessed December 6, 2003, from: http://www.informationweek.com/story/showArticle.jhtml?articleID=16101259.

PR Newswire. (2001). *Success in leveraging technology and e-business applications, integration of business processes still elusive for most companies.* February 28.

Whyte, W.H. (2002). *The Organization Man.* Philadelphia, PA: University of Pennsylvania Press.

Acknowledgments

The editors would like to acknowledge the assistance of all involved in the preparation of this book without whose support the project could not have been successfully completed. This preparation included collation, review, and modification of the submitted chapters. In addition, a special note of thanks is extended to all the staff of Idea Group Inc., whose contributions throughout the entire process from the genesis of the idea of the IT Skills Portfolio to the final publication have been incalculable.

Most of the authors of the chapters also served as referees for articles written by other authors. Thanks go to all who provided constructive and comprehensive reviews. Some reviewers need to be mentioned because their reviews set such high standards. Reviewers who provided the most inclusive and insightful comments include: John E. Anderson of East Carolina University, Susy S. Chan of DePaul University, Elizabeth Lahey formerly of the Computing Technology Industry Association, Ryutaro Manabe of Bunkyo University, Cheryl Maranto of Marquette University, Abdulrahman A. Mirza of King Saud University, Paul H. Schwager of East Carolina University, Yoko Takeda of Yokohama National University, and Diana J. Wong-MingJi of Eastern Michigan University.

We especially want to give heartfelt thanks to the publishing team at Idea Group Inc. Michele Rossi gave us valuable advice on the publishing process. Jan Travers helped us in keeping progress on track. Mehdi Khosrow-Pour graciously extended an invitation to write this book.

We also want to thank our families for their unwavering support throughout this project. In particular, we want to thank J.J. Gata who was unfailing in his ability to cheer us with his charm and help us with his insights on the essentials.

Editors
Makoto Nakayama, PhD
Norma Sutcliffe, PhD
Chicago, Illinois, USA
December 2003

Chapter I

Skills, Management of Skills, and IT Skills Requirements

Makoto Nakayama
DePaul University, USA

Norma Sutcliffe
DePaul University, USA

Abstract

Information technology (IT) skill shortages appear at the market level occasionally—usually for emerging technologies, unanticipated challenges, and/or unresolved issues such as systems security. Even when a market-level skill shortage does not exist, a firm can still suffer from skill shortages for its critical information system (IS) project and/or IT operations unless the firm plans and manages its needs for IT skills. This chapter first surveys IT skills at the market level and then at the firm level to gain a perspective on the issues. Attention turns to the nature and characteristics of skills in general—not just IT skills—by reviewing past literature. The management of skills is deeply rooted in the management of knowledge, skills, and abilities (KSAs) and human resource practices of the firm. Key issues and lessons are drawn from the literature in those areas. We conclude by considering the nature and characteristics of IT skills in developing an agenda for the effective management of IT skills.

Introduction

The employment issues for information technology (IT) professionals are sources of considerable debate. While the economy may be on its way to the recovery, many firms still struggle to contain costs. IT has especially been impacted by the tidal waves of changes in the economy.

The 1990s enjoyed an economic boom due to the Internet and its killer application, e-commerce. At the turn of the 21st century, the Bureau of Labor Statistics (2000) estimated that between 1998 and 2008 the demand for IT professionals, such as computer engineers, computer support specialists, database administrators, and systems analysts, would grow at rates exceeding 70%. In 2001, industry surveys estimated that there were 850,000 IT positions open in the U.S. and that Europe had 1.7 million vacant IT positions (Fisher, 2001). Along this line, industries and nations recognized the IT skills shortage as a major problem needing a resolution. For example, the Sector Skills Development Agency (SSDA) in the United Kingdom (UK) funds, supports, and champions the new UK-wide network of influential, employer-led Sector Skills Councils (SSCs). One of the SSCs is e-skills, designed to foster skill availabilities for the IT, Telecoms, and Contact Centre sectors. The U.S. government also had similar initiatives and produced reports on this matter (Rada, 1999).

However, a drastic shift in the economic climate occurred particularly after the September 11 attack. Firms were forced to slash operational costs by streamlining their business processes. Unemployment rates went up. All of a sudden, the IT skills shortage disappeared in firms. A good number of IT professionals were forced out of their positions.

According to the U.S. Labor Department, the number of workers filing for unemployment benefits rose to 439,000 as of July 2003. A recent press release by the Information Technology Association of America (ITAA) (2003) says, "[P]redicted demand for hiring IT workers has reached a historic low of only 493,000 positions over the next 12 months—down from 1.6 million at the start of 2000 and less than one-half of the predicted 1.1 million positions needed at the start of 2002." In addition, ITAA estimated that more than 200,000 IT workers are jobless (King, 2002). Thus, not only did we overestimate the demand for IT skills, but also about half of those filing claims for unemployment benefits are IT workers!

Behind such not-so-sanguine facts is the relentless economic pressure on containing IT operational costs. Firms not only try to accomplish the same amount of work with lower headcount, but they also increasingly rely on offshore outsourcing. According to a recent ITAA survey (2003), "Sixty-seven percent of respondents already outsourcing IT work overseas say that jobs most likely to be moved offshore are programming or software engineering positions, followed by 37% moving network design, and 30% moving Web development jobs."

Demand at Market and Firm Levels

If firms are downsizing their internal IT workforce, the question is whether we should be concerned about IT skills shortage in the first place—at least for now. To address this issue, we need to examine the demand for IT skills at two levels—the market level and the firm level.

According to a 2002 survey done by META Group (2002), 62% of the survey participants replied "not at all" to the question, "Are you experiencing a 'skill shortage' in your IT organization?" Twenty-two percent said "somewhat" and only 16% said "yes." Such results are not surprising given that many firms reduced their IT workforce to cut costs. If there is so much "excess" supply of IT labor, then one should conclude that there is no skills shortage at the market level.[1]

However, the supply and demand of IT skills look different if we take a closer look at them at the firm level. Although a skills crisis is not evident at the market level, "the concept of a skills shortage is not always the same as a hard-to-fill vacancy" (Green, Machin, & Wilkinson, 1998). According to a recent survey by *people3* (a subsidiary of Gartner) (Marlin, 2003), the most difficult jobs to hire include: database administrator, Internet architect, network engineer, security analyst, project manager, and Web application programmer, whereas among the most difficult skills to hire are Oracle administrator, PeopleSoft, Unix, Java, Oracle development, and Microsoft SQL server. Although the results from such surveys change quickly as markets and technology change, what those results imply are twofold: (1) the demand and supply of skills vary from one skill to another skill, as well as from one firm to another; and (2) *competent* skills are usually not easy to hire and retain.

The current economic pressures notwithstanding, it does not seem that firms soon will cut or slow down their efforts to improve IT skills among their employees. According to IDC, the IT training and education market is expected to increase at a compound annual rate of 5% from 2002 to 2007 in the United States (D'Antoni, 2003). Moreover, IDC predicts that corporate training will increase at twice such rate over the same period. What do firms want from their IT skills? They are not interested in bringing in new hires or increasing their headcount, but they are interested in more efficiently managing their human resources.

In addition, IT skills are not exclusively executed by IT professionals. Because so much business work cannot be done without IT, increasingly IT skills are an integral part of end-user skills. For instance, in the 2003 *InformationWeek* survey, 34% of CFOs valued IT knowledge as the most important complementary skills for accountants, while 23% of them regard general knowledge of business as most important (Foley & Murphy, 2003). This is not surprising as more and more accountants rely on IS for their work. The majority of Fortune 500 companies already use ERP systems that require from the user some level of systems familiarity, if not IT skills. In contrast, if a firm uses a systems development method requiring intensive user involvement such as prototyping, as opposed to the conventional system development life cycle (SDLC), the distinction between IT personnel and non-IT personnel becomes the matter of degree rather than a clear line of demarcation.

Firms frequently have critical IT projects that are at risk when IT skills are lacking. The critical IT projects might be updates to legacy systems or an overhaul of an existing business process by using new IT. No matter the type of project, it will fail to meet planned completion time, systems functionality, and/or costs when lacking critical IT skills including IS project skills (Jiang & Klein, 2001; Lemon, Bowitz, Burn, & Hackney, 2002; META Group 2003). Moreover, recent research shows that IT professionals value leadership and management skills to support teamwork more than non-IT business professionals (McGee, 2003). Losing such talents is fairly costly to the firm.

Thus, firms can always use better talents and skills in critical areas of their business operations so they can become more competitive. A skills shortage becomes salient or non-existent, as the supply and demand of IT workers fluctuates with technology changes and business economic climates. For the firm, what is important is knowing what it needs for getting their IT systems competitive by using human and capital resources most efficiently. Offshore outsourcing may not be the right option depending on the skills areas involved. In addition, skills planning should also be considered at the user level. What might be the criteria for skills planning?

The following sections consider how firms know what IT skills they need, and how they actually obtain and retain them. First, we look in-depth at what skills generally are, in terms of their definition, characteristics, and management processes. Then, we examine the nature and management process specific to IT skills.

What Do We Know About Skills?

Before we discuss IT skills planning, how much do we already know about skills planning in general? What are some important lessons learned in the past? Towards this end, we first review what a skill really is, and the nature and characteristics of a skill. Then, we look at what strategic human resource management (SHRM) is, some of its important methodologies, and then we end with what we know about skills planning and management.

What is a Skill?

According to *American Heritage Dictionary* (2000), skill is "(1) Proficiency; dexterity, (2) An art, trade, or technique, esp. one requiring use of the hands or body." Skill pertains to the *delivery* of tasks by human workers, or simply *task performance*. Examples of skills include Swiss watch makers' manual dexterity skills, industrial data analysts' quantitative analytical skills to Hollywood movie makers' marketing skills, and CEOs' crisis handling skills. Along this line, Welford (1968, as referenced by Proctor & Dutta, 1995) defined skill as "being concerned with all the factors which go to make up a competent, expert, rapid, and accurate performance. Skill in this sense thus attaches, to a greater or lesser extent, to *any* performance and is not limited to manual operations but covers a wide range of mental activities as well." Thus, our starting definition of skill is the delivery of competent, expert, rapid, and accurate behaviors to complete tasks.

Characteristics of a Skill

Because there are so many kinds of tasks and also numerous skills to accomplish them, can we identify some common characteristics of all skills? According to Proctor and Dutta (1995, p. 18), some of these critical characteristics include:

- A skill is not innate, but must be learned.
- A skill behavior is goal directed. A skill develops in response to some demand imposed by the task environment.
- A skill is acquired when the behavior is highly integrated and well organized. Through experience, the components of the behavior become structured into coherent patterns.
- Cognitive demands are reduced as skill is acquired.

Then, a skill is something that results from *learning* and something that is *shown* in task performances. Taking such "process" view of skill, Proctor and Dutta (1995) define skill as "goal-directed, well-organized behavior that is acquired through practice and performance with economy of effort."

Along the line of learning theory, the process of skill acquisition is often based on the three-phase model proposed by Fitts (1964, 1962/1990; Fitts & Posner, 1967; as referenced by Proctor & Dutta, 1995):

- *Cognitive Phase*
  One understands the nature of the task and how it should be performed.
- *Associative Phase*
  Inputs are linked more directly to appropriate actions, the need for verbal mediation is diminished, errors decrease and performance time improves.
- *Autonomous Phase*
  The requirements for conscious attention to performing the task decrease, and task performance no longer requires conscious control.

In this model, a skill is continuously developed over time, following the learning curve, until one can deliver task performance with the minimum amount of conscious effort. So, our definition of skill is now revised to be the delivery of competent, expert, rapid, and accurate behaviors to complete goal-directed, pre-defined tasks.

Assessment of Skill

If we take the *task-oriented perspective* of skill, the measurement of skill becomes basically the matter of assessing *task performance*. As long as the task is simple and measurable, we can easily assess one's skill by looking at the quantity and quality of task performance as well as time and costs of task delivery. In contrast, skill assessment becomes more difficult when:

(a) The task is complex.

(b) The task goals (also known as deliverables) are not easy to define.

(c) Task outcomes are either not evident or are ambiguous.

(d) Task outcomes are not immediately available (outcomes appear over time).

(e) Task outcomes are embedded in other task outcomes.

(f) The task is done with other tasks, and they are interdependent.

Then, the definition of a skill is revised to be the delivery of competent, expert, rapid, and accurate behaviors to complete goal-directed, pre-defined tasks that can be assessed through observation.

Classification of Skills

Having our working definition of what a skill is, we now look into the substance of skills. Because skills can be associated with many kinds of tasks, the classification of skills is complicated. There are numerous tasks, and tasks can be divided into sub-tasks. Also in some contexts, sub-tasks are known as tasks. Tasks and their sub-tasks are often interdependent with each other.

In addition to skill classifications, we are also interested in what the "fundamental" or "foundational" skills are, given that skills can be hierarchically classified according to their dependency on each other. If we can identify fundamental skills, the common belief is that enhancing those fundamental skills can result in enhancing numerous "terminal" skills to deliver "final" tasks. One example is the impact of academic skills (fundamental skills) on the labor market performance (terminal skills). Indeed, past studies show that the level of schooling and the level of wages are positively associated with each other (Stasz, 2001).

From the standpoint of firms, the pressing questions are: What are the most important skills? What are the fundamental skills that result in competitive advantage?

Unfortunately, those questions are not easy to answer. According to Stasz (2001), we have "no consensus as to the definition and measurement of 'fundamental' skills" although skills can be categorized broadly in four areas such as: (1) academic/cognitive skills (skills primarily acquired in schooling); (2) generic skills (problem solving, communications, working in teams); (3) technical skills (specific skills needed in an occupation); and (4) work-related attitudes/soft skills (motivation, volition, dispositions). She also reports, "[S]ince the literature on non-academic skills is somewhat undeveloped conceptually, direct or even indirect measures of these skills have not been fully developed."

As an alternative to the "objective" view of skills, she suggests that we take what she calls a "sociocultural perspective" on skills, where skills are basically understood within the particular context of work and its social setting. This situational perspective is "a practice-based perspective of work that is open to broader characterizations of skill and other conceptions of knowledge which are less tied to formal schooling (e.g., tactile understanding, social understanding, artisan skills, improvisational skills, etc.)."

While each work setting provides unique circumstances for skills, the sociocultural perspective itself unfortunately does not give easy-to-follow, common guidelines for managing the workforce skills.

For firms, the unit of focus is often the human worker rather than skills, because skills are embedded within human workers. Organizational psychologists traditionally categorized different types of learning outcomes as knowledge, skills, and abilities (KSAs) (Blanchard & Thacker, 1999, pp. 4-5). Using such categories, the human resource (HR) department conducts job analysis to identify what KSAs are needed for the organization's tasks. The organization then allocates its employees who have the KSAs to where they are needed. In addition, KSAs are used to screen and evaluate new hires. To assess employees' job performance, HR managers can rate the knowledge needed to execute their tasks, the skills demonstrated in their task delivery, and the abilities to conduct their current or future tasks.

Skill vs. Performance

Like skills, KSAs can directly pertain to task, job, and/or organizational performance. If so, KSAs ultimately impact on the value of the firm itself through how KSAs are acquired and utilized based on human resource management practices. Youndt, Snell, Dean, and Lepak (1996) summarize such linkage under the *human capital theory* as follows:

> "From micro economics, human capital theory suggests that people possess skills, knowledge, and abilities that provide economic value to firms. Since firm investments to increase employee skills, knowledge, and abilities carry both out-of-pocket and opportunity costs, they are only justified if they produce future returns via increased productivity (Duncan & Hoffman, 1981; Rumberger, 1987; Tsang, 1987). In other words, increased productivity derived from human capital investments depends on the contribution of employees to a firm. Therefore, the higher the potential for employee contribution in a firm, the more likely it is that the firm will invest in human capital (via human resource management activities) and that these investments will lead to higher individual productivity and firm performance (Becker, 1976; Parnes, 1984). As many contemporary manufacturers are said to be increasing the potential for employee contributions in their production equations (Walton & Susman, 1987), human capital theory would suggest that HR practices can directly influence firm performance."

Interestingly, past studies noted that task performances are influenced not only by KSAs, but also by the motivation of workers and the environment where those tasks are executed (e.g., London, 1983; Murray & Gerhart, 1998; Noe, 1986). For example, Blanchard and Thacker (1999) formulated the factors that determine human performance as: **Performance = Motivation x KSAs x Environment**, where the A in KSAs is the worker's Attitudes rather than Abilities. In Blanchard and Thacker's view, "ability" cannot easily be differentiated from "skill" partly because they define skill as capacity. Indeed, "skill" and "ability" are often used interchangeably in our daily lives. They also raise a good point in that a person's attitude influences job performance. So the definition of a skill is the delivery of competent, expert, rapid, and accurate behaviors to complete goal-directed, predefined tasks that are usually assessed through observation.

Figure 1: Performance Delivery and KSAs

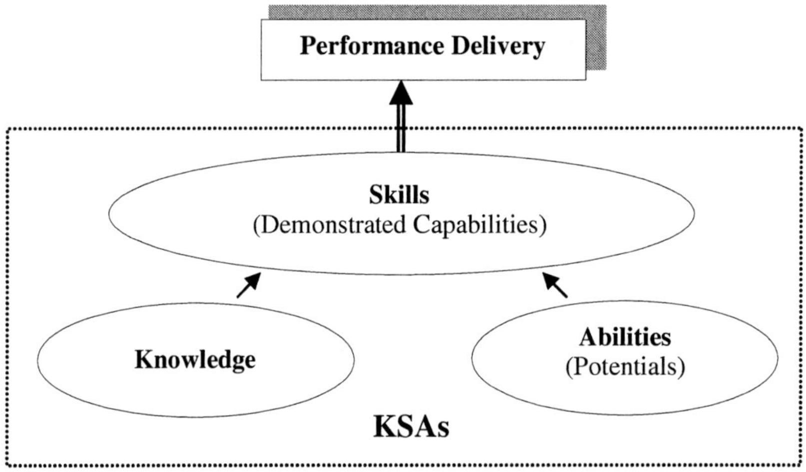

That is, skill is a *demonstrated* capability to accomplish a task. In contrast, ability is a potential—that is, a latent factor for the skill (see Figure 1). Attitude generally refers to a state of mind and feeling, which includes "motivation." Attitude is a holistic state or posture that is formulated through a variety of factors including genetic inheritance, upbringing, mental state, education, family situation, and so forth. Interestingly, Waldman and Avolio (1993; as referenced by Tesluk and Jacobs, 1998) report that non-work experience can also influence work-related knowledge, skills, abilities, and motivation. After all, a person can be viewed as a system consisting of body and mind. It is also known that mind affects the body and vice versa. Thus, we "loosely" view skill as the actual performance delivery, which is supported by knowledge and ability.

In this view, knowledge and ability enable performance delivery, which is the exercise of skill. Also, we would like to integrate the above performance formula by Blanchard and Thacker with non-work factors such as our social life, hobbies, family situation, and so forth—taking a view that our personal lives do affect how we perform at work. Then, we can summarize, for the time being, the factors that impact worker performance as:

Performance=Motivation x KSAs x Work Environment x Non-Work Factors

A Strategic Approach to Skills Management

The 1990s saw us revisit the question of what really differentiates a successful firm from the less successful ones. One answer was the notion of strategic human resource management (SHRM), which focused our attention to the criticality of human resource management. Under SHRM, individual workers are viewed as a *source* of the firm's competitive advantage rather than as *complementary* or *limiting factors* of the firm's success. Moreover, SHRM places people in the core of management.

Pfeffer (1998) notes that the source of competitive advantage shifts over time, as some firms succeed in one period and fade in another. However, certain firms such as Plenum Publishing, Circuit City, Tyson Foods, Wal-Mart, and Southwest Airlines enjoy *sustained* competitive advantage; "they rely not on technology, patents, or strategic position, but on how they manage their workforce."

As a guideline, Pfeffer, Hatano, and Santalainen (1995) suggested the 13 collective practices for SHRM: (1) employment security, (2) selectivity in recruiting, (3) high wages, (4) incentive pay, (5) employee ownership, (6) information sharing, (7) participation and empowerment, (8) self-managed teams, (9) training and skill development, (10) cross-utilization and cross-training, (11) symbolic egalitarianism, (12) wage compression, and (13) promotion from within. While these practices are desirable, the question remains whether the practice of SHRM really results in better firm performance. Several studies report that SHRM makes a positive difference in firm performance (e.g., Becker & Gerhart, 1996; Delaney & Huselid, 1996; Youndt et al., 1996).

While skills are part of SHRM, how do skills relate to firm, group, and/or individual performance? After all, "[s]killed behavior is fundamental to all human activities" (Proctor & Dutta, 1995, p. 1). For this reason, it is not surprising that "[s]ystematic research on skill acquisition and human performance has been conducted since the late 1800s" (Proctor & Dutta, 1995, p. xv).

In the spirit of SHRM, the performance equation (Performance = Motivation x KSAs x Work Environment x Non-Work Factors) has a twofold implication. First, a firm's SHRM should establish systems to enhance and/or change performance favorably through such factors as worker motivation, work environment, and non-work factors. Second, management strategically plans and enhances KSAs. While the former goes beyond the scope of this chapter, we will investigate what we already know about the management of KSAs, and then what we can apply to the management of IT-related KSAs.

The general process of strategic staffing is:

(1) job analysis;

(2) KSA acquisition through training and/or hiring; and

(3) management of KSAs considering the rates of attrition and retention, the assessment of KSAs, and the pace of KSA obsolescence.

While there are many studies covering job analysis (e.g., Levine, Ash, Hall, & Sistrunk, 1983; Schneider & Konz, 1989), job analysis generally involves the following two steps: (1) defining what the job needs to accomplish (in the present and future), and (2) identifying what KSAs are needed to accomplish the job, together with any needed equipment.

The definition of "job," according to the *American Heritage Dictionary* (2000), is "(1) A regular activity performed for payment. (2) A position in which one is employed." So long as one's job is simple and repetitive (e.g., attaching a part to the casing of equipment), job analysis is easy at the individual level. Nevertheless, job analysis becomes more complex when a job involves more tasks—a mortgage broker (job) needs to maintain the information on what mortgage suppliers provide and what mortgage buyers look for currently (several major task steps) and in the future, and successfully complete the transaction (several major task steps). Moreover, there are more job positions today demanding that professionals play different job roles simultaneously—an IT director who coordinates the work to be done in her IT department (department manager), oversees a major enterprise system implementation project (project manager), and participates in a corporate-level strategy reformulation project (corporate director).

According to Campbell (1988), the four fundamental attributes of complex tasks are:

(1) multiple potential paths to arrive at a desired end state;

(2) multiple desired end states to attain;

(3) conflicting interdependence among paths to multiple desired outcomes; and

(4) uncertain or probabilistic links among paths and outcomes.

Further, Campbell classifies the major task types as: (a) simple tasks, (b) decision tasks, (c) judgment tasks, (d) problem tasks, and (e) fuzzy tasks.

The combination of economic pressures and progress in business management certainly put more incentive on firms to make IT and non-IT professionals more versatile in their work. One result is increasing complexity of jobs along with the job complexity dimensions Campbell outlined.

In contrast, what are the important or significant skills needed to perform simple to complex jobs as well as the tasks within those jobs?

A Focused Approach to Skills Management

If we recall our working definition of skill—"the delivery of competent, expert, rapid, and accurate behaviors to complete goal-directed, predefined tasks"—there are potentially numerous skills because there are countless tasks. Thus, the fundamental problem for strategic skills management is how we should classify skills and what the fundamental skills are. For example, Clarkson (2001, p. 130) provides an example of a seemingly simple task that can consist of numerous KSAs:

> "[G]iving presentations is commonly seen as interpersonal skills. Yet the process of creating and delivering a presentation or technical briefing calls on several abilities:
>
> - Conceptual thinking and analytical ability in deciding what to include.
> - Planning and communication in ordering the contents.
> - Some kind of design skills in creating the supporting visual aids for the presentation or briefing.
> - Communication in delivering the material.
> - Reading the body language in gauging audience reaction.
> - Active listening and quick thinking in answering the questions."

From the standpoint of strategically managing skills, what would be the important abilities and/or skills? Clarkson claims that they are "competencies [that] are hidden inside the person but influence how he uses his skills." She lists those important competencies as: analytical ability, conceptual thinking, communication, self-development, adaptability, and initiative (p. 134).

The term "competency" usually refers to the level of KSAs, especially that of making a competitive advantage. This leads us to the notion of "core competency" proposed by Prahalad and Hamel (1990) (see Figure 2). They think that the firm's competitive advantage is rooted in the core competencies, which are "the collective learning in the organization, especially how to coordinate diverse production skills and integrate multiple streams of technologies."

Core competencies are an abstracted set of skills at the group level. Core competencies are the driving force behind the creation of core products, which will lead to the boundary of business units. For example, 3M's core competencies are "substrates, coating, and coated abrasives and devised various ways to combine them" to produce "Post-it" notes, as well as magnetic tape and photographic film products. It is important to note that such core competencies are not necessarily particular patents and/or technologies, but more about the abilities to integrate and coordinate different products and work units to create products.

So far, we looked at skills in general. To summarize, the key lessons we can apply towards the effective management of IT skills are:

Figure 2: Core Competencies, Products, and the Organization (Prahalad & Hamel, 1990)

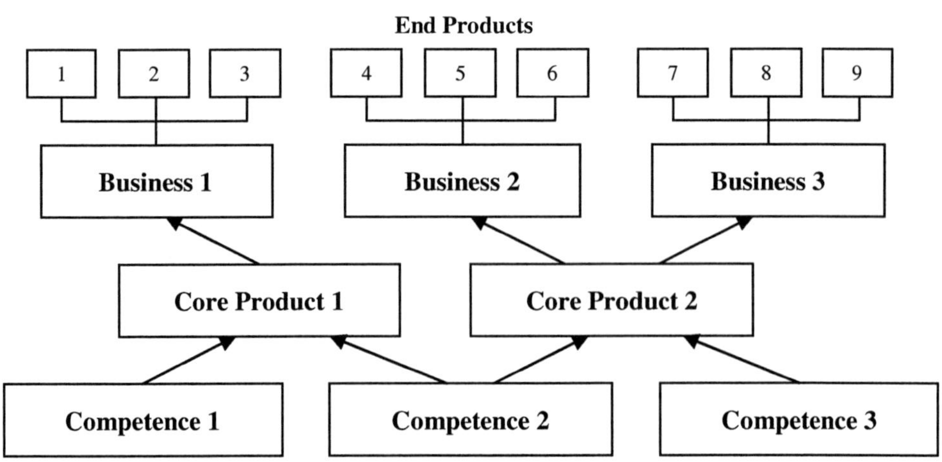

- Skill is goal-oriented, demonstrated capability.
- Skill can be associated with any performance and defined in many ways.
- Skill delivers performance, mediated by knowledge, abilities, motivation, work environment, and non-work-related factors.
- Skill is acquired and enhanced through work.
- A firm can enjoy sustained competitive advantage and, in turn, higher performance through strategic management of human resources.
- Workers should be regarded as a main enabler of the organization rather than costs and/or constraints.
- Recognizing what core competencies the firm possesses and translates into products and supporting organizational structures are critical for the management of skills at the firm level.

Management of IT Skills

Above, we reviewed business and management skills in broad terms. The next logical questions are:

(1) Are IT skills different from non-IT skills? If so, how?

(2) What are the implications of these differences for managing IT skills strategically?

To examine how unique IT skills are, we must first define what IT skills are, and then compare them to non-IT skills.

In a narrow sense, IT skills are the demonstrated proficiency in using IT tools such as personal computers, programming languages, and sales management systems. IT skills can be viewed at many levels (see Table 1). For example, we can attribute skills to different types of hardware, software, telecommunication, network, and information systems.

Focusing on the roles of those who use IT, we can frame skills by development tasks (e.g., development tool design such as compiler design, systems analysis, systems design, project management, programming types, programming languages, testing, maintenance, helpdesk, end-user training and education) and end-user tasks (e.g., using developer platforms/tools such as IBM WebSphere,

Table 1: Examples of IT/IS Skill Classifications

Classification	Skill Examples
IS elements	hardware skill, software skill, network/telecommunication skill, organizational skill, people skill
managerial functions & roles	CIO skill, departmental coordination skill, IT architecture design skill, IT resource planning skill, change management skill, security skill, end-user training skill
work types	project management skill, administrative skill, technical support skill
industry/firm	industry-specific (e.g., grocery retailing, automotive manufacturing) skill, firm-specific skill
IS development process	survey skill, interview skill, feasibility study skill, systems analysis skill, systems design skill, systems development skill, debugging/troubleshooting skills, IS training skill, IS maintenance skill
programming languages	C++ skill, Java skill, COBOL skill, Visual Basic skill, SQL skill, HTML skill
business process related	business analysis skill, operational planning skill, process design skill, project coordination skill
e-commerce	Web page design skill, Web graphic design skill, site design & coordination skill, ASP skill, JSP skill, Perl skill, Flash skill, DreamWeaver skill
database related	database design skill, database programming skill, relational database skill, object-oriented database skill, DB2 skill, Oracle skill, Sybase skill
product vendors	IBM skill, Microsoft skill, Oracle skill, Cisco skill
product types	ERP skill, mainframe skill, Web server skill, middleware skill, router skill
products	Lotus Domino skill, MQ Series skill, SAP R/3 skill, NetWare skill, Access skill
development platform/tools	WebSphere skill, Visual Studio .NET skill, Rational Rose skill, UML skill
business related	business skill, "soft" skill, interpersonal skill, writing skill, communication skill
IT types	PC skill, backend system skill, PDA skill, WAN skill, LAN skill, global IT skill

using application software ranging from Microsoft Office, Photoshop to enterprise systems).

Skills can be categorized into domains of development tasks (e.g., business process application, website design and management, database design and reporting). Skills can also be categorized by numerous IT product types, vendors, and particular products (e.g., publishing document software, Macromedia Flash, 3-D simulations). Alternatively, skills can be categorized by industries, firm types (e.g., large/small, regional/global), individual firms, managerial levels, and organizational structures and functions.

The number of ways to classify IT skills is virtually limitless because the use of IT continues to grow in business operations, public services, and private lives.

While past studies note that the number of skills has no limit, professional skills are usually attributed to managerial roles or types of professions and any equipment if used. In addition, the pace of change in these attributes is relatively slow compared to those in the IT domain. In IT, the norm of speed is well characterized by Moore's Law—the capability of microprocessors doubles every 18 months. An advancement of one product, say the version-up of the Windows operating system, triggers a whole new set of consequential changes in numerous related products. As technologies evolve, their levels of sophistication increase. The operating environment of IT skills does seem different from that of general business skills in the past. The universe of IT grows faster—or even explodes occasionally.

What then makes IT skills different from non-IT skills (see Figure 3)? First, IT skills are directly subject to the rapid speed of technological innovations. Thus, particular IT skills may soon become obsolete. Certain non-IT skills also become obsolete over time, when they are impacted by various technological and/or non-technological innovations. However, IT skills are often directly impacted by the pace of technological innovations. Thus, the half-life or volatility of IT skills utility is in general higher than non-IT skills.

Second, as technologies evolve, the internal complexity of IT tools and products tends to increase so it can realize greater flexibility and usability. In the 1970s, the engineers of personal computers (PC) could be involved in the development of various hardware and software aspects. In 2000, each technology element is much more sophisticated because types of technologies involved in the PC literally exploded. For example, Windows 3.1 had three million lines of code; Windows XP now has 45 million lines of code.[2] According to Microsoft, their PC operating system doubles its lines of code every 866

Figure 3: Characteristics of IT Skills

- Numerous ways to define IT skills by different attributes and tools
- Driven directly by continuous IT innovations
- Shorter half-life for IT skills
- Complex interactions between IT, organization, tasks and individuals
- A wide spectrum of users

days.[3] The inference is that the types of technical expertise are growing exponentially. As the universe of IT gets more sophisticated and complex, the IT professional can get buried in one narrow range of a technical domain and too preoccupied with one technology domain to have a broader perspective on the entire IT cosmos.

Third, many IT skills are focused on with the complex interactions between IT, the organization, tasks, and individuals. In one sense, IT skills are the skills to use tools. Work tools include home building tools (e.g., saw, hammer, wrench), construction tools (e.g., crane, bulldozer, roller), and so forth. While traditional tool skills tended to focus on particular task domains, many IT skills are concerned not only with the knowledge of the IT tools, but also with how those tools are used at the organization and/or work group level. An additional concern is whether and how IT tools benefit the organization. For example, even programming skills are not simply self-contained skills on syntax use. Often, effective programming cannot be done without knowing how computers generally work, having an insight on how the system software is constructed, and understanding how particular modules are designed and interact with other modules (e.g., system function/object interfaces, class/layered module hierarchies). Many IT tools, especially for IS development tasks, are used to automate or facilitate business processes. Thus, IT skills inherently intermingle with the elements of business activities and resources.

Lastly, IT skills have a wide spectrum of "owners." It is not just IT engineers who use IT skills. With the continuous diffusion of IT, professional, educational, and personal environments require their workers to use the equipment powered by microprocessors. Thus, IT skills are no longer held by a select few technical specialists.

Given the unique characteristics of IT skills, the critical questions for the management of IT skills at the individual, work group, firm, and societal levels include:

- What are "fundamental" IT skills?
- What are "critical" IT skills for those involved?
- How should we acquire and maintain IT skills at the various levels?
- How should we plan and manage IT skills strategically?

The last question hinges on identifying the firm's strategies and goals. In the next chapter, we give guidelines on using the firm's strategy for IT skill portfolio management. The question of skill management at the societal level involves efforts between national, state, and municipal institutions, together with the educational institutions. And such efforts need to be based on the current and future thinking of the first two questions above.

While the research community continues to examine what constitutes fundamental and critical IT skills are, we believe the business community needs to pursue a more goal-driven approach (see Figure 4). As reviewed earlier, skills are tied to task performances (also known as deliverables) and, in turn, to strategic business goals. The benefit of the goal-driven approach is that the "fundamental" or critical business goals and objectives can dictate and/or

Figure 4: The Goal-Driven, Context-Specific Approach for IT Skill Management

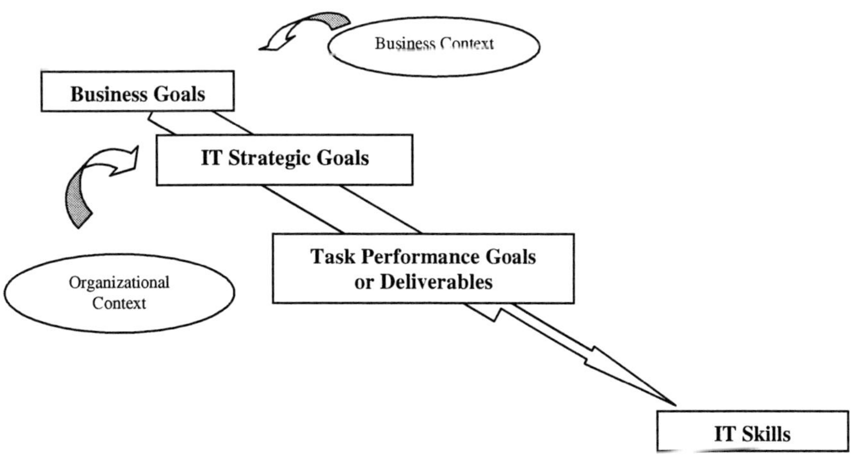

translate into "fundamental" IT skills. Whatever needs to be done to accomplish the important strategic business goals determines the task performance goals (also known as deliverables), which then define skills. Thus, the prevailing skill classification does not constrain our planning; we can name skills after specific task goals such as "Chicago Air enterprise system integration skills," "Los Angeles Municipal COBOL/legacy system upgrade skills," "supplier data integration skills," and so forth, as opposed to "programming skills," "Visual Basic skills," and "SAP skills."

When planning for the capabilities of the firm's IT/IS unit, the nine core capabilities model proposed by Feeny and Willcocks (1998) provides an excellent starting point; it is a checklist to "soul-search" critical skills for the IT/

Table 2: IS Core Capabilities vs. Key Skills (Feeny & Willcocks, 1998)

IS Core Capabilities	Skills to Achieve Core IS Capabilities
IS/IT Leadership Integrating IS/IT effort with business purpose and activity **Business Systems Thinking** Envisioning the business process which technology makes possible **Relationship Building** Getting the business constructively engaged in IS/IT issues **Architecture Planning** Creating the coherent blueprint for a technical platform which responds to present and future business needs **Making Technology Work** Rapidly achieving technical progress—by one means or another **Informed Buying** Managing the IS/IT sourcing strategy that meets the interests of the business **Contract Facilitation** Ensuring the success of existing contracts for IS/IT services **Contract Monitoring** Protecting the firm's contractual position, current and future **Vendor Development** Identifying the potential value of IS/IT service suppliers	**Technical Skills** **Business Skills** **Interpersonal Skills** **Time Horizons** Skills for identifying and protecting the future position **Motivating Values** Motivation or individual's value set to be multi-talented

IS unit (see Table 2). It is important to stress that the process of identifying firm-specific, critical IT skills (or IT competencies) itself provides a meaningful opportunity for managers to identify the firm's strategic business objectives and to devise complementary strategies and tactics for the IT/IS unit.

The goal-driven approach is also a context-specific approach. Goals, firm resources, and business situations create a unique context, which dictates a set of specific skills that enable goal accomplishment. Such a context is never static—it changes and evolves. This means that skills management is based on moving targets. On the one hand, we need to identify critical business goals, critical IT objectives, and, in turn, critical IT skills or IT competencies. On the other hand, we need a system in which skill acquisition and development are done dynamically through the evolving work context. That is, skills and work-based learning go together.

Green, Ashton, and Felstead (2001) also emphasize "the indispensability of work-based learning," while they note schooling can complement such work-based learning with somewhat diminishing return of efforts. Situational learning enables us to acquire "important skills that were hard or impossible to codify (and hence teach in a classroom)" while giving us opportunities to socialize with other workers. They also note, "The ability to learn is indeed sometimes seen as an important skill in itself."

At the individual level, IT professionals should be cognizant of their "core" competencies. Clarkson (2001) states that "the individual's job requirements drive the interpersonal skills and behavioral competencies that he needs." She suggests that we call driving factors of those skills "competencies," and identifying such competencies is a staring point of skills development.

At both firm and individual levels, it is important to recall that skills are acquired through experience. Until we discover—if there exists—"fundamental" IT skills, it makes more sense at present to take a (situational) task/job-driven IT skills planning and management approach.

Conclusion

In this chapter, we looked at past studies on skills in general, then at how firms manage skills. We also considered the unique characteristics of IT skills compared to non-IT skills. Based on these reflections, we reached the insight where the goal-driven, context-specific approach for managing IT skills makes more sense to give firms core competencies. In looking towards the next chapter, key insights and issues we recognized in this chapter include:

- Task goals drive skills.
- Skill and learning are two sides of the same coin.
- How the firm plans and manages its human resources not only affects its performance, but also impacts the sustainability of its competitive advantage.
- Human resources are the source of competitive advantage, not the factors of costs and/or limitations.
- Some characteristics of IT skills pose challenges to both firms and individual workers. The fast pace of technological innovations brings more complexity and diversity to IT tasks and skills. While individual workers aspire to be an expert in a certain domain of work, it is not easy to have a broader perspective of KSAs in the entire IT cosmos. As IT evolves, IT skills are important for not only IT professionals, but also for IT users—almost everybody nowadays.
- Plan and manage IT skills with a goal-driven, context-specific approach.

Endnotes

1 Some industry experts predict, however, that there will be a mass-exodus of mid-level managers seeking a better position once the economy solidly recovers (McGee, 2003).

2 http://www.tessier.com/2001/Life/08/28/opensource/

3 http://research.microsoft.com/acm97/nm/tsld027.htm

References

The American Heritage Dictionary of the English Language (4th edition). (2000). New York: Dell Publishing.

Becker, B., & Gerhart, B. (1996). The impact of human resource management on organizational performance: Progress and prospects. *Academy of Management Journal, 39*(4), 779-801.

Becker, G.S. (1976). *The economic approach to human behavior.* Chicago: University of Chicago Press.

Blanchard, P.N., & Thacker, J.W. (1999). *Effective training: Systems, strategies, and practices.* Upper Saddle River, NJ: Prentice-Hall.

Bureau of Labor Statistics. (2000). *2000-01 Occupational Outlook Handbook.* Washington, DC: U.S. Department of Labor.

Campbell, D.J. (1988). Task complexity: A review and analysis. *Academy of Management Review, 13*(1), 40-52.

Clarkson, M. (2001). *Developing IT staff: A practical approach.* London: Springer-Verlag London Limited.

D'Antoni, H. (2003). Behind the numbers: IT professionals cash in on company training. *InformationWeek,* (June 30), 67.

Delaney, J.T., & Huselid, M.A. (1996). The impact of human resource management practices on perceptions of organizational performance. *Academy of Management Journal, 39*(4), 949-969.

Duncan, G., & Hoffman, S. (1981). The incidence and wage effects of overeducation. *Economics of Education Review, 1,* 75-86.

Feeny, D.F., & Willcocks, L.P. (1998). Core IS capabilities for exploiting information technology. *Sloan Management Review,* (Spring), 9-21.

Fisher, A. (2001). Skills shortage puts job market out of balance. *Financial Times,* (May 2).

Fitts, P.M. (1964). Perceptual-motor skill learning. In A.W. Melton (Ed.), *Categories of human learning* (pp. 243-285). New York: Academic Press.

Fitts, P.M. (1990). Factors in complex skill training. In M. Venturino (Ed.), *Selected readings in human factors* (pp. 275-295). Santa Monica, CA: Human Factors Society. (Original work by Fitts published 1962.)

Fitts, P.M., & Posner, M.I. (1967). *Human performance.* Belmont, CA: Brooks/Cole.

Foley, J., & Murphy, C. (2003). 6 myths. *InformationWeek,* (June 30), 30-42.

Green, F., Ashton, D., & Felstead, A. (2001). Estimating the determinants of supply of computing, problem-solving, communication, social, and teamworking skills. *Oxford Economic Papers, 53*(3), 406-433.

Green, F., Machin, S., & Wilkinson, D. (1998). The meaning and determinants of skills shortages. *Oxford Bulletin of Economics & Statistics, 60*(2), 165-187.

ITAA. (2003). New ITAA study shows tech job outlook to remain soft in 2003. Information Technology Association of America, Press Release, May 5. Accessed August 4, 2003, from: www.itaa.org/news/pr/PressRelease.cfm?ReleaseID=1052157509.

Jiang, J.J., & Klein, G. (2001). Software project risks and development focus. *Project Management Journal, 32*(1), 4-9.

King, J. (2002). Hard times: Tech workers trying to find jobs face a bleak future. *Computerworld,* (April 29). Accessed August 4, 2003, from: www.computerworld.com/careertopics/careers/recruiting/story/0,10801,70626,00.html.

Lemon, W.F., Bowitz, J., Burn, J., & Hackney, R. (2002). Information systems project failure: A comparative study of two countries. *Journal of Global Information Management, 10*(2), 28-40.

Levine, E.L., Ash, R.A., Hall, H., & Sistrunk, F. (1983). Evaluation of job analysis methods by experienced job analysts. *Academy of Management Journal, 26*(2), 339-348.

London, M. (1983). Toward a theory of career motivation. *Academy of Management Review, 8*(4), 620-630.

Marlin, S. (2003). IT compensation gets a dose of performance. *InformationWeek,* (July 14/21), 22.

McGee, M.K. (2003). Good as gone. *InformationWeek,* (September 8), 18-20.

META Group. (2002). *2003 worldwide IT benchmark report.* Stamford, CT: META Group.

META Group. (2003). *Best practices in project estimation and performance management.* Stamford, CT: META Group.

Murray, B., & Gerhart, B. (1998). An empirical analysis of a skill-based pay program and plant performance outcomes. *Academy of Management Journal, 41*(1), 68-78.

Noe, R.A. (1986). Trainees' attributes and attitudes: Neglected influences on training effectiveness. *Academy of Management Review, 11*(4), 736-749.

Parnes, H.S. (1984). *People power.* Beverly Hills, CA: Sage Publications.

Pfeffer, J. (1998). *The human equation: Building profits by putting people first.* Boston, MA: Harvard Business School Press.

Pfeffer, J., Hatano, T., & Santalainen, T. (1995). Producing sustainable competitive advantage through the effective management of people. *Academy of Management Executive, 9*(1), 55-72.

Prahalad, C.K., & Hamel, G. (1990). The core competence of the corporation. *Harvard Business Review, 68*(3), 79-91.

Proctor, R.W., & Dutta, A. (1995). *Skill acquisition and human performance.* Thousand Oaks, CA: Sage Publications.

Rada, R. (1999). IT skills standards. *Communications of the ACM, 42*(4), 21-26.

Rumberger, R.W. (1987). The impact of surplus schooling on productivity and earnings. *Journal of Human Resources, 22,* 24-50.

Schneider, B., & Konz, A.M. (1989). Strategic job analysis. *Human Resource Management, 28*(1), 51-63.

Stasz, C. (2001). Assessing skills for work: Two perspectives. *Oxford Economic Papers, 53*(3), 385-405.

Tesluk, P.E., & Jacobs, R.R. (1998). Toward an integrated model of work experience. *Personnel Psychology, 51*(2), 321-355.

Tsang, M.C. (1987). The impact of underutilization of education on productivity: A case study of the U.S. Bell companies. *Economics of Education Review, 6,* 239-254.

Waldman, D.A., & Avolio, B.J. (1993). Aging and work performance in perspective: Contextual and developmental considerations. In K.M. Rowland & G.R. Ferris (Eds.), *Research in personnel and human resources management* (pp. 133-162). Greenwich, CT: JAI Press.

Walton, R.E., & Susman, G. (1987). People policies for the new machines. *Harvard Business Review, 65*(2), 98-106.

Welford, A.T. (1968). *Fundamentals of skill.* London: Methuen.

Youndt, M.A., Snell, S.A., Dean, J.W. Jr., & Lepak, D.P. (1996). Human resource management, manufacturing strategy, and firm performance. *Academy of Management Journal, 39*(4), 836-866.

Chapter II

An Approach for Managing an IT Skills Portfolio

Makoto Nakayama
DePaul University, USA

Norma Sutcliffe
DePaul University, USA

Abstract

In this chapter, the focus is on best practice for IT skills portfolio management. To begin, we formulate the key principles or mission statement for IT skills portfolio management based on the previous chapter. Under the principles enumerated there, this chapter outlines how to build an IT skills portfolio, and then looks at how to apply the portfolio at the firm and the individual IT professional levels.

Introduction

From the discussion of past studies in the preceding chapter, we develop a framework for managing IT skills at the firm level. The gist of such a framework is summarized in *Appendix A: Birds-Eye View on IT Skills Portfolio Management* as well as in *Appendix B: The IT Skills Portfolio Management Framework*. Appendix A summarizes what this chapter presents in a figure. Appendix B shows the skeleton of the managerial steps for planning and managing IT task forces at the firm level.

At the beginning, we derive key guiding principles for IT skills management from the past lessons and today's business and IT environments. The first principle (*people-centered organization*) is drawn from human resource management. We derive the second principle (*multi-mission capability*) from two phenomena. First, today's economic and competitive conditions are forcing us to do more work with fewer people. Second, the growth of new IT technologies has brought us more complex interactions between IT devices and systems, as well as between IT and organizations. The third principle (*work-based learning*) comes from two directions. As the pace of technological innovations gets faster, IT professionals have no choice but to keep learning to stay current with IT innovations. Also, the preceding chapter emphasizes the importance of anchoring IT skills to business and task goals. Consequently, it is important that we use these three guiding principles to construct a framework for managing IT skills.

The main thrust of the IT skills portfolio management framework is to focus on business goals and the critical tasks for accomplishing these goals. As the appendixes show, the proposed framework binds business goals to what IT professionals have to do to accomplish them. The framework consists of the following four steps:

(1) Clearly recognize business goals.

(2) Translate business goals into what IT projects have to accomplish.

(3) Define IT skills based on deliverables of IT projects.

(4) Determine the best option for IT skill sourcing.

In these four steps, we use 2x2 matrices with the time dimension (now vs. future) and the criticality assessment dimension (how crucial, how difficult, and how risky) to optimally allocate resources. Those matrixes are the heart of managing the IT skills *portfolio.*

Key Principles

A key underlying principle in strategic human resource management (SHRM) is to regard people as a main enabler for the organization rather than as a cost and/or a constraint. Under the 13 collective practices for SHRM that Pfeffer, Hatano, and Santalainen (1995) listed, the organization views the IT professional as the fundamental value creator who can orchestrate the successful application of IT to meet the organization's needs. With this mindset, organizations not only train managers and workers with new skills, but go further by changing the structure in which the new skills are used. For example, at Advanced Micro Systems' submicron development facility, most workers came from their older, closed facilities. Before transferring to the new facility, these workers were fully paid while attending a seven-month training program that gave them the needed new skills.

Another collective practice is cross-utilization with cross-training. Traditionally, when the market conditions deteriorate, people with unneeded skills are laid off to free up resources for hiring new people with needed skills. The downside is that the new people do not have the firm specific skills that the layoffs had, and it will take time for them to get those skills. But with cross-training and cross-utilization, people have skills in several areas and can be used where the need exists.

In the 1980s, Mazda was not selling cars at the same pace they were producing cars. So Mazda took factory workers off the production lines and sent them out selling cars, which in Japan are often sold door to door. At the end of the year, Mazda found that all of the top 10 sales people came from the factory. Why were they so effective? They had the specific knowledge on the products and services that can only be gained at the firm. They knew the cars so well because they had made them and could answer customer concerns very effectively. When sales had improved and these employees went back to the factory, they then used their sales knowledge to improve auto production.

Principle 1: People-Centered Organization

Think of people before thinking of IT skills and KSAs, which are the essential building blocks for delivering performance. Whereas skills are demonstrated capabilities or "goal-directed, well-organized behavior that is acquired through practice and performed with economy of effort" (Proctor & Dutta, 1995), the abilities of people are the growth potential. Thus, the wise managers start with looking at abilities of the people available. When they hire, they hire IT professionals for the firm, rather than for just a specific set of tasks. They utilize their IT professionals for their abilities, or their potentials, before looking outside for talent.

From the first programmable computers of the 1940s to now, the skills needed to use computers constantly change. The skills needed to program the early "Univacs" are vastly different from the skills needed to develop software for today's inter-organizational application systems, such as supply chain management. Keeping up to date with such changes is daunting.

The impact of change appears at three levels. First, a new computing innovation arrives, with existing computing hardware and software improving marginally or significantly over time in response to the innovation (Hock, Roeding, Purkert, & Lindner, 2000, pp. 259-271). Thus, mostly technical skills are needed to respond to such changes (*the first-order effect of IT change*). In addition, new, improved IT is applied in business, economic, and social

Figure 1: Knowledge, Skills, and Abilities (KSAs)

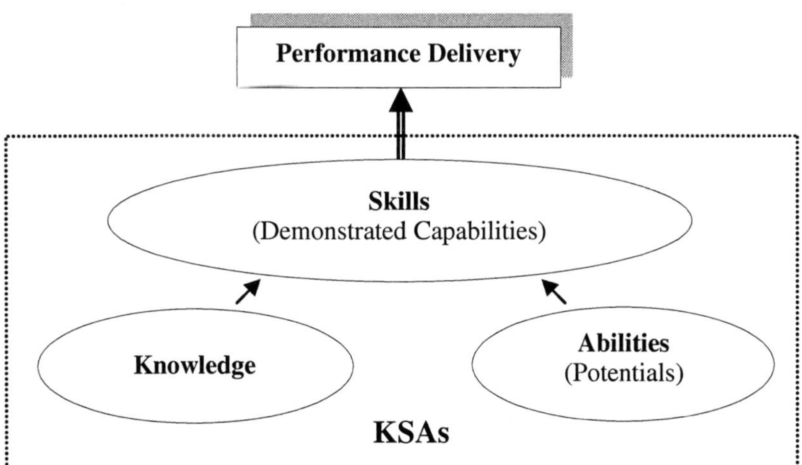

contexts, and the skills of how to apply IT in turn change over time (*the second-order effect of IT change*). Those changed business, economic, and social practices consequently loop back to the future requirements or desires for IT innovations, or the change planning (*the third-order effect of IT change*). The result of such spiraling evolution is inevitable uncertainty. Also, under a tight fiscal environment, IT and business innovations result in efficiencies of work at all levels—that is, IT and non-IT professionals accomplish the same or more with fewer resources (e.g., time, man-hours, budget) than they did in the past. The implication is that IT professionals are asked to have what the military calls "multi-mission capability."[1]

Principle 2: Multi-Mission Capability

IT professionals are capable of playing several critical roles for the firm. They are capable of performing tasks from one critical skill domain, but they are also capable of performing tasks from other critical skill domains as well.

In the dawn of the Internet era, IT professionals already started facing increasingly complex tasks. For example, a narrow, "traditional" definition of "programmer" is not quite indicative of what the current "programmer" is required to do (Mack & Dec, 1997). The recent squeeze on the economy further pushed companies to combine the responsibilities of several positions, so that work can be done with a lower headcount (McGee, 2003).

With a multi-mission capability, an IT professional may be an expert and valued contributor on a database management system, but she also possesses the skills to lead an inter-organizational IT project involving her firm's trading partners. In other words, she has industry knowledge and experience to manage a project while honing her competency in database systems.

Oftentimes in traditionally managed IT organizations, the idea that IT professionals are multi-dimensional in their personal skills portfolio is alien to upper IT management, partly because they lack in-depth knowledge of the IT staff's abilities. The project managers know, but their managers lack this knowledge. We will discuss more on this lack later.

Consequently, IT managers do not consider their current pool of talent when a new IT need arises. These managers usually consider only hiring new personnel, the "doing without" option, using consultants, or outsourcing to fill the need. By recognizing and utilizing the multi-mission capability of their IT professionals, management can strengthen individual and team motivation, reduce coordination costs, and increase productivity.

Finally, we constantly need to frame skills in terms of task and project goals. The focus on the aims that the skills will fill is often lost or blurred if the skills are not framed in this fashion. Thus, tying skills to project goals reinforces attention. Another reason is that the learning takes place best in the context of work where people perform using skills supported by knowledge and abilities. Therefore, it is important to have programs in place to foster applied, ongoing learning in the workplace.

Principle 3: Work-Based Learning

IT professionals are capable of constant learning in several critical skill domains. They learn as they work and through their work. They also learn from one another while also improving their firm-specific skills through their application of technology to their organization's problems.

What we need now is an HRM approach to realize the "best practice" of IT skills management by following the above three principles. The following sections describe how we can.

IT Skills Portfolio Management

We first look at some background behind IT skills portfolio management. We then look at how a firm develops its IT skills portfolio and how a firm can use the portfolio. In finance, a *portfolio* is a collection of investments held by an institution or a private individual. By extension, here we are looking at the collection of IT applications that an institution holds.

Background

Why is IT skills portfolio management an important tool? To answer this question, a little background is needed. Most firms today organize IT systems development efforts on a project basis rather than on the traditional functional basis. Under this functional structure, projects were divided between the systems group whose analysts specified what was to be done and the programming group whose programmers actually developed and tested the system. Now under the project structure, all personnel working on the project are together on one team with a project leader/manager whose primary responsibility is to keep the project on schedule.

In contrast, when projects moved between different functional groups, each functional manager's primary responsibility was to operate efficiently by leveraging all available resources. The programming manager knew each programmer's expertise and could match skills to particular tasks regardless of the project. So, a programmer could and often would work on several applications during the same timeframe. The downside of this functional arrangement was that project deadlines often slipped because no one was accountable for the project. They were only responsible for getting particular deliverables accomplished. Now, with the project orientation, the overall project schedule is kept better.

However, the downside of using a project structure is leveraging IT skills across a number of projects. It is very problematic because no one has detailed knowledge or has the responsibility for matching skills to deliverables from multiple projects. Project leaders do have detailed knowledge of the skills on their project team, but also have powerful incentives to keep that knowledge to themselves. If that knowledge became known, their project deadlines could be compromised with the loss of those skills to a higher priority project. Better to keep quiet until the end of the project.

IT skills portfolio management solves this problem. From the IT Projects Set, the IT Deliverables Set is built which is the basis for establishing the IT skills portfolio. All members of the IT management team are involved in all steps of portfolio construction. With this tool, management can see what skills are needed for the most important deliverables and when they are needed, what skills are in abundance, what skills can be developed, what skills to obtain through outsourcing and in-sourcing, and what skills are no longer needed.

A logical starting point for effective IT skills management is to focus on the deliverables from the projects aimed at satisfying the firm's business and IT strategic goals. In other words, consolidating the project deliverables from all the projects becomes the basis for building the IT skills portfolio. Deliverables are also known as task performance goals for skills to aim at satisfying. However, the examination of deliverables is not enough. It is also important to rank the deliverables based on how important they are to the organization, how dependant they are on external factors, and how risky they are. Yet, before examining the deliverables, it is important to step even further back to a firm's strategy and strategic goals.

The Steps to the IT Skills Portfolio

The major thrust of IT skills portfolio management is the management of goals and project/task deliverables (Figure 2). It is business goals that determine what deliverables the current and future IT projects should provide. And these deliverables dictate what IT skills portfolio the firm must have.

Both current IT applications and planned future IT projects determine such deliverables. This framework assumes that all IT projects are approved because their implementation will further the achievement of the organization's strategic business goals. Why is this assumption important? When IT is negotiating with top management for scarce resources, the link to strategic business goals is an essential justification. So, by extension, all IT strategic goals are linked to the strategic business goals.

Figure 2: The Goal-Driven, Context-Specific Approach for IT Skills Management

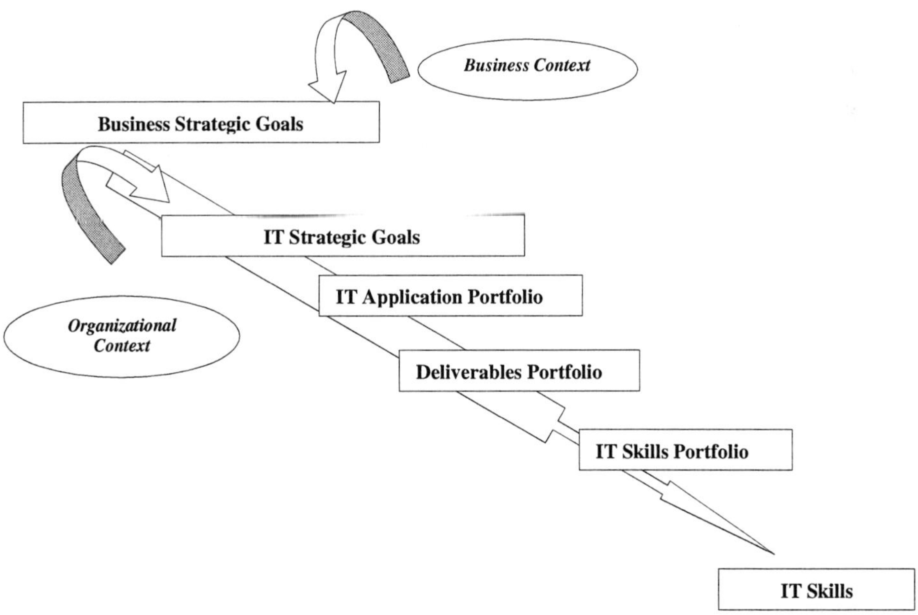

In the NIBCO case (Brown & Vessey, 2001), top management of this mid-sized manufacturer of valves and pipe fittings determined that their major strategic thrust was to increase customer service capabilities. The primary business goal then became reengineering their supply chain to increase flexibility in meeting customer needs. That strategic business goal necessitated the replacement of the current IS systems with integrated ERP suites for finance, materials management, production, and sales/distribution (IT strategic goal). Thus, the IT goal for replacing existing legacy systems with integrated ERP application suites determined the deliverables.

Hence, to define and rank IT deliverables, which are also known as the task performance goals that IT skills accomplish, we need to use a top-down approach. In response to its business context, the organization formulates its business strategic goals. Along with the organizational context, these goals are the basis for the IT strategic goals that the current and future IT applications aim to satisfy. From examining the IT Projects Set, the IT Deliverables Set is assembled. Because the deliverables are task performance goals that the IT skills satisfy and the deliverables determine the specific needed skill, the Deliverables Set is used to determine the IT skills portfolio (see Figure 2).

Overall Classification Scheme

When delivering the hierarchy of goals, one critical issue is how to strike a balance between the current and the future. The other critical issue is the criticality. When assessing projects, deliverables, or skills, the level of *criticality* is assessed along the following three dimensions:

- How *crucial* is the item for accomplishing the defined goals in business strategy, project, and deliverables, respectively?
- How *difficult* is the item to accomplish because it is inherently complex, has numerous integration points with other IT applications, or uses new technology?
- How *risky* is the item due to its reliance on scarce resources?

In other words, projects, deliverables, and skills are assessed in the two-dimensional matrix consisting of the time dimension and the criticality dimension of impact on goals, difficulty in doing, and reliance on scare resources. This approach is IT skills portfolio analysis. To gain an appreciation of the power of portfolio analysis, we now look at how it is used in finance.

The concept of portfolio analysis is rooted in financial investment portfolio analysis (e.g., Ellis, 1971; Moore, 1971). Such analysis provides investors with a bird's eye view on their financial resource allocations, together with the information on returns and risks. Boston Consulting Group (BCG) applied portfolio analysis for managing strategic business units at the corporate level (Hax & Majluf, 1983; Porter, 1980, pp. 361-367). Using their Growth-Share Matrix (see Figure 3), the firm can assess risk and return, from now and the future, dynamically. Somewhat similar is Ansoff's Matrix (Ansoff, 1965) that gives an overall picture on the firm's marketing strategies. This matrix (see Figure 4) shows what marketing strategy to use depending on whether the products are for existing or new markets, and also depending on whether the products are new or existing.

Figure 3: BCG Growth-Share Matrix

		Relative Market Share	
		High	**Low**
Market Growth Rate	**High**	**Stars** 	**Question Marks** 
	Low	**Cash Cows** 	**Dogs** 

Figure 4: Ansoff Matrix

	Existing Products	New Products
Existing Markets	**Market Penetration**	**Product Development**
New Markets	**Market Development**	**Diversification**

Firms use the BCG matrix to categorize their strategic business units (SBUs) on two dimensions—the market growth rate and the relative market share—so they can rationally distribute their resources to those units with the best potential.

Those SBUs that have a high market share in a growing market are "stars." They deserve the most resources to assure they keep and expand their position.

In contrast, SBUs that have a low market share in a growing market are "question marks." Because they lack share but are in a growing market, making additional resource investments is questionable and requires careful analysis. A careful analysis of an SBU's potential against its competitors might show that investing additional resources translates into growing market share. In contrast, if the competition has sustainable advantages that are difficult to combat, then moving the SBU into markets with more potential or selling the SBU are the most viable options.

With SBUs operating in markets with only low growth potential, substantial resource investment is not advisable. The "cash cows" have high market share and have profits that can be diverted to either the "stars" or "question marks."

The "dogs" have low market share in a low growth potential market. The most viable options are either moving into different markets, or closing or selling the SBU.

Just as the BCG matrix is used to clarify resource investment strategies, the Ansoff Matrix provides a specific growth strategy dependent on the SBU products and markets. There is less risk with existing products than with new products.

When an SBU has existing products in an existing market, then the market penetration strategy is appropriate. The aim is to increase market share, leveraging existing resources.

Unfortunately there is a saturation point for any product in any market. When reached, either expanding into new markets and/or new products is the next step. If the firm wants to stay in existing markets and leverage their reputation and core competencies, then product development is the appropriate marketing strategy.

In contrast, when an SBU takes existing products into new markets, then market development is appropriate. This is often risky because the knowledge of the new markets is scant.

However, the most risky is diversification where new products are being brought into new markets. Not only is there scanty market knowledge for the new products, but there is also scanty product knowledge.

To summarize, both BCG and Ansoff matrices are mechanisms for ranking entities for the potential risk and gains. They clarify for managers where the payoffs are most likely, where investments have potential, and where they do not. They are tools for portfolio analysis.

The spirit of portfolio analysis is to *prioritize resource allocations* at the firm level. Portfolio analysis is a great tool to assess *the current and future prospects of risks and returns*. However, just using portfolio analysis alone does not end the ongoing management of skills. It has to be complemented with guidelines on the best IT skills management practices.

The IT Skills Portfolio Process

Developing and using an IT skills portfolio consists of four main steps. The first step is to clearly define strategic goals for the business and for IT. The second step is to develop the IT Projects Set along with the IT Deliverables Set. The third step is to translate the task goals from the Deliverables Set into the IT skills portfolio. The final step is managing IT skills using the IT skills portfolio guidelines. As mentioned earlier, this process requires the participation of the entire IT management team, not just its top level.

Step 1: Clarifying Strategic Goals—Business and IT

- **Strategic Business Goals.** Prepare a statement defining each *strategic business goal*. Although a goal does not have to be quantitative, it is important that the goal's evaluation method is clearly stated. There is an old adage that all goals are important, but specific, measurable goals are superior to vague goals, which are superior to no goals. Thus, goal statements are superior in that are specific and clearly detail how progress is measured towards attaining the goals.

  Those goal statements that rely on vague aspirations, such as, "We want to be known as the best in the market," are almost doomed to failure before they start. Why? Best in what? How would anyone know if they are the best or the worst? Asking those questions often clarifies strategic goals.

In contrast, look at this excellent goal" "Within five years we will have at least 25 Fortune 500 clients with a minimum of $5,000,000 in annual billings." This goal has a timeline, a quantitative measure, and a clearly defined target. Every month it is easy to determine how close the firm is getting to attainment. Another good business goal is: "Within two years we will bring five new products to market every month."

- **Strategic IT Goals.** Prepare a statement defining each *strategic IT goal* emphasizing goals specific to the IT domain. A business goal does not necessarily have associated IT goals, but an IT goal should have at least one associated business goal. For IT, it is useful to document explicitly the relationship between an IT goal and its associated business goals, when competing for business resources with others in the organization.

  Just as business goals aim for specificity, so should IT goals. An excellent IT goal is: "Within three months after going into production, the new call center will process a minimum of 3,500 calls per day, averaging less than five minutes per call for satisfactory resolution." While not monetary, this goal is still measurable with a timeline, the number of units (calls), and the size of the ideal unit (less than five minutes). The related strategic business goal is to "raise the customer retention rate to 40% by the end of the fiscal year."
- Rank the strategic business goals in importance to the firm, with "5" being most important and "1" being trivial.
- Rank the strategic IT strategic goals using the same scale.
- Pitfalls and how to avoid them.
  - A major pitfall is formulating IT strategic goals that are unaligned to any current business strategic goals. The obvious difficulty is that support is usually ephemeral and weak. Gaining support outside of IT is nearly impossible because the rest of the organization cannot relate to the goals.
  - Weak or vague strategic goals make execution difficult. Whereas specific goals motivate efforts, weak goals are not easy to communicate and are difficult to monitor.

Step 2: Developing the IT Projects Set & IT Deliverables Set

- **Projects:** List all known IT projects. This list is the foundation for the Projects Set and Deliverables Set, and then the IT skills portfolio.
- **For Each Project:**
  - o **Project Identifier:** Unique and descriptive.
  - o **Strategic IT Goal Link:** List all goals that the project aims to fulfill.
  - o **Timeframe:** Identify whether *ongoing* (0-2 years from now) or *future* (starting from 2-5 years).
  - o **Resources:** Identify the level of resources (**RC**) needed (1-5 for few to extensive) and the length of time the resources are needed (in years).
  - o **Criticality:** Score the **Criticality** (**C**) of the project for the success of its underlying IT strategic goals (1-5 from not important to very important).

    This score is later used for a project Assessment Score (**AS**), which also needs the project's difficulty (**D**) and project's risk level (**R**). The latter two scores are based on all deliverables for a project. Attention now turns to an examination of each deliverable. It then becomes possible to calculate the project's AS.
- **Deliverables:** List all known deliverables on each IT project. This list is the foundation for the Deliverables Set and then the IT skills portfolio.
- **For each Deliverable within a project** and then for the project, calculate scores on two attributes:
  - o **Deliverable Descriptor (dp):** Unique for every deliverable, but substantially the same for the same performance tasks in different projects.
  - o **Project Identifier:** For the deliverable.
  - o **Difficulty:** Rank (0: not applicable, 1-5: from easy to impossible) for each deliverable its current level of difficulty (**d**), then calculate the project difficulty (**D**) score as the average of all the deliverable difficulty scores.

Examples of high difficulty are a dependence on an enterprise-wide database; a dependence on new, unproven technologies such as grid computing; and a high level of integration with other systems.

- **Risk Level:** Rank (0: not applicable, 1-5: from low to high) for each deliverable (**r**), then calculate for the project the risk level (**R**) score as the average of all the deliverable risk level scores.

  Examples of high risk level are a reliance on scarce resources, reliance on resources controlled by others, and inadequacy of contingency plans.

- **Deliverables Set:** To recap, the list of deliverables for each project now has each deliverable's descriptor (**dp**) risk level (**r**) and difficulty score (**d**). It is now possible to group all the same deliverables from different projects together.
- **Projects Set continued:** To recap, each project now has:
  - resource needed score (**RC**) which is "1" to "5" for few to extensive,
  - difficulty (**D**),
  - risk level (**R**),
  - criticality score (**C**), and
  - the length of time needed (in years).
- Now it is possible to calculate the project **Assessment Score** (**AS**)—which is the average of **Criticality** (**C**), project **difficulty score** (**D**), and project **risk level score** (**R**)—and note results in the Project Portfolio.
- This **Assessment Score** (**AS**) is a quick indication of what projects require more managerial oversight for successful completion. Also, the pattern of **D = difficulty**, **R = resources,** and **C = criticality** indicates the appropriate managerial actions to take.
  - When **C** is much higher than **D** or **R**, accelerating the schedule without adding excess resources is a very sound decision because it increases IT credibility with other parts of the organization.
  - When **C** and **D** are higher than **R**, adding more resources can make sure the project is well covered. However, if adding resources is not feasible, then a careful analysis that clarifies the risks with tactics for mitigating them is very important.
  - When **C** and **R** are higher than **D**, it is a flag that outsourcing the project may be feasible. If the project is not highly integrated with

other IT applications, then using an outsourcer can free up scarce human resources for other projects.

- o When **C** is lower than **D** and/or **R**, it is a clear indication that the success is problematic. It is difficult and it needs resources, but is not strategically crucial.

- **Potentialities:** List potential factors in the Projects Set that may positively and negatively affect project success. Some factors are: application of organizational changes, business climate changes, technology changes, labor market changes, and so forth.
- Pitfalls and how to avoid them.
    - o IT projects not clearly linked to IT strategic business goals. Without that link, success is very problematic.
    - o The inability to group similar deliverables because of the use of idiosyncratic descriptions. To avoid this problem, use generic deliverable descriptions that can be used in a large number of different projects. Ideally before starting the skills portfolio management process, IT staff will examine all project plans, and code the deliverables and skills using the same descriptions.

Step 3: Developing IT Skills Portfolio

- Using the Deliverables Set developed above, develop the IT skills portfolio.
    - o List each major skill (**SK**) needed for each deliverable within a project.
    - o Determine and note for each **SK** the following scores in range (1-5: from little to much):
        - its criticality (**sc**) score for its deliverable;
        - its difficulty (**sd**) score for its deliverable;
        - its risk level score (**sr**) for its deliverable;
        - its assessment score (**sas**) for its deliverable as the average of sc, sd, and sr;
        - its timeframe—current (within 2 years) or future (2 to 5 years);
        - its requirements—how much of the skill is needed (**sq**).

- Now, group together all **SK**. This gives the picture of what projects are currently using that skill, what projects need that skill in the future, and how many projects need that skill.

- Pitfalls and how to avoid them.
  - Having too many skills. To avoid, you need to look at a group of tasks together and figure out what are "common" skills. If needed, define skills in your own way.
  - Having too many Projects and Deliverables sets. The number of sets should be in scale with the size of the organization.

Step 4: Using the Skill Portfolio Sourcing Matrix

Based on the timeframe and assessment score **sas** (see Figure 5, Skills Portfolio Sourcing Matrix), management can determine the best approach for acquiring the needed skill.

When the skill is needed currently and has a high assessment score (**sas**), management needs to use *critical sourcing*. In other words, management buys the best possible skill level available. It can be outsourcing or hiring or transferring from within. Management's goal is to make sure that the schedule and level of quality are kept at a high level.

When the assessment score is low for current projects, best sourcing is the appropriate approach. Under best sourcing, there are two options. If the skills are already available at the firm, then those skills are used, otherwise outsourcing is the choice.

Figure 5: Skills Portfolio Sourcing Matrix

		Timeframe	
		Current	**Future**
Assessment Score (sas)	**High**	**Critical Sourcing**	**Training/Hiring**
	Low	**Best Sourcing**	**Outsourcing**

When the skills are for future projects that have a high assessment score, management has time to plan for either training for and/or hiring those skills.

When there is a low assessment for the skill, outsourcing is appropriate for future projects. There is no need to hire or train for these skills.

- Reviewing skills with high assessment scores, identify IT personnel who possess those skills, and who possess multi-mission capabilities that can play key roles in leadership, critical task/skill delivery, group management, and crisis management.
- Around critical IT personnel are IT professionals who need to further their skill development and/or their multi-mission capability. Devise a system where KSAs are continuously enhanced through work and supporting mechanisms such as *knowledge management* and HR practices, especially *mentoring*.
- Pitfalls and how to avoid them.
    - o Premature skill sourcing decisions. They are typically due to short changing process in the first three steps. It is essential that strategic goals, IT projects, and deliverables are analyzed carefully and thoroughly.
    - o Ignoring technology and product life cycles. Periodically management must monitor and re-evaluate technology and product life cycles, particularly for highly assessed projects.
    - o A lack of occasional revisions. The management should revise their *Projects Set, Deliverables Set,* and *IT skills portfolio,* whenever there is a significant change in business goals, IT goals, organizational situations, key technologies, and/or important products/tools.

Best Practices for the Firm

The following practices and insights are important as the foundation for good skills management.

- While skills are important, they are not the end but the means to the end, which is strategic goal attainment. Therefore, organizations need to emphasize and communicate the business and IT strategic goals with IT professionals. The IT professionals need to know the critical deliverables for a five-year timeframe so they can see what skills are important to the firm.

- Let IT professionals self-manage their skill levels and give them the incentives to do so. It is important that management communicate the incentives to all employees along with the critical deliverables mentioned above. In this way, organizations can guide employees towards the most needed skills; the organization can also determine who is most motivated.
- Reward the attainment of deliverables, not just possession of desired skills. That does not mean that the organization should not give tuition support; rather it means that bonuses and promotions are tied to the successful attainment of goals through the application of skills.
- Analysis of major skills or job/task categories.
  - List major skill categories, ideally somewhere between 5 and 20.
  - List key requirements (including a few critical ones, but no more than 5 in total) for each category.
  - If your firm has more than 20 categories, consider consolidating them into fewer than 20. The idea is to keep the household tasks of IT workforce management as simple and flexible as possible. This also forces the use of job rotations to build a more flexible IT workforce.
- Pay particular attention to those KSAs that are specific to the core business operations in your firm. Those KSAs can never be outsourced; they can only come from within the organization.
- Conduct an assessment analysis and prepare contingency plans when unfavorable events are likely, and their impact level and probability can be estimated.
- Hire and develop IT professionals for the firm, rather than for a position.
- Emphasize to the IT professionals the importance of possessing multi-mission capability.
- The most important skill is the skill to learn.
- Identify the few critical IT personnel; prepare retention *and* succession plans.

Skills Portfolio Management for the Professional

Just as the firm needs to manage the various skills available, so the IT professional needs to keep an eye on the current needs for skills, the desired level of expertise for the skills, and what the future desired skills are. Thus, the professional uses the following process to keep up-to-date.

- Determine your skills at the following three levels:
    - o *industry/firm specific* KSAs, such as expertise in health care claims processing, accounting systems for non-profits, and so forth;
    - o *technology specific* KSAs, such as expertise in database servers, Linux-based online transaction procession, C#/VB .NET programming, and so forth;
    - o *organizational* (team, project, management) KSAs, such as project planning, manpower planning, and so forth.
- Assess your current level of competency in the above three KSAs.
- Define your career skill path (not the same as "career path") for the next five years. That is, where are you weak and need additional training? Where do you want more experience? What areas do you want to avoid?
- Make sure that you have more than one competency so you have flexibility.
- Identify the gap between your current competency and required competency for the areas you want to work in.
- To summarize, your most important skill is your skill to learn.

Conclusion

This chapter started with a discussion of the principles that guide the development and use of a skills portfolio. Then attention turned to management of the portfolio. Background was presented on how the portfolio answers real problems in managing the skill needs for a multi-project IT organization. A detailed plan for developing the IT skills portfolio follows that starts with the business strategic goals for the organization. With the IT skills portfolio built, it is now possible to answer the IT skills sourcing concerns. With that done, the chapter ends by looking at the best practices for the firm and for the IT professional.

Endnote

1 Under limited budgets, the U.S. military often stresses the importance of "multi-mission capability" when it develops and deploys equipment and task forces. For example, some aircraft such as the F/A-18 Hornet of the Navy have the combined capability of both fighting (dog-fighting) and attacking (bombing) against the opponents. The Joint Strike Fighter (JSF) program of the U.S. military aims to deliver the next-generation aircraft that can be deployed for a variety of military objectives in the Air Force, Navy, and Marine Corps.

References

Ansoff, H.I. (1965). *Corporate strategy.* New York: McGraw-Hill.

Brown, C.V., & Vessey, I. (2001). NIBCO's big bang. *Communications of the Association for Information Systems, 5*(1). Accessed September 2003 from: http://cais.isworld.org/articles/default.asp?vol=5&art=1.

Ellis, C.D. (1971). Portfolio operations. *Financial Analysts Journal, 27*(5), 36.

Hax, A.C., & Majluf, N.S. (1983). The use of the growth-share matrix in strategic planning. *Interfaces, 13*(1), 46-60.

Hock, D.J., Roeding, C.R., Purkert, G., & Lindner, S.K. (2000). *Secrets of software success.* Boston, MA: Harvard Business School Press.

Mack, R., & Dec, K. (1997). *Transition strategies (TS), building a strategic plan for an information technology transition.* Gartner Group, April 25.

McGee, M.K. (2003). Good as gone. *InformationWeek,* (September 8), 18-20.

Moor, R.E. (1971). Economics and investment analysis. *Financial Analysts Journal, 27*(6), 63.

Pfeffer, J., Hatano, T., & Santalainen, T. (1995). Producing sustainable competitive advantage through the effective management of people. *Academy of Management Executive, 9*(1), 55-72.

Porter, M.E. (1980). *Competitive strategy.* New York: The Free Press.

Proctor, R.W., & Dutta, A. (1995). *Skill acquisition and human performance.* Thousand Oaks, CA: Sage Publications.

Appendix A: Birds-Eye View on IT Skills Portfolio Management

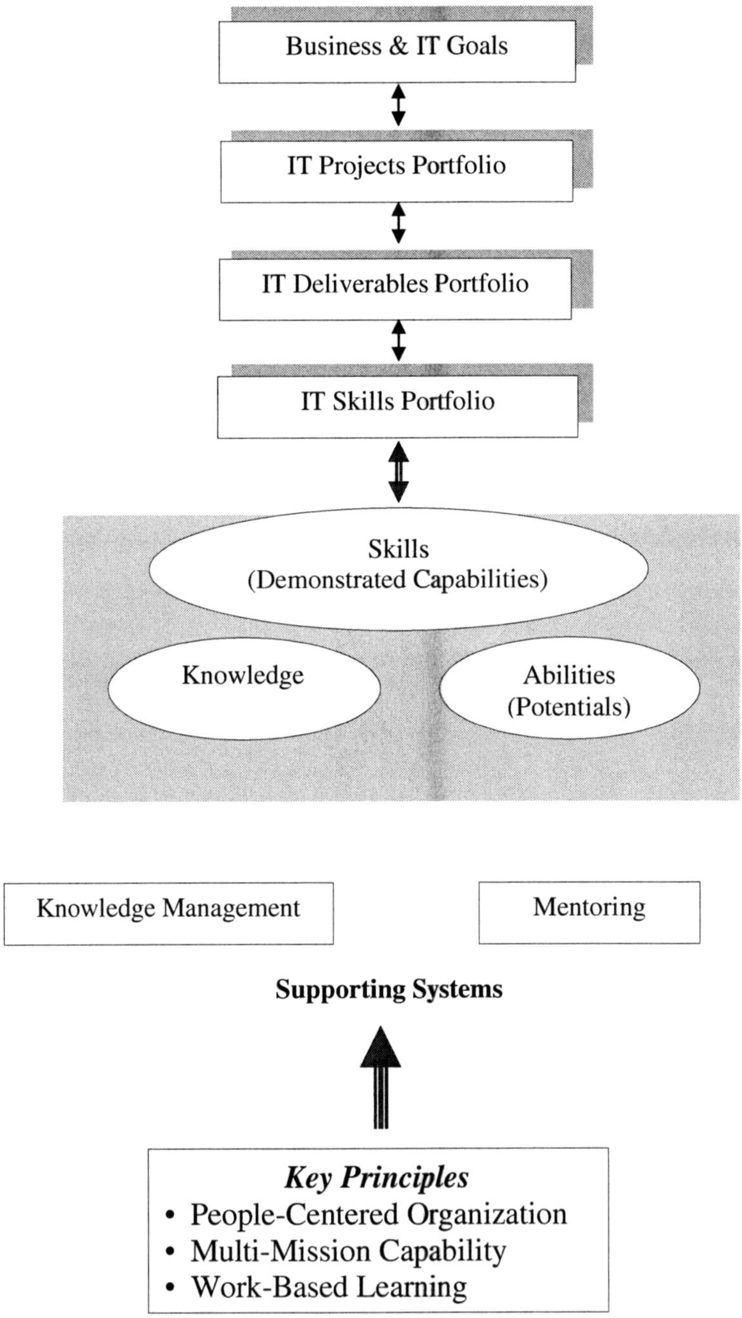

Appendix B: The IT Skills Portfolio Management Framework

Three Key Principles

Principle 1: People-Centered Organization

Think people ahead of IT and KSAs. IT professionals are hired for the firm, rather than for a specific set of tasks.

Principle 2: Multi-Mission Capability

IT professionals are capable of playing several critical roles for the firm. They are capable of performing tasks from one critical skill domain, but they are also capable of delivering critical tasks from other critical skill domains.

Principle 3: Work-Based Learning

IT professionals are capable of constant learning in several critical skill domains. They learn as they work and through their work.

The Process of IT Skills Portfolio Management

Step 1: Clarifying Strategic Goals—Business and IT

- Prepare a statement on each *strategic business* goal.
- Prepare statements on each *strategic IT* goal.
- Rank the business strategies and goals in importance to the firm.
- Rank the IT business strategies and goals within the associated business strategies using the same scale.

Step 2: Developing IT Projects Set & Deliverables Set

- Develop IT Projects Set.
  - List all known projects with unique identifier.
  - Identify whether a project is *ongoing* (0-2 years from now) or *future* (starting from 2-5 years).
  - Identify the level of resources needed (1-5 for few to extensive) and the length of time needed in years.
  - Score the Criticality of the project (C) for meeting the strategic goals (1-5 for from trivial to crucial).
  - Score the Assessment (AS) of the project after developing Deliverables Set as below.
- Develop Deliverables Set.
  - List the project's Deliverables with a descriptor, and its scores on difficulty and risk levels.
  - Summarize the list of deliverables, with each deliverable's risk level (r) and difficulty score (d), along with deliverable's project criticality score (c).
  - Identify the level of resources needed (1-5 for few to extensive) and the length of time needed (in years).
- Calculate the project Average Scores from the project's deliverables:
  - Risk Level (R) as the average of deliverables risks (r)
  - Difficulty (D) as the average of deliverables difficulties (d)
  - Criticality (C) as the average of deliverables criticalities (c)
- Calculate the project *Assessment Scores (AS)* as average of C, D, and R.
  - Based on the *Assessment Scores*, evaluate resource acquisition options.
  - List contingencies, and evaluate their probability.

Step 3: Developing IT Skills Portfolio

- Using the *Deliverables Set* developed in Step 2, develop the IT skills portfolio.

- o List each major skill (SK) needed for a deliverable.
- o Determine and note for each SK its criticality, difficulty, and risk level scores, as well as its timeframe and how much and how long the skill is needed.
- o Assess those skills (sas) by using the three criteria: criticality, difficulty and risk level.
- o Summarize the assessments in the IT skills portfolio.

Step 4: Using Portfolio Matrix

- Based on the IT skills portfolio, assess and determine the best skill sourcing option.
- Identify (or define if it does not exist) critical IT personnel.
- Around critical IT personnel, devise a system where KSAs are continuously enhanced through work. Consider using knowledge management and mentoring if appropriate.

		Timeframe	
		Current	**Future**
Assessment (sas)	**High**	**Critical Sourcing**	**Training /Hiring**
	Low	**Best Sourcing**	**Outsourcing**

Chapter III

Challenges for Managing IT Skills Portfolio for E-Business

Abdulrahman A. Mirza
King Saud University, Saudi Arabia

Susy S. Chan
DePaul University, USA

Abstract

Organizations are under increasing pressure to adopt Internet-based e-business solutions for improving internal efficiency and collaboration with partners, suppliers, and customer firms within the environment of e-business webs. To realize these benefits, companies must transition towards an e-business organization. Such transformation demands IT knowledge and expertise at different levels. Each level requires special IT skills introduced as a result of the complex and dynamic nature of an e-business environment. In this chapter we examine the e-business environment and its implications for firm-level IT skills portfolio management. We then present five levels of challenges related to an e-

business firm's IT skills requirement. We further present: (1) future trends relating to the changing landscape for e-business IT skills; (2) activities that support acquisition, development, and maintenance of these skills; and (3) the gap between academic programs and e-business needs. In conclusion, we propose a research agenda.

Introduction

In spite of recent economic slow down and dot-com failure, e-business continues to grow at a consistent rate. A 2002 projection by Forrester Research forecasts online retailing to grow at a cumulative annual growth rate of 25% to reach a sales volume of $217.8 billion by 2007 (Hirsh, 2002). Recent estimates of B2B transactions for 2003 stand close to $2.4 trillion, nearly doubling the 1999 Forester Research projection of $1.3 trillion by 2003 (Mullaney et al., 2003). In Europe, B2B e-commerce transactions have grown at an annual rate of 100%, reaching $200 billion in 2002, a fourfold increase from B2B transactions in 2000 (Reinhardt & Majidi, 2003). In China, the number of Internet users is expected to increase 1,184% by 2006 (Vinas, 2002). These figures affirm the continued growth of the Internet and e-business.

Global corporate adoption of Internet-based initiatives has accelerated the movement towards a tighter collaboration among companies along the industry value chains. By implementing integrated enterprise systems, partner firms aim to improve the quality of services and products, and the speed of market entry and penetration. These types of business relationships, established mainly for the improved customer experience, are called e-business webs (Kalakota & Robinson, 2001; Tapscott, Ticoll, & Lowy, 2000). The impact of the Internet has expanded from the initial phase of transaction-based e-commerce, to firm-based integration of Internet strategies, to industry-wide collaboration. Such transformation demands firms to undertake different approaches to managing information technology (IT) services and human resources.

Rapid advancement of information technology further complicates the difficulty of managing IT personnel. Researchers have advocated an IT skills portfolio approach to managing a firm's IT skills and developing appropriate strategies for meeting its changing needs (Nakayama & Sutcliffe, 2001). For companies transitioning towards an e-business environment, IT skills portfolio management has to go beyond the organizational boundaries to consider requirements imposed by the collaborating partners in e-business webs.

We propose to examine IT skills portfolio issues within the context of emerging e-business webs from a firm's perspective. Specifically, this chapter will: (a) identify the unique characteristics of e-business and its implications for firm-level IT skills portfolio management; (b) discuss specific skills requirements to support e-business transformation at five levels; (c) examine relevant trends affecting the dynamic nature of e-business IT skills management; and (d) propose research questions.

Background

The E-Business Environment

The Internet has a profound impact on companies. Industry-wide adoption of Internet-based business solutions has moved information systems beyond enterprises boundaries (Alter et al., 2001). These e-business initiatives have contributed to significant economic growth through cost reduction, process improvement, customer satisfaction, and increased profitability (Varian, Litan, Elder, & Shutter, 2002)

E-business, a major driving force in today's economy, is seen as the top concern among the 10 hottest issues of information technology (Kanter, 2003). Kalakota and Robinson (2001) define e-business as the "complex fusion of business processes, enterprise applications, and organizational structure necessary to create a high-performance business model" (p. *xx*). In the context of supply chain integration, e-business refers specifically to "the planning and the execution of the front-end and back-end operations in a supply chain using the Internet" (Lee & Whang, 2001, p. 2).

Firms seeking to leverage the full power of the Internet in conducting and growing their businesses need to transform themselves into e-business organizations. E-business transformation "requires dramatic changes in strategy, organization, process, and systems. It also involves rethinking the entire order fulfillment process, extending from customer to supplier, requiring significant changes in the way employees do work, and how a company organizes its supply chain and purchasing processes" (Neef, 2000).

For e-business organizations, intra- and inter-organizational processes and communications are managed through Internet-based enterprise systems. Enterprise systems include systems for enterprise resource planning (ERP), customer relationship management (CRM), supply chain management (SCM), e-procurement (EP), business intelligence (BI), and enterprise application integration (EAI). These systems make the enterprise-wide sharing of information much more effective and efficient. For example, e-procurement enables a firm to handle value chain management processes such as requisition, purchase order, invoice, and payment more efficiently through horizontal or vertical B2B e-hubs. Application service providers (ASPs) such as salesforce.com provide companies with sales force management software that can be leased and used through the Internet. Furthermore, ERP systems are no longer used only for integrating internal business functions. These systems can extend beyond enterprise boundaries to link to supplier, partner, and distributor firms' ERP systems for supply chain integration.

In today's e-business web environment, the customer is seen as the most critical driving force for organizational success. A satisfied customer is a loyal customer willing to return for repeat purchases. Customers are becoming increasingly intelligent in defining their expectation for the desired products and/or services, quality, price, and speed of delivery (Barua, Konana, Whinston, & Yin, 2001). As illustrated in Figure 1, in this "customer-centric web environment," suppliers, manufacturers, distributors, retailers, and transport-

Figure 1: Customer-Centric E-Business Web

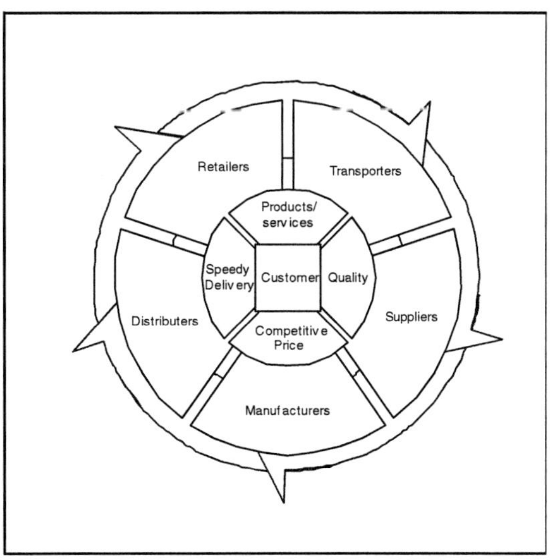

ers collaborate together in a continuous cycle towards satisfying the customer's need.

The e-business environment is characterized by the dynamic interactions among its member firms. As illustrated in Figure 2, a member firm in the e-business web environment may represent any player along the path of a given industry's supply chain. An e-business firm in such a dynamic environment may have most, or all, of its primary value chain activity systems, such as operations, logistics, marketing, and sales, virtually linked to systems of other members of the e-business web. A firm may also have most, or all, of its secondary value chain activity systems, such as administration, human resources, accounting, and procurement, run or administered by ASPs who are members of the e-business web environment. Therefore, firms interact with one another in a semi-borderless network through one-to-one and one-to-many direct relationships, or through consortia and online marketplaces.

Evolving business models and technologies affect the state of e-business and cause it to be in a constant state of change. One simple example of such new developments is what is known as Web services (Lim & Wen, 2003). Web services promise to provide a new technological solution where firms can search for and consume services provided by other firms, eliminating the need to develop those services internally. Such technology advancement creates

Figure 2: E-Business Dynamic Environment

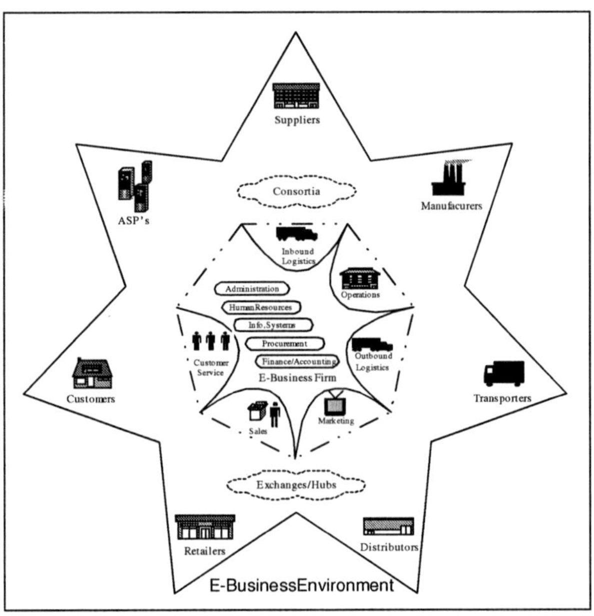

new demand on the IT staff responsible for running a firm's e-business technology infrastructure. It is a complex operation for them to meet different requirements of partners, suppliers, distributors, and customers. Additionally, they have to ensure the security of confidential data and organizational strategies in view of competitors' activities.

The e-business web environment poses many challenges for a firm's IT staff (Atler et al., 2001). In-house IS specialists have to shift their focus from building and maintaining internal systems to system integration. Increasingly, they have to provide IT support for both internal users and heterogeneous external customers. Systems that were traditionally developed and managed as internal resources are now increasingly being developed and managed as external resources. These changes imply that system developers need to acquire a better understanding about inter-organizational behavior and the value chain essential to an e-business web. Chan and Mirza (2003) have proposed a framework for identifying IT skill sets essential to e-business transformation. As shown in Table 1, companies need to acquire new IT

Table 1: A Proposed Framework for E-Business IT Skills Portfolio (Chan & Mirza, 2003)

Factors	*Issues*	*IT Skills Requirements*
Architecture	Application architecture; Distributed systems; Infrastructure architecture Collaboration; Information structuring & architecture	Internet/Web architecture; Application architecture; Network administration; Database management; Middleware; Security; Document management; Information management; Knowledge management; Technology planning; E-business strategy
Implementation	ERP and Web systems integration; Effective project management; Process change management; Enterprise systems; Integration of Web systems and enterprise systems	Systems integration; SCM, CRM, IM; Data warehousing, Data mining; Project management; Interpersonal skills; Process re-engineering
Organization Change	Process change driven by external demand; Permeable organizational boundaries; External users and consumers; E-collaboration	ERP, CRM, SCM; Change management; Human factors
Application Development	A shift of development efforts from simple Web development to analytic capability and system/application integration; Web-based interface design	Project management; E-business analysis; Structured programming methods; Web development and design; Object-oriented development; Data mining Human computer interaction; Workflow analysis; Domain knowledge
Tools and Technology	Wide-range of tools and technology; New tools and technology; Lack of standardization; Proper education and training	Unix, Linux, Windows; .Net technologies; CGI, Perl, C++, C#, ASP; PHP, SQL, MySQL, XML, Java, SOAP, UDDI, WSDL, ebXML

knowledge and skills in distributed systems architectures; prototyping in Web-based systems development; and business and systems integration, enterprise systems, integration of Web-based systems, and enterprise systems.

IT Skills Portfolio Management

Rapid technology advancement has made the shortage of IT skills a chronic problem for firms. For better control of a firm's IT human resources, Nakayama and Sutcliffe (2001) propose a skills portfolio approach to managing its IT skill needs. They emphasize that acquiring the right mix of skills is far more challenging than simply getting IT workers. Furthermore, firms are experiencing increasing difficulty in determining their optimal skills portfolio, and in acquiring and managing that portfolio in turbulent times. A two-year study by *CIO Magazine* (2002) attests to the difficulty of finding the right mix of skills, even in the time of economic slowdown and reduced demand on IT staff.

Nakayama and Sutcliffe (2001) define three managerial foci for IT skills portfolio management: skills acquisition, development, and maintenance. Skills acquisition addresses skills recruitment, building of skills inventory, and skills acquisition through outsourcing. Skills development considers determining desired skills requirements, designing and implementing skills enhancement plans at the firm level, designing programs to allow skills transfer, and developing a roles rotation process. Skills maintenance focuses on talents retention and updating skills.

The approach of IT skills portfolio management seems especially necessary for the more complex and dynamic e-business environment, as many variations exist between traditional IT and e-business implementations, teams, and management (Lientz & Rea, 2001).

IT Skills for E-Business

The shortage of appropriate IT skills may delay e-business transformation for many companies. Forrester Research (2000) indicates that, in one study, 31% of e-business groups were understaffed, and this staff shortage caused the delay of 41% of e-business projects. The latest study by the Information Technology Association of America (ITAA) indicates that demand for IT staff has reached an historic low of 493,000 jobs for the next 12 months, compared with 1.6 million jobs demand in 2000 and 1.1 million jobs demand in 2002 (ITAA, 2003).

Based on a series of surveys conducted by *CIO Magazine* (2002), IT managers have found that the difficulty of IT hiring and retention has eased since 2000. However, in mid-2002, 56% of the IT executives surveyed agreed that they're still experiencing a skills crisis, having difficulty matching available skill sets with their companies' IT needs. But only 2% of the respondents noted staffing crisis. ITAA studies (2000, 2001, 2002) also reveal that IT positions remained unfilled at a constant rate of 50% over the last three years due to the lack of qualified workers. These results, combined with the declining demand of IT workforce, indicate that a gap exists between available skills sets and desired skills sets. Rapid technological advancement contributes to this gap. Recent Internet boom renders older skills obsolete and increases the difficulty in finding and keeping the newer skills (Agarwal & Ferratt, 2002; Tiwana & McClean, 2002).

Most companies are under pressure to leverage enterprise systems for forging a greater role in the e-business environment (Bartol et al., 2002). Enterprise systems, such as CRM, SCM, and ERP, now capture a larger share of IT budget than they did in prior years. Companies are seeking IT skills that support e-business initiatives such as supplier-facing extranets, customer-facing Web-based applications, and collaboration on industry exchanges and marketplaces (Goff, 2000a). However, many of these skills are in short supply. Most companies have to retrain their current IT staff to support CRM systems, data warehousing, data mining, e-commerce applications development, Internet applications development, and ERP. The continued growth of e-business requires a company to pay closer attention to its e-business IT skills portfolio. A capable IT staff is essential to the transformation and integration of legacy and enterprise applications into viable e-business solutions.

In early 2000, skills most in demand included application development, networking, Internet development, e-commerce, and data mining (Goff, 2000b). The *CIO Magazine* 2002 survey reports that the in-demand IT skills were application development (53% of respondents), project management (50%), database management (47%), and networking (48%). These four IT skills have remained the "most in-demand" over the two-year period between November 2000 and July 2002 (*CIO Magazine,* 2002).

As IT roles are changing at an increasingly rapid pace, technical skills alone are insufficient for enabling e-business transformation. Based on a multi-company case study by Bailey and Stefaniak (2000), it is increasingly important for an

IT staff to possess both soft skills and business skills. Soft skills include communication, problem solving, adaptability to new technology, and teamwork. Business skills include understanding the customer mentality, investigative skills for asking probing questions, idea initiation, and project management.

Process redesign and change management are critical to successful implementation of enterprise systems. The Electronic Commerce (EC) Institute (2001) has defined a body of knowledge for e-business. This knowledge base encompasses skills for managing business transformation, process reengineering, integration, and relationship management. In-house skills in these areas are often in short supply. The demand for integrated enterprise applications and collaboration systems implies that companies will need more IT talents with solid foundation in project management, systems integration, and change management.

The above section highlights some of the challenges created by the e-business web environment. One main challenge is the difficulty in managing and operating a wide-range of inter-connected enterprise systems across the e-business web. Another challenge is the shortage in e-business skills for supporting the evolving organizational relationships, tools, and technologies. Thirdly, companies are facing the challenge of proper IT skills portfolio management for member-organizations of an e-business web environment. In the following section, we analyze these challenges from a firm's interactions with its e-business web environment at five levels.

Five Levels of Challenges

Firms transitioning towards an e-business environment are facing five levels of challenges in managing IT skills. These five levels of challenges are: strategy, architecture, systems, project, and tools and technology (see Figure 3). Challenges present in each level are influenced by the e-business environment and will demand special strategies for IT skills portfolio management with regard to skills acquisition, development, and maintenance.

Table 2 presents an overview of these five levels of challenges as related to e-business IT skills portfolio management. At each level of challenge, we propose a set of skills, critical for the success of the e-business web firm. The ensuing discussion analyzes issues pertaining to each level of challenges.

Figure 3: Levels of Challenges for an E-Business Firm

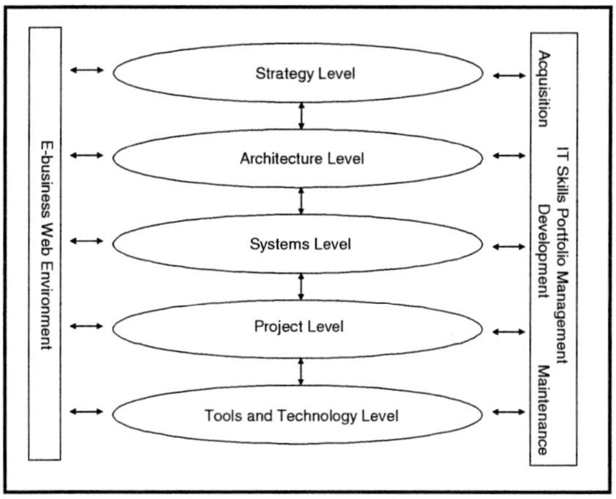

Table 2: Necessary Skills per Level of Challenge

Levels of Challenges	*Necessary Skills*
Strategy	Strategic planning. Leadership, governance, and decision making. Knowledge about technology. Understanding of e-business webs complexity.
Architecture	Architecture knowledge as part of IT planning skills. Distributed systems knowledge. Application architecture and systems integration. Knowledge about technology standards.
Systems	Deep knowledge in business process (intra- and inter-organizational processes). Technical knowledge in systems integration. Vendor and product knowledge. Application architecture.
Projects	Deep knowledge in process related to industry value chain. Deep knowledge in inter-department process. Change management. Web-based system development. Integration of legacy systems, enterprise systems, and Web-based systems. Project management. Interpersonal and communications skills.
Tools and Technology	Multiple operating systems. Wireless. Web services. XML; Java. DBMS and networks. Client-side programming tools; Server-side programming tools.

The Strategy Level

A well-defined strategy is critical to the success of any e-business firm. Pinker, Seidmann, and Foster (2002) stress the idea that, without a sound e-business strategy, any firm venturing in this arena is at a serious disadvantage. Evans (2001) states that a "business vision is vitally necessary for developing an e-business strategy because the structure and components of this strategy determine where the business is today and where the business will be in the future." Becoming an e-business is a major decision for any organization. Strategic planning for developing a vision of the firm's future is the responsibility of upper level management, most specifically the CEO of the firm.

A CEO is not only responsible for developing an e-business strategy, but must also champion such a strategy. Executive leadership is considered a critical success factor for developing a firm's e-business strategy (Viehland, 2000). Typical executives do not have the strong technological background to understand their implications on the business. In order to succeed, however, these executives need to understand modern technological developments, and their implications on the firm and the industry in general. A CEO who champions an e-business transformation will see to it that all the necessary resources for the success of e-business operations are provided.

Of main concern here is what an e-business strategy offers when it comes to IT skills portfolio management. One possible step in the right direction is the institution of a specialized chief e-commerce officer (CeCO) position (Pinker et al., 2002), or a chief e-business officer (CeBO). Many organizations have developed similar positions with varying titles. A major role of this person is in the formulation and implementation of a firm's e-business strategy. Several organizations used the CIO as the CeBO. Nevertheless, it may be more appropriate to fill the CeBO position with a different individual. A CIO is typically more attuned to the internal needs of the organization, with a traditional operations mindset, and following traditional means of IT workforce acquisition, development, and maintenance. A CeBO, on the other hand, expected to have both internal and external focus, with transformational goals, may approach IT skills management issues more effectively in accordance with the dynamic IT workforce market.

Whether a CeBO position has been created in a firm or not, successful development and management of an IT skills portfolio depends greatly on upper management policies and strategy. An e-business IT staff should be viewed as a strategic advantage that needs to be nourished and maintained. In the new e-business web environment, IT talent can easily be lost to competitors if not given proper attention and resources. Skills retention could be accomplished through the application of several retention practices, including competitive salaries and benefits, skills development through training or continued education, and other job perks such as telecommuting (Gill & Pidduck, 2001).

Additionally, upper management must invest sufficiently in acquiring critical IT skills. Settling for second best, or trying to simply bring the skill level of current staff to accomplish more advanced jobs, a firm may be missing great business opportunities. On other occasions, it may be more logical to outsource certain jobs. This requires that upper management understand values added through outsourcing in the long run, in spite of apparent high cost associated with it (Rozwell & Krammer, 2001).

Furthermore, upper management must recognize the difference between an IT culture within a traditional business and that of an e-business. In an e-business firm, the IT staff needs to collaborate with other firms' IT teams. Those firms could have been recent competitors. Interactions among various IT staffs may pose threats to some firms. Such relationships require trust and capable management. Experience of collaboration with other partner firms could be emphasized as a skills development and retention mechanism rather than a threat.

In short, at the strategic level, IT skills essential to an e-business include:

- strategic planning,
- leadership,
- decision making,
- knowledge about technology, and
- understanding of e-business webs' complexity.

The Architecture Level

A firm's technology architecture typically includes computer networks (intranets and extranets), legacy systems running on a mainframe, client/server systems running newer types of applications, database management systems (DBMSs), decision support systems (DSSs), data warehousing, and ERP systems. A firm's e-business architecture also emphasizes integration of enterprise systems for SCM, customer CRM, e-procurement, and EAI with ERP as the backbone. Beyond the enterprise boundaries, the e-business architecture supports interactions with trading partners and customers through public and private e-marketplaces and transaction-based online retail sites.

An efficient architectural design is critical for a firm to perform effectively in an e-business web environment. In the 1990s, many organizations failed to achieve the desired benefits of integrating systems and applications through ERP systems (Krasner, 2000), thus unable to create architecture to support data sharing. E-business architecture is much more complex to manage since it is not limited to inward facing systems. Customers and suppliers are granted access to a firm's enterprise systems. Additionally, e-business architecture includes partner systems not controlled by the firm. EAI packages try to integrate internal enterprise systems with external systems. However, this is a very complex proposition considering the large number of systems and applications that need integration (Lee, Siau, & Hong, 2003).

For the e-business IT staff, different skills are required for dealing with such complex application and technology architecture than those required in a traditional IT environment. E-business webs link tens, hundreds, and even thousands of customer and supplier firms (Laudon & Traver, 2001). Different customer firms' systems may impose different data and interface requirements. Access to supplier systems may also need special applications and programming. This complexity poses great challenges to a firm's IT staff and its capability for information management (Mendonca, 2003).

In short, IT staff must possess the following skills to handle the complexity of e-business architecture:

- architecture knowledge as part of IT planning skills,
- distributed systems knowledge,
- application architecture and systems integration, and
- knowledge about technology standards.

The Systems Level

At the systems level of an e-business are the different enterprise applications such as data warehousing, ERP, SCM, CRM, BI, e-procurement, and EAI. Some of these systems extend beyond the enterprise boundary to facilitate collaboration across the supply chain. These systems are normally supported by a number of different vendors. Vendor applications typically offer generic solutions that require fine-tuning, customization, and integration with other applications and/or legacy systems within the enterprise. Different vendor solutions use different standards of development and, hence, each new application requires a new set of skills.

The greatest challenges facing an e-business IT workforce with regard to enterprise systems are those concerning inter-organization systems. SCM and CRM systems allow suppliers and customers to access a firm's enterprise systems. EAI systems tie a firm's ERP with supplier and partner ERP systems.

Therefore, an e-business firm needs to acquire the following IT skills for handling challenges at the systems level:

- deep knowledge in business process (intra- and inter-organizational processes),
- technical knowledge in systems integration,
- vendor and product knowledge, and
- application architecture.

The Project Level

E-business project implementation differs from traditional IT project implementation. Lientz and Rea (2001) identify 12 different characteristics that distinguish between e-business project management and traditional project management. These differences stem from the dynamic nature of e-business projects themselves and the nature of the e-business web environment.

E-business projects at the intra-organizational level typically are not well defined. Requirements change at a very fast pace, and the development period is expected to be very short. These characteristics represent conflicting objectives. Having to complete a project in a short period when requirements are not clear at the onset of the project can cause great confusion in the implementation process. Project management must be able to quickly define a clear end-result and work towards achieving it. Internal e-business projects typically involve many different divisions within the firm, some of which may be at dispersed locations. The complexity in project coordination increases when different divisions need to agree on the desired project results. Furthermore, a firm's employees may receive internal e-business projects with resentment. They may see the new project as a threat to their own positions in the firm, and hence, may be reluctant to cooperate fully.

For inter-organization projects, the challenges for project implementation are more complex. IT staff must deal with technical and non-technical personnel of partner firms. A manager in this type of projects typically has little control over what goes on in the partner firms. Therefore, it is difficult to manage cross-boundary projects. Participating organizations must have the same level of understanding about a project's objectives, requirements, and benefits. Failure to maintain close interactions and continuous communications may lead to wasted efforts and resources. Communication and interpersonal skills are highly important in these types of projects.

The state of IT staffing also affects the implementation of an e-business project. An e-business IT staff often has to concurrently support traditional systems and e-business projects (Agarwal & Ferratt, 2002). Companies have to confront the lack of skilled workforce by staffing e-business teams with outsourced consultants or freelancers possibly working from remote locations. Gomolski (2001) indicates that for a typical e-business IT project team, 50% will come from outside resources. This staffing pattern definitely creates a project management nightmare. Developing project management skills for such situations becomes a necessity.

Skill sets essential to the successful implementation of e-business projects include:

- deep knowledge in process related to industry value chain;
- deep knowledge in inter-department process;
- change management;
- Web-based system development;
- integration of legacy systems, enterprise systems, and Web-based systems;
- project management; and
- interpersonal and communications skills.

The Tools and Technology Level

The accelerated pace of technology advancement exacerbates a firm's capability to manage IT human resources. It has become a norm that, almost every year, a new "hot" technological development is introduced promising to solve most problems of previous tools or technologies. New applications and business models may also arise out of these new developments. Operating system wars continue to wage on, with both Windows and Linux trying to grab a larger share of the market. Enterprise systems are continuously upgraded as support for older versions soon expires. Lack of standards on many programming languages and technologies, such as wireless, increase the complexity of systems development. Functional codes often need to be re-written several times to run correctly on different vendor applications. A simple case in point is the difference between Internet Explorer and Netscape Navigator Web browsers.

Back at the e-business firm, collaborative systems and the desire for greater integration with partner, supplier, and customer systems demand advanced skills for IT tools and technology. Familiarity with a diverse range of vendor tools and technologies may be necessary to work effectively with other firms. Rejecting the adaptation of a certain vendor tool or technology may not be a productive option.

How can an e-business firm prepare for new tools and technologies imposed by partner firms? How can a firm determine if a new technological development is worth investing in skills development? Waiting to adopt a new technology when it matures may leave the firm at a disadvantage. By the time the staff is brought up to speed, it is time for a new technology, leaving the now "old" technology of a year or two ago behind.

These issues cause serious problems for most e-business firms. Several technologies, such as HTML, Java, and XML, have been widely adopted and have remained as viable e-business development tools (Smith, 2001). However, even with these popular tools, some vendors insist on developing varying versions that do not adhere to standardization efforts.

Based on our review of skills in demand discussed earlier in the chapter and of industry trends, skills that are valuable for the next few years include:

- multiple operating systems,
- wireless,
- Web services,
- XML,
- Java,
- DBMS,
- networks,

- client-side programming tools, and
- server-side programming tools.

Future Trends

The rapid pace of change in IT led by increased vendor competition has caused poor quality in application development, incompatibility, and management confusion within a firm (Benamati & Lederer, 2001). Technology changes heighten the demand for IT skills training. CIOs are also struggling to find and retain skilled employees (Santosus, 2002). Dynamic and complicated inter-organizational collaboration, combined with ever-evolving technologies and shortage of skills, makes it necessary for firms to take an approach of skills portfolio management. In this section we examine five trends related to an e-business firms' IT skills portfolio management. These trends are: the changing landscapes of IT skills, skills acquisition, skills development, skills retention, and the gap between academic programs and industry needs.

A Changing Landscape of IT Skills

E-business has introduced many changes in a firm's IT skills requirements. These changes span the firm's upper management and the IT workforce, starting at the CIO level and reaching all the way down to the analyst, programmer, and quality assurance levels.

A CEO needs to have a solid understanding of a firm's IT resources and how to leverage those resources for strategic advancement. New executive positions, such as chief e-business officer (CeBO), chief knowledge officer (CKO) (Herschel & Nemati, 1999), and chief algorithm officer (CAO) (Kane, 2002), have been introduced to support new e-business functions. These technology-savvy executives shall play an influential role in driving e-business transformation and the strategic use of IT resources.

The integration of enterprise systems globally and across organizational boundaries requires a firm to possess skills of systems architecture, distributed systems, systems integration, and change management. E-business also demands IT talents with knowledge of multiple enterprise systems and business processes.

The external interactions with partner firms' systems increase the requirements of business and soft skills of an IT staff. The ability to communicate well with other firms' IT staff is critical to achieving the desired goals and objectives of e-business web relationships. IT teams, as a result of the distributed development and collaborative environments, must be able to effectively work together in a way that is previously unfamiliar to them.

However, obsolete and legacy systems remain and demand old skills to support continued operation and maintenance of these systems (McKeen & Smith, 2002). A firm's existing IT personnel may have to be trained to support new technology while maintaining legacy systems. Placing too much pressure on a firm's IT staff may lead to burnout and loss of key IT staff (Huarng, 2001).

E-Business IT Skills Portfolio Management

Such changes in the landscape of IT skills make a skills portfolio approach critically important during e-business transformation. The ensuing discussion will examine trends affecting IT skills acquisition, development, and retention. A checklist of required skills and proposed activities for IT skills acquisition, development, and maintenance is provided in Appendix 1.

IT Skills Acquisitions

An e-business places a high demand for IT skills in systems architecture, systems integration, distributed systems, and change management. For a firm to succeed in the dynamic environment of e-business webs, it must strategically plan for the acquisition of those skills as part of a comprehensive plan for skills portfolio management.

Acquisition of skills for e-business may be accomplished through different means. The most obvious method is through training current IT staff. Offering training in new technologies, tools, and techniques, as well as rotating IT staff across jobs and technologies, are considered among the most attractive personnel retention practices (Agarwal & Ferratt, 2002). However, many newly skilled IT e-business experts soon flee for higher-paying jobs (Gomolski, 2001). To avoid such occurrences, e-business IT staff may be trained in specific skills through one- or two-week intensive courses rather than training for specific roles.

For certain e-business projects that require years of experience, which may not be easily attained through short-term training, hiring of skilled IT staff is necessary. This requires the firm to be willing and capable of offering attractive compensation packages to recruit expert IT workers.

In other cases, a firm may manage its strategic skills portfolio by acquiring a specific level of expertise on a part-time or temporary basis to complete short-term tasks. According to Gomolski (2001), half of a firm's e-business expertise will come from external resources. These may include "former employees, freelancers, interns, retired employees, and those seeking part-time or seasonal work," as well as outsourcing service providers. Even though the use of outsourced IT staff may help accomplish the desired tasks, this approach is costly and generates no immediate benefit in the development of a firm's internal IT skills.

Certain e-business projects may be accomplished through teams assembled from different partner organizations. This type of effort requires strong trust between participating firms, and the IT staff's ability to communicate and collaborate across organizational boundaries.

Increasing cost pressure and the need for business agility has motivated many companies to seek offshore outsourcing as an alternative means of meeting their IT skills requirements. It is likely that more than 80% of U.S. companies will explore this option of IT services, and 40% will engage in pilot initiatives in the coming years (Thibodeau, 2003). Industry projections suggest that offshore outsourcing will focus initially on low-end "commodity" work, such as legacy application maintenance, ERP enhancement, and help desks. Increasingly, companies may also use offshore services for project-based work in Web services and in enterprise application integration and implementation (Morello, 2003). The ITAA 2003 survey finds programming and software engineering jobs are most likely to go overseas (67%), followed by network design (37%) and Web development (30 %) (ITAA, 2003). These findings suggest that the offshore development trend is both real and expanding to more sophisticated, value-added jobs. This trend presents opportunities for firms to acquire skills economically, but also creates difficulty for maintaining staff morale and talents.

Skills acquisition includes the activities of recruiting for skills, building skills inventory, and outsourcing for skills (Nakayama & Sutcliffe, 2001). In addition, IT managers need to determine desired talent profiles, retool existing IT skills, determine the effectiveness and impacts of skills outsourcing, and determine the effectiveness of various compensation methods based on skills. The choice of skills acquisition activities should support an e-business firm's strategies, requirements, and goals. Appendix 1 includes a checklist of required skills per level of challenge and the activities for acquiring those skills.

IT Skills Development

The development of requisite skills for e-business transformation should be determined by a firm's strategic plan for IT skills portfolio management. The first step is to determine the required skill sets. This initial step is critical and should address both short-term and long-term skill requirements, as well as different levels of challenges.

Skills development involves activities for determining the desired skills portfolio, designing and implementing skills enhancement plans at the firm level, designing programs to allow skills transfer, and developing a roles rotation process (Nakayama & Sutcliffe, 2001). As shown in Appendix 1, it is also important to consider skills measurement and evaluation, commonalities and heterogeneities among different skills, the impact of job/position rotation, and the effectiveness of different skills development activities. Skills development activities include internal training, education, self-study, on-the-job training (OJT), and industry certification (IC).

IT Skills Maintenance

Skills maintenance consists of talent retention through different retention methods such as benefits, compensation, work conditions, and the updating of skills (Nakayama & Sutcliffe, 2001). IT managers should also evaluate the use of skill sets, factors for retaining talent, needs for skill updates, and the effectiveness of training methods.

Maintaining IT talents is essential to an IT skills portfolio management plan. The dynamic nature of the e-business web creates an attractive work environment for skilled IT professionals to move about, especially since firms collaborate closely and their individual environments are exposed to employees of other firms. E-business firms are hence subject to a high rate of employee turnover and must take the necessary measures to reduce the IT staff's need to seek alternative jobs. Hacker (2003) considers IT staff turnover to be the silent profit killer of an organization.

Agarwal and Ferratt (2002) have conducted a study of 32 organizations on their retention practices of IT professionals. They identify 11 categories of retention practices and 32 detailed practices. The categories are: compensation and benefit systems, employability training and development, sense of community, work arrangements, quality of leadership, performance measurement, opportunities for recognition, opportunities for advancement, lifestyle accommodations, longer-term career development, organizational stability, and employment security. Some of these categories represent qualitative factors, while others are more action oriented. Appendix 1 incorporates a checklist of required IT skills with corresponding maintenance activities.

Gap Between Academic Programs and E-Business Needs

The shift in the marketplace presents new pressures on the academy. Fast-paced technology and business evolution dictates that IS and EC curricula must closely follow the application of technology in business and industry (Augustine, Surynt, & Jeancola, 2002). Universities also need to undertake continuous curricular innovation in order to meet the demand of changing e-business needs (Chan, 2001). Two trends are emerging. E-business transformation requires advanced skills in architecture, systems integration, collaborative systems development, and complex business processes. Offshore outsourcing will reduce the demand on traditional IT jobs in programming, systems development, ERP maintenance, and technology support. These two trends combined will have significant implications for academic programs.

What do academic programs currently teach? A study by White, Steinbach, and Knight (2003) reveals that technical graduate e-commerce programs give business education equal importance to technical education in the category of essential courses. However, the same cannot be said about graduate e-commerce programs in business schools, where the greatest emphasis is placed on business education, with a 2.5-to-1 ratio favoring business courses. Courses in networking, project course, and marketing were found to be most essential in both graduate and undergraduate technical e-commerce programs. Surprisingly, courses in database and server-side Web application development were found less essential, being offered at only 58% and 50%, respectively, of technical graduate e-commerce programs. This represents a gap between what the industry needs and what educational institutions see as important.

A study by Lomerson and Schwager (2002) has identified the most popular technical courses on e-commerce technologies taught in IS programs. On the client-side technologies, using a six-point scale to indicate degree of coverage, website design (average = 3.3), XML (3.3), Web design tools (3.0), and JavaScript (3.0) have received more attention than HTML (2.7), DHTML (2.5), and CSS (2.5). On the server side, the most frequently covered technologies are SQL (3.4), Active Server Pages (3), Java (3), ODBC (2.8), Apache (2.6), Unix/Linux (2.6), PHP (2.6), and Java Server Pages (2.6). These findings suggest that most academic programs only cover basic Web development skills and technologies. Students are not prepared to address advanced technologies and systems development.

Researchers and educators have voiced the importance to expand curricular offerings in systems integration (Chan, 2001) and enterprise systems beyond ERP (Lederer-Antonucci et al., 2003). Students need to develop a solid understanding of strategies and processes as well as technology know-how. Nevertheless, the majority of IS and e-commerce programs only address the business side of these complex e-business developments. These educational programs need to continuously monitor and understand the changing requirements of e-business firms. In the fast and dynamic e-business web environment, review and assessment of curriculums must be done almost on a yearly basis.

Efforts to bridge the gap were taken by the EC Institute, which recently initiated a project aiming to determine the body of knowledge for e-business (EC Institute, 2001). The resulting document provides a comprehensive list of topics and skill sets aimed for certification of the e-business professional.

Conclusion

In this chapter we have introduced the emerging e-business web environment, and described its dynamic nature and impact on the IT skills portfolio of e-business firms. IT managers are faced with five levels of challenges (strategy, architecture, systems, projects, and tools and technology) to which proper skills portfolio management is necessary. By implementing IT skills portfolio management activities of skills acquisition, development, and maintenance, we believe that a firm will have a better grasp of its e-business operations and IT human resources. The checklist of activities, as summarized in Appendix 1, may serve as a guide for managing IT skills required for e-business firms.

In conclusion, we recommend further studies to verify our proposed levels of challenges and their associated skills. It is also important to determine the most

Table 3: Research Questions Regarding IT Skills Portfolio Management Practices

Level	*Skills Acquisition*	*Skills Development*	*Skills Maintenance*
Strategy	- What efforts are taken to attain strategic e-business IT know-how? - Is upper management playing a leadership role in e-business decisions? - What new positions are created to support e-business strategies?	- Is upper management being educated on e-business technology and benefits? - What skills development strategies are planned or used?	- What is being done to update IT management skills with e-business skills? - What is being done to keep e-business IT management on board?
Architecture	- How are architecture skills acquired?	- What architecture skills are required? - What measures are taken to develop architecture skills?	- What measures are taken to update and maintain architecture skills?
Systems	- How are systems skills acquired?	- What systems skills are required? - Which activities are conducted to develop systems skills?	- What measures are taken to update and maintain systems skills?
Project	- How are project skills acquired?	- What project skills are required? - Which activities are conducted to develop projects skills?	- What measures are taken to update and maintain project skills?
Tools and Technology	- How are tools and technology skills acquired?	- What tools and technology skills are required? -Which activities are conducted to develop tools and technology skills?	- What measures are taken to update and maintain tools and technology skills?

effective activities for the acquisition, development, and maintenance of e-business IT skills. How a firm's skills portfolio changes during e-business transformation will merit a close look. A list of possible research questions on skills acquisition, development, and maintenance is presented in Table 3.

References

Agarwal, R., & Ferratt T. W. (2002). Enduring practices for managing IT professionals. *Communications of the ACM, 45*(9), 73-79.

Alter, S., Ein-Dor, P., Markus, M.L., Scott, J., and Vessey, I. (2001). Does the trend toward e-business call for changes in the fundamental concepts of information systems? A debate. *Communications of the Association for Information Systems, 5*(10).

Augustine, F., Surynt, T., & Jeancola, M. (2002). Implementing an e-business curriculum: Opportunities and issues, issues and trends of information technology management in contemporary organizations. *Proceedings of the 2002 IRMA International Conference* (pp. 179-181).

Bailey, J. & Stefaniak, G. (2000). Preparing the information technology workforce for the new millennium. *Proceedings of ACM SIGCPR 2000 Conference* (pp. 1-7).

Bartol, K., Williamson, I., Venkatesh, V., and Liu, W. (2002). A study of entry-level information technology workers: Employee expectations and job perceptions. *Proceedings of the 23rd International Conference on Information Systems* (pp. 797-801).

Barua, A., Konana, P., Whinston, A., & Yin, F. (2001). Driving e-business excellence. *MIT Sloan Management Review, 43*(1), 36-44.

Benamati, J., & Lederer, A. (2001). The effect of rapid IT change on the demand for training. *Proceedings of the 2001 ACM SIGCPR Conference* (pp. 37-47).

Chan, S. (2001). Challenges and opportunities in e-commerce education. *Proceedings of the 7th AMCIS Conference* (pp. 1-7).

Chan, S.S., & Mirza, A.A. (2003). Towards defining IT skills portfolio for e-business. *Proceedings of the 2003 Information Resources Management Association (IRMA) International Conference* (pp. 63-65).

CIO Magazine. (2002). Mid-2002 IT staffing update. *CIO Magazine*, (August 5). Accessed online at: http://www2.cio.com/research/surveyreport.cfm?id=8.

EC Institute. (2001). *The EC Institute body of knowledge for electronic commerce.* Accessed online at: http://www.ecinstitute.org/ecinstitute/education.htm.

Evans, C. (2001). An e-strategy for online e-business. *Information Systems Management, 18*(4), 8-21.

Forrester Research. (2000). *Pumping up internal eBusiness talent.*

Gill, B., & Pidduck, A. B. (2001). IT staffing and retention: A success story. *Proceedings of the 2001 ACM SIGCPR Conference* (pp. 97-92).

Goff, L. (2000a). ComputerWorld's 7th annual skills survey: The skills that thrill. *Computerworld, 34*(49), 54-59. Accessed online at: http://www.computerworld.com/careertopics/careers/story/0,10801,54596,00.html.

Goff, L. (2000b). The e-lusive staff: Computerworld's 4th annual hiring forecast. *Computerworld, 34*(1), 90-93.

Gomolski, B. (2001). *Assembling e-business skills at wrap speed.* Gartner. COM-13-2614.

Hacker, C. (2003). Turnover: A silent profit killer. *Information Systems Management, 20*(2), 14-18.

Herschel, R., & Nemati, H. (1999). CKOs and knowledge management: Exploring opportunities for using information exchange protocols. *Proceedings of the 1999 ACM SIGCPR Conference* (pp. 42-50).

Hirsh, L. (2002). E-commerce: A better Q3? *E-Commerce Times.* Accessed January 8, 2003, from: http://www.ecommercetimes.com/per/story/19301.html.

Huarng, A. (2001). Burnout syndrome among information system professionals. *Information Systems Management, 18*(2), 15-20.

Information Technology Association of America (ITAA). (2000). *Bridging the gap: Information technology skills for a new millennium.*

Information Technology Association of America (ITAA). (2001). *When can you start? Building better information technology skills and careers.* City, Country.

Information Technology Association of America (ITAA). (2002). *Bouncing back: Jobs, skills and the continuing demand for IT workers.* City, Country.

Information Technology Association of America (ITAA). (2003). *ITAA 2003 workforce survey.* City, Country.

Kalakota, R., & Robinson, M. (2001). *E-business 2.0: Roadmap for success.* City: Addison-Wesley.

Kane, M. (2002). Amazon hires algorithm guru. *CNET News.com,* (November 8). Accessed online at: http://rss.com.com/21001017965068.html?type=pt%E2%88%82=rss&tag=feed&subj=news.

Kanter, J. (2003). Ten hot information technology (IT) issues and what makes them hot. *Information Strategy: The Executive's Journal, 19*(3), 23-36.

Krasner, H. (2000). Ensuring e-business success by learning from ERP failure. *IT Pro, 2*(1), 22-27.

Laudon, K., & Traver, C. (2001). *E-commerce: Business, technology, society.* Addison-Wesley.

Lederer-Antonucci, Y., Muehlen, M., Shoemaker, M., Wagner, W., Steward, G., and Kirchmer, M. (2003). Beyond enterprise systems curricula: Perspectives on the integration of next generation ERP technologies into curricula. *Proceedings of the 2003 Information Resources Management Association (IRMA) International Conference* (p. 1181).

Lee, H., & Whang, S. (2001). E-business and supply chain integration. *Proceedings of the Stanford Global Supply Chain Management Forum.* Available online at: http://www.stanford.edu/group/scforum/Welcome/EB_SCI.pdf.

Lee, J., Siau, K., & Hong, S. (2003). Enterprise integration with ERP and EAI. *Communications of the ACM, 46*(2), 54-60.

Lientz, B., & Rea, K. (2001). *Dynamic e-business implementation management: How to effectively manage e-business implementation.* City: Academic Press.

Lim, B., & Wen, J. (2003). Web services: An analysis of the technology, its benefits, and implementation difficulties. *Information Systems Management, 20*(2), 49-57.

Lomerson, W., & Schwager, P. (2002). Technical foundations of e-commerce curriculums: An exploration of the importance, content, and extent of topics. *Proceedings of the 2002 Americas Conference on Information Systems* (pp. 816-824).

McKeen, J., & Smith, H. (2002). New developments in practice IV: Managing the technology portfolio. *Communications of the Association of Information Systems, 9,* 77-89.

Mendonca, J. (2003). Change and challenge: The impact of e-business from an organizational management perspective. *Proceedings of the 2003 IRMA International Conference* (pp. 420-423).

Morello, D. (2003). *CIO alert: 2003 offshore outsourcing predictions focus on impact to the IT profession.* Gartner. IGG-01012003-03.

Mullaney, T., Green, H., Arndt, M., Hof, R., & Himelstein, L. (2003). The e-biz surprise. *BusinessWeek Online,* (May 12). Accessed online at: http://www.businessweek.com.

Nakayama, M., & Sutcliffe, N. (2001). Skills portfolio management for information systems professionals: Managerial issues and research topics. *Proceedings of the 2001 Americas Conference on Information Systems* (pp. 1917-1921).

Neef, D. (2000). Hiring and e-team. *Journal of Business Strategy, 21*(6), 17-21.

Niederman, F., & Sumner, M. (2001). Job turnover among MIS professionals: An exploratory study of employee turnover. *Proceedings of the 2001 SIGCPR Conference* (pp. 11-17).

Pinker, E.J., Seidmann, A., & Foster, R.C. (2002). Strategies for transitioning 'old economy' firms to e-business. *Communications of the ACM, 45*(5), 77-83.

Reinhardt, A., & Majidi, N. (2003). Europe's borderless market: The net. *BusinessWeek Online,* (May 12). Accessed online at: http://www.businessweek.com.

Rozwell, C., & Krammer, M. (2001). *Advice to the e-business czar: Consultants can help.* Gartner. TG-13-0814.

Santosus, M. (2002). Loyalty, shmoyalty. *CIO Magazine, 15*(13), 40.

Shuman, J., Twombly, J., & Rottenberg, D. (2001). *Collaborative communities: Partnering for profit in the networked economy.* City: Dearborn Financial Publishing.

Smith, R. (2001). Trends in e-business technologies. *IBM Systems Journal, 40*(1), 4-7.

Tapscott, D., Ticoll, D., & Lowy, A. (2000). The rise of business webs. *Ubiquity, 1*(3), Article 2.

Thibodeau, P. (2003). Offshore outsourcing is relentless. *Computerworld,* (June 27).

Tiwana, A., & McLean, E. (2002). Knowledge integration and individual expertise development in e-business project teams: From the pod to the peas. *Proceedings of the 2002 ACM SIGCPR Conference* (pp. 120-123).

Varian, H., Litan, R., Elder, A., & Shutter, J. (2002). *The Net impact study: The projected economic benefits of the Internet in the United States, United Kingdom, France and Germany.* Accessed July 10, 2003, from: http://www.netimpactstudy.com.

Viehland, D. (2000). Critical success factors for developing an e-business strategy. *Proceedings of the 2000 Americas Conference on Information Systems* (pp. 10-13).

Vinas, T. (2002). China embraces the Internet. *Industry Week, 251*(5), 11-12.

White, J., Steinbach, T., & Knight, L. (2003). E-commerce curriculum: After the fall. *Proceedings of the 2003 Information Resources Management Association (IRMA) International Conference* (pp. 611-614).

Appendix I: IT Skills and Portfolio Management Activities Checklist

Levels of Challenge	Skills Sets	Skills Acquisition Activities			Skills Development Activities					Skills Maintenance Activities				
		Recruiting	Building	Outsourcing	Internal Training	Education	Self-Study	OJT	IC	Compensation & benefits	Training & Development	Work Arrangements	Performance Measurement	Recognition & Advancement
Strategy	Strategic planning													
	Leadership													
	Decision making													
	Knowledge about technology													
	Understanding of e-business web complexity													
Architecture	Architecture knowledge													
	Distributed systems													
	Application architecture and systems integration													
	Technology standards													
Systems	Business process (internal and inter-firm)													
	Systems integration													
	Vendor/product knowledge													
	Application architecture													
Project	Industry value chain process													
	Inter-departmental process													
	Change management													
	Web-based systems development													
	Systems integration													
	Project management													
	Interpersonal and communications skills													
Tools and Technology	Multiple Operating systems													
	Wireless													
	Web services													
	XML													
	Java													
	DBMS													
	Networks													
	Client-side programming tools													
	Server-side programming tools													

Chapter IV

Skills and the Worker: Let's Get Real

Elizabeth Lahey
Elizabeth Lahey and Associates, USA

Abstract

Technology professionals have real lives, interests, and desires that are affected by rapid changes in the industry. With the decline of the "Organization Man" model, workers are now expected to maintain their skills and manage their careers without employers' help. With skills that rapidly become obsolete, technologists must prepare continuously for the future. Yet, to maximize the utility of new skills, they cannot prepare too far ahead. This reality creates a dilemma for skills portfolio development. The TechCareer Compass® (TCC) website was designed to solve the problem. The sponsors are industry-leading firms, so workers know the skills portfolio and career information is accurate and reliable.

Introduction

The information and communications technology (ICT) industry gestated in a business environment that supported lifetime employment. When young employees entered a company, they took entry-level jobs with decent pay and excellent benefits, with the expectation of continuous growth and development until retirement at age 65.

Changes in skills or knowledge needed to perform advancing levels of work within the organization were a benefit of long-term employment in the organization. The company provided both the education and time necessary to address the developmental needs of their employees. Training was both a classroom and on-the-job experience that was built into the organization's structure. Successful employees were encouraged to train their own replacements so that in turn they might prepare to move up when a higher-level position became available.

The "Organization Man" was the business model of the post-World War II generation (Whyte, 2002). It is not the model in today's business world. It had all but disappeared by the early 1990s, and Generation X never saw it at all. Generation X entered the workplace with the explicit message that each employee was an independent entity responsible for defining, sculpting, and continually reevaluating his or her own career. This included opportunities both internal and external to the organization.

Members of the baby boom generation, caught between business models, were in a dilemma. They attended schools that taught the Organization Man model of the business world, but what they found instead was that the competitive nature of business was forcing firms everywhere to rethink the Organization Man premise that had been at the core of post-war growth. That older model included the concepts of employability for life and compounding benefits for longevity and loyalty. Employers willingly went outside the four walls of the organizational family to bring in new skills, novel thoughts, and ideas. Buzzwords like "out-of-the-box" thinking expressed values management believed internal employees lacked.

Leading-edge technology skills were lacking as well. For most companies it was cheaper and easier to hire outside expertise to seed ICT efforts than it was to gear up their employees for leading-edge software development. Many feared that costly software skills training would quickly become obsolete on hardware rapidly being replaced. The learning curve for employees was great, the return on the employer's investment in training was questionable, hiring outside consultants was expedient, and frequently employees reluctantly learned new skills they knew were of fleeting value.

The workplace underwent a major revolution. The responsibility for careers and career development shifted. The changes came fast and were implemented with little concern about their impact on employees. Businesses told employees, often explicitly, that it was not the company's role to manage employee careers, and employees were responsible for maintaining their value within the organization. The business model was completely shifting to the individual. Monitoring skill needs and maintaining employability became the sole responsibility of the individual. Some employees only reluctantly accepted the role of keepers of their own career growth. They desperately held onto the Organization Man model. They believed in it until faced with the massive layoffs and early retirement packages that came after 9-11.

Other workers willingly accepted ownership of their career and personal development. But they faced challenges as well. The speed at which the ICT industry evolved made it impossible to predict with accuracy what skills would be needed in the marketplace. The lead-time needed to prepare oneself for future career opportunities was offset by the time needed to determine the validity of the available information on the skills the industry desired.

A significant skill mismatch developed between workers' skills (or those they were in the process of developing) and the skills the industry planned to hire to over the next year. All players recognized the need to bridge the gap. The industry could not continue its growth without properly skilled workers, and educators could not prepare curriculum without advance knowledge of the industry's needs. Technology workers planning career growth and development activities required information from reliable resources. All stakeholders needed access to the trendsetters in the technology industry. Trend-setting ICT companies and ICT think-tank gurus needed to be part of the input process. This made the information being disseminated credible, an important consideration for individuals and support organizations making life-altering career decisions.

When companies make poor ICT decisions, their operations can be seriously harmed. The decisions are financially significant and create nightmares for the technology staff. The decisions frequently lead to repeat expenditures aimed at "band-aiding" the problem. The decisions may even result in the cost of transitioning to different, better platforms.

But, if a family of four "bets the farm" on the same decision, it can mean financial ruin. If the worker's skills are suddenly no longer in demand, the family loses its stability. And as an aside, during the period when the chosen ICT platform is operational, the worker is in extreme demand. The opportunity to develop new skills is at a cyclical low. The free time to develop new skills comes only after the employee is no longer needed; impending doom is not even recognized and leaves the family unprepared.

ICT professionals have a unique perspective on the problem of skills in the industry. They see themselves as responsible for filling the gap between supply and demand, and in most cases they willingly assume that responsibility. As computer "geeks" they welcome the challenge of new technology. But, the need for valid direction is critical to ICT professionals meeting that goal.

Our objectives in exploring a worker's perspective on skill issues are to:

1) Discuss the Organization Man model and its impact on business.
2) Consider a case study of an information technology department.
3) Provide an overview of adult learning theory in the context of careers.
4) Share personal skills perspectives with three workers.
5) Learn how the industry supports workers.

The Organization Man Model

The end of World War II brought about a period of personal and worldwide prosperity. Organizations expanded, and employees were part of the growing company family. The typical professional worker was willingly shaped by the needs and demands of the employer. It was an equitable trade-off between the two parties. The employee expected and received regular pay increases, routine promotions with increased responsibilities, and excellent employment and retirement benefits. In exchange, the company received loyalty and depth of expertise.

William H. Whyte's best-selling book, *The Organization Man*, first published in 1956, became a classic in popular culture (Whyte, 2002). It is the standard by which all models of employer-employee relationships are compared. The Organization Man model (and at the time it was just men, so, I apologize to the feminists out there) played to workers' fears of the day. The model stereotyped individuals as "yes-men," unable and unwilling to innovate. It portrayed employees as singularly focused on advancing through the organization and consequently improving their status on the domestic front. The author simply contrasted these trends to the traditional American values of competition, originality, and individualism (Smith, 2002). Whyte succeeded at fueling debate over American values during the 1950s. But Whyte managed to spark even more significant discussions on employee-employer roles in career development—discussions that continue today.

Typically, employees entered the workforce immediately after high school. They might follow the previous generation into the same firm and career. There was little need for career planning or skill development. The company played the role of big brother. It gave the employees the classroom instruction and tools needed. It apprenticed younger workers with senior staff who passed along details of the job. Management expected the senior workers to teach the junior persons. An older employee taught understudies how to perform exactly as it was done in the past. No innovation was needed and the wheels of the business continued to rotate smoothly.

It was in a senior worker's best interest to train the new hire well. By being a good mentor, he demonstrated the increased value he brought to the firm. He trained his own replacement and was now free to be trained for the next higher position. As a bonus, the senior worker was gradually developing supervisory skills.

The transition away from the Organization Man model of business was not rapid. Most of us remember relatives or family friends who retired after service records spanning 25 to 30 years with the same firm. The retiree likely received a farewell gala, a gold watch, and medical and pension benefits for life, all paid for by the company. A few larger companies even provided benefits to spouses who never worked at the firm, despite the possibility the spouse would survive the employee. It seems an appropriate trade-off for those of us not born into the Organization Man generation. A lifetime of secure employment and regular salary advances in exchange for professional loyalty. However, this post-war reality did not last.

Somewhere in the midst of the baby boom generation, the rules changed. Sadly, many baby boomers believed in the old standards. Their parents taught them the value and virtues of working for the same company for their entire lives. They thought they should do just as their fathers had done. Employers and employees approached the 1980s believing life and the economy would just keep improving for each succeeding generation. But, the market crash in October of 1987 made it crystal clear that "the times they was a changing," as Bob Dylan so passionately expressed.

ICT Department Case Study

In late 1992, I faced a challenge. I was McDonald's Corporation's ICT training expert for approximately 600 professionals. A large portion of the staff was dedicated to application development, maintenance, and support on large mainframe computer software and hardware. Lead times were long. The delivery of products was slower than desired by management, both in the ICT department and at the corporate level. I received a reasonable budget to pilot a boot camp, transitioning employees from mainframes and COBOL to personal computers and early Web-based tools. I felt competent putting the boot camp training program together, but I was unsure of its prospects for success. The reason for my uncertainty was the continuing prevalence of the Organization Man model in McDonald's Information Services Department, even though this was not the case in all parts of McDonald's organization.

Factors working against the program were:

- McDonald's never had a lay off at the corporate level in its 40-year history.
- When different skills were needed in the past, new employees or consultants were hired to fill the void.
- Approximately one-third of the employees to be trained had over 15 year's seniority.
- Workers received above-average wages and benefits, and enjoyed high levels of independence and flexibility in their jobs.
- When interviewed, many employees believed they would not be required to change.
- No incentive was attached to skills attainment.
- No disincentive was given for lack of transition to new skills.

I decided on a small pilot to test the boot camp concept before applying it to the 600 employees. I observed the selected group of students throughout a 30-day period of training, exercises, and hands-on assignments. My assumptions about the employees' willingness to adopt new skills were neither entirely wrong, nor entirely correct. The Generation X participants all embraced the new skills with enthusiasm. They looked at this as an opportunity to learn leading-edge technology at no personal expense. They were obviously not children of the Organization Man model. The oldest workers—those approaching retirement in one to three years—had little interest in learning new skills. They used the training time as an escape from the daily routine of the office. But, the group of employees in the middle was more difficult to understand. Some followed the pattern of the workers nearing retirement, despite many fruitful years ahead of them. Others were thrilled with the opportunity to finally do something leading edge. These employees clearly had gone into the ICT field to do exciting things, but they were extremely bored. It was time they got the chance to learn new skills; they even questioned why McDonald's waited so long to let them learn new technology.

My analysis was not scientific, but I nevertheless concluded that the Organization Man model was affecting both groups of baby boomers in their middle career years. Members of one group wanted to work their way up the organization ladder one rung at a time. They believed in learning only the information needed to get the next job, felt entitled to that higher position when it became available, and could not face the possibility of learning an entirely new set of skills. Change upset the apple cart and threw the traditional hierarchy into chaos. There was a chance that today's mid-career employees would be tomorrow's has-beens. That was change many mid-career employees chose not to accept.

On the other hand, there were an equal number of mid-career employees who genuinely enjoyed learning new technology. But they too believed that the organization was key to their future. The believed the company was responsible for employee skill growth and career development, and were blind to the fact it had always been within their power to update their skills. From their perspective, the organization was the responsible party. They hired into McDonald's, planning to spend their entire careers there. McDonald's *should* determine what skills and career growth opportunities best suited them. They never considered changing firms as an option to enhance and enrich their work life, despite dissatisfaction with the lack of variety in their jobs.

At the end of the pilot boot camp, the recommendation made to the senior management of the Information Services Department was far different from what they expected. The program funds were redirected into touting a message on the importance of adopting life-long learning and ongoing skill development. The department would no longer be an employer for life. Employees became responsible for maintaining their employability. The department became an employer of required skills portfolios. Employees with obsolete skills portfolios got reasonable opportunities to update their skills before receiving layoff packages for non-compliance. The department published the skill sets required of their employees and funded 90 hours of employee training per year. The training was at the employee's discretion, on or off work hours. This training would supplement, not replace, the corporate-wide tuition reimbursement program.

The program finally developed was not a boot camp at all, but a series of mandatory management-led "rap sessions." The employees got the opportunity to understand the purpose of the new training, ask their questions, and vent their anger. Within months, employees saw uncooperative colleagues leaving the organization. The message was clear. Skill growth and career development were no longer the company's responsibility. Employees were the keepers of their own careers, and should take responsibility for them.

McDonald's realized the need for support mechanisms. The company did not blindly turn its ICT employees loose to manage their careers. The ICT Department developed an entire human resource (HR) function around these 600 individuals. The HR team helped them with every aspect of their career planning. The HR professionals provided the necessary infrastructure, which allowed employees willing to take the initiative to successfully navigate their technology careers in McDonald's.

Adult Learning Theory

Does it matter whether employees develop skills under the Organization Man model or the individualist model? In the Organization Man model, employees know exactly why they learn a skill and when they will use it. In the individualist model, employees learn a skill for the sake of learning. The employee attempts to stay ahead by predicting future skill needs. Employees try to possess leading-edge skills at the exact point in time that these skills are likely to be in demand. Therefore, individuals learn skills that lack immediate application. Does this difference in approach matter?

The Organization Man model matches human learning theory closely. The transfer of training from the classroom to the job is practically perfect. Therefore, the ability to directly and successfully pass job skills from one generation of workers to the next is a major benefit of learning under the Organization Man model. The immediate transfer of training to a job is not the approach in individualist learning. Many of the skills are stored for application at a later point in time. The acquired skills are shelved, retrieved, and dusted off before being transferred to a real job. Some loss of ability is inevitable due to the time delay. Passing job skills between generations of workers is counter-intuitive to an individualist learning approach. Individualist learning functions best in settings where skills are evolving and shifting; passing along the last generation's skill sets provides no value.

Organization Man learning most closely provides skill development opportunities centered on the concept of andragogy. Andragogy is the conceptual framework best suited for the adult learner. We will look at components of the andragogical theory of adult learning to assess the relative value of the two learning styles.

Andragogy basically affirms ideas most readers take for granted. It states that adults do not learn in the same way that children learn. Adults are not empty jars into which knowledge can be poured. Adults approach educational opportunities with a different level of involvement and interest from that of the average child. Adults know how to learn better than children due to life experience.

The learning model for children is called the pedagogical model and differs from the andragogical model is some key ways. Adults feel responsible for their own decisions and lives. As a result, adults have a strong need for self-directed learning. Adults ask more questions and quickly fill in gaps between what the instructor provided and what is needed to perform properly. Adults have a self-concept children lack. Adults bring a variety of experiences to the learning situation that younger individuals cannot bring. Adults incorporate similar experiences, assumptions, and even alternative viewpoints into the learning situation. This adds greater depth of understanding. One particular experience adults possess cannot be understated. It is through the completion of the schooling process itself that adults know better how to learn. They consciously through years of struggle figured out how they learn best (Knowles, 1990).

Adults need to know why a skill is valuable before beginning the learning process. Employees training to do activities performed on the job clearly understand the need to learn and willingly begin the learning process. The concept taught is not abstract, it is concrete. Success in learning the task will be reflected in their paychecks. So, adults with training tied directly to job performance are motivated to continue skill growth over a lifetime (Knowles, 1990).

This fits neatly with the Organization Man model. Employees are hired to do specific jobs in specific ways. They are apprenticed on the task to a senior employee. They are under direct supervision by the employee they will eventually replace. Success is clearly defined. What the employee must learn and why they need to learn it are directly related to effective job performance. The employee's motivation is pay, job enrichment, and movement up the company hierarchy, whereas individualist learning is exploratory and success is not guaranteed—the "why" behind skill acquisition is unclear. No employment motivation ties to successful completion of the skill development effort.

The Organization Man learning practices—apprenticeship, mentoring, and on-the-job training—are all excellent ways for an adult to learn quickly and successfully. Each learning practice applies principles of the andragogical model for adult learning. They are all based upon links between successful employees and younger workers. Thus, another positive aspect of Organization Man learning is the effective transfer of training from one employee to another. The older workers are free to prepare themselves for higher-level positions once their skills are transferred to younger workers. There is a continuous "ratcheting up" of skills in the organization. Entry-level workers feed the pipeline, and everyone moves up the corporate ladder. These same results are not found in the individualist approach.

The Organization Man approach to career advancement works well in a stable and growing economy like that of the post-war era. Expenses associated with junior and senior employees working in tandem are easily buried in the cost of goods sold. Apprenticeship type learning techniques work especially well when three market conditions apply. Demand for products and services must continue at a steady pace, allowing cost pressure masking. Worker supply must remain constant to feed the pipeline. Finally, job responsibilities must remain stable to maximize the value of skill transference. If any of these conditions shift, the Organization Man learning approach becomes less appropriate.

Technology is the quintessential case study for shifts in all three of the above market conditions. The introduction of the radio into the consumer market in the 1920s was just the beginning of the flood to come. Technology appeared rapidly with everything from wireless laptop computers, to cellular phones with color video games, to vehicles with satellite global positioning devices. The plethora of products and services offered by ICT companies expanded at ever-increasing rates.

The availability of ICT workers is not constant. In the early 1990s there were not enough workers to fill open positions in most companies. Educators scrambled to develop curriculums that prepared students for lucrative high-tech careers. The dot.com boom sapped the best and brightest ICT professionals. Workers went to startup firms offering large stock option packages.

Conferences sprang up across the globe addressing the issue. Firms needed help attracting and retaining high-tech professionals. Then, as quickly as the boom started, the bubble burst. The supply of ICT professionals now exceeded the demand. But, a new problem emerged—the available workers had the wrong skills to fill the available positions.

The mismatch was an example of the final market condition that impacts Organization Man learning techniques—rapidly changing job responsibilities. The skills and knowledge a worker needed to remain a valuable commodity changed at an accelerating pace. A company's ICT skill needs shifted away from its employees' expertise. Few companies maintained the pace of skill development necessary to ensure their employees continued adaptability to the market. Companies found it cheaper to dispose of their depreciated human capital and made investments in fresh resources. In extreme cases, companies were so far out of touch, they folded or were bought by more successful competitors. So the labor market was flooded with improperly skilled employees.

The ICT industry was one of the largest, fastest growing industrial sectors in the world. Its impact on the world economy and world employment continued to expand because of the instant information demands of businesses and consumers. But by 2000, many high-technology companies found their growth rates unsustainable for the long haul. The firms became victims of the dot.com fiasco. As a result, many ICT workers were laid off. These ICT professionals were victims of companies that dropped the Organization Man model without informing and supporting their employees. The economic slowdown through 2003 continues to affect the need for ICT workers. But, despite the experience of some high-technology companies, the worldwide need for a steady supply of new and properly skilled workers continues to grow.

Although the information and communication technology industry sector began with telephones and computers, the future appears to be in information mobility, content-rich broadband applications, and intelligent devices. Government legislation, enormous network capacity, and the digitization of information fostered the convergence of computer, telephone, cable TV, Internet service provider, satellite, TV and radio broadcast, and wireless companies worldwide. This created the need for workers with more diverse skills than any one organization required in years past. Companies required skills portfolios that few employees possessed. The diversity of ICT companies and the impact of the skills portfolio needs of ICT professionals were profound. This added additional layers of complexity to the skill set workers in the industry must possess to continue to be marketable.

In addition, the technology worker could no longer enter the ICT field planning to remain separate from the core activities of the business. Most organizations positioned ICT workers as key business advisers. The technologist's skill set included business acumen and the ability to partner with the decision makers in the company's strategic business units. Technology raised many levels in an organization's strategic planning. It no longer served as a support function that responded to corporate directives. ICT workers needed to feel competent to sit at the table with other decision makers. Their input guided the future of the business. So, the skills portfolio of today's technology worker included expertise from areas including communications, media, entertainment, marketing, business, strategic planning, and client relationships. Understanding which of these skills were needed at any point within a career was key to advancement.

Individual Perspectives

Case Study Number 1: Matthew was a male, over 50, employed in the technology department of a large retail organization for over 20 years. He began his career as a computer operator, but worked his way up the ladder to a director position over software application development activities. He raised his children and was now an empty nester. Fortunately, during his career he earned an MBA and took advantage of the company's other generous education and career development opportunities. Although he had been able to maintain many of his technical skills, his career advancement primarily focused on strategic activities. He built up a strong business network both inside and outside the company. He nurtured and maintained the network through frequent contact. He was compensated well and was considering his retirement options when he was laid off.

As devastating as the news was, the timing worked in Matthew's favor. He leveraged the approaching Y2K "crisis" to get a foot in the door with some of his contacts. With a combination of technical and strategic business skills, he turned the negative situation into a successful consulting company. His decision early on in his career to focus on business skill development, instead of strictly technical skills, positioned him to add value to a variety of clients. Had Matthew chosen to direct his career on a completely technical dimension, the results would have been vastly different. And in his case, I suspect, much less lucrative.

Case Study Number 2: Jamie was a male approaching 55. He worked in the networking group of a large telecommunications firm until 2001. He was the stereotypical technology "geek." A quick learner, as a younger man he taught himself the latest the ICT industry offered. His nose was always buried in a technical manual of some sort or other, and he was valued highly in his company. He could be counted upon to learn anything on-the-job if the need arose. But, Jamie's home life was tumultuous the last few years. His daughter married and moved away. Jamie now realized he and his wife had nothing in common. It affected his interest in learning new skills and his career in general. He stopped exploring the latest and greatest tools and techniques. His performance slipped. When asked about his change in attitude, he responded flippantly, suggesting, "old age was just creeping in" or that he was "just sick of all the changes forced on him by the technology giants. What was so bad about version 6.1 anyway?" When telecommunications companies contracted and merged, he lost his job. The layoff left him without a job *and* with outdated skills. Jamie realized he was no longer the hot commodity he had once been. He needed a strategy to make himself appealing to technology employers once more. That was difficult given the number of unemployed telecommunication workers out in the marketplace and his advancing age. Could he gain the edge needed to get interviews? Or was retirement his only option? Jamie could not bear staying home every day with the wife he now saw as a stranger. His motivation levels were high, but he had no idea where to begin. He searched the Internet for career advice. Fortunately, there was a tool available. He found the TechCareer Compass® at http://tcc.comptia.org.

Case Study Number 3: Lynne began her professional career as a management trainee in a warehouse distribution facility. She was a single woman in her twenties when her boss asked if she would act as a subject matter expert (SME) on a systems project. The project would automate the product ordering and inventory process for the distribution firm's largest customer. She jumped at the chance, though she had no idea what the project meant for her career. Lynne transitioned from warehouse management trainee into an ICT career. She held technology-related positions for over 20 years. In 2003, she was the mother of a pre-teen and was recently widowed. She had not led an easy life. The industry ups and downs only added to the pain. But, the skills she acquired assure her on-going value to her employer. She had a variety of mini-careers within her overall technology career. Lynne was a systems analyst on her first project. She taught herself a variety of programming and business analysis skills since they were not part of her existing toolkit. She also did some technical writing for that project, a role she truly despised and felt poorly trained to perform. She grew her role on the first project into a supervisory position. She acquired budgetary and client relationship responsibilities as a supervisor. The skills portfolio she acquired on her first project was daunting. But, from the very beginning she accepted all new skill sets as her personal responsibility, and she took honing her skills portfolio seriously. Lynne took advantage of educational opportunities provided by the company, but also tapped the expertise of the business and technology resources on the team. She developed (and still has) quite an extensive network of personal and professional contacts. She identified those possessing certain knowledge and felt comfortable asking them to share it.

Lynne's next assignment required her to learn the intricacies of database, as she served in the role of a database technician. She used her client relationship skills from the prior assignment and expanded them to include the classroom training of users. She utilized her technical writing skills to develop complete sets of user manuals and technical documentation for the project. She further demonstrated both skills by designing training programs for the project.

She excelled at training management activities so much that when the inevitable layoff occurred in the mid 1990s, she sold herself to a small technology company as training manager. Her technology skills and her general training expertise served as a springboard for a totally new career in a heavyweight ICT firm. She addressed employees' technology needs, as well as their broader developmental needs. In general education courses she used examples relevant to technologists. After establishing herself as a credible talent in the training field, she moved to a similar job in a large training department at a major retail firm. Although her focus was now management, she always kept her technical skills on the leading edge. She was ready to walk into a classroom at a moment's notice if an instructor called in sick.

She did well until the downsizing struck again in 2000. But, again her technology skills proved invaluable. Although she preferred a full-time position (her husband was ill and she needed the income), all that was available was a consulting job with a telecommunications firm. The position demanded many of her leading-edge technology skills. The job description dealt with the convergence of the computer and telecommunications fields, and required someone to effectively deal with client relationships. The position also prepared user documentation and provided user classroom training. Lynne was a perfect fit. That part-time position evolved into a permanent one for Lynne. She described it as the job of her dreams. The company was extremely accommodating with her recent widowhood and single parenting situation. It allowed her the type of flexibility and independence most people never find. She defined the permanent job to fit her greatest skills, interests, and ambitions. Was this the end of the story for Lynne? Not likely...she believes in lifelong learning. And, technology is constantly changing. That combination is limitless.

What do these three case studies illustrate? No two individuals follow exactly the same career path. There are a great variety of jobs within the technology arena. The skills that each person needs to develop over a career are diverse. They include both technical and business skills. Even when one's career path remains within a narrow technical specialty, the skills change over time. Often career advancement requires an individual to move between technology and related business units. And, ultimately, skills must be portable and verifiable from one organization to another.

As a professional in the ICT industry, your reaction to the amount of effort required to manage your career might be, "Get real! I have work to do, a family to nurture, and I want some quality time for myself. Unless someone can make this easy, my career will just ebb and flow on its own."

Most people do not approach their careers in such a laissez-faire manner. But neither do they know how to solve the problem. They stand in an ocean of conflicting and overlapping information. Individuals feel powerless to sort and decide which information is valid. They then must further analyze which facts are relevant at the current stage in their career. The demands of analyzing and synthesizing information in the technology arena are relentless.

When organizations abdicated their role of employer for life and career manager, they placed a huge burden on their employees. Organizations took a function once performed by a group of trained people with a targeted budget and external resources, and dropped it squarely in the lap of the individual. The individual had no budget, no staff, no training, and no trusted resources to support the process. Was there any wonder a large skill gap plagued the ICT industry?

All the rhetoric around skill development, taking responsibility for maintaining employability, and preparing oneself for leading-edge technology trends can be confusing to any individual. Without a structured road map—with buy-in from all key stakeholders—caprice might easily determine an individual's chances for success. Just as likely, the individual might simply waste valuable time and resources.

Solutions

Technology firms had ICT professionals at the highest levels on their corporate ladders. These individuals faced the very same issues as unemployed ICT professionals in navigating their careers. They were also experiencing the flip side of the problem as hiring managers. They advertised for ICT professionals, only to discover a lack of qualified applicants for open positions. But as leaders of the ICT industry, they were better positioned to address the issue than most. Several giants in the industry decided to find a solution. They decided to address the lack of credible information for career planning and skill development.

Organizations facing similar challenges often choose to join industry associations so they can pool their resources. They can also address issues that require a single industry-wide solution to avoid ineffectual splintering. The ICT skills mismatch problem was one such issue. The industry leaders asked CompTIA[1], their industry trade association, to convene a task force to find a solution.

The industry leaders knew there were critical ICT positions that went unfilled due to lack of qualified individuals. Yet they realized workers were unemployed and wanted to work. The dilemma was how to communicate to ICT professionals the skills portfolios needed to qualify them for the open positions. Their shared belief was ICT professionals, and the agencies that trained and supported them, had misinformation on skills. No single organization could accurately define ICT skill requirements for the industry overall. The industry consortium decided the best solution was to take group responsibility for a solution. It planned to provide the necessary information on an ongoing basis.

Now workers managing their skills portfolio have a comprehensive ICT industry solution actively helping and supporting them. The solution the industry developed, released, actively expanded, and maintains is named the TechCareer Compass®. It can be accessed on the Internet at http://tcc.comptia.org.

The TechCareer Compass (TCC) is an expansive website dealing with ICT industry skills. TCC contains a uniform set of job definitions and skill standards for careers in the industry. TCC maps industry-supported certifications to specific jobs. TCC identifies knowledge and skills required to do each job. TCC maps learning providers to certifications to assist those interested in formal courses of study. In addition, TCC has a variety of value-added resources, such as career assessment tools, skill gap analysis tools, and a technology dictionary.

The mission of the TechCareer Compass is to eliminate the ICT worker demand and skill mismatches on a worldwide basis. TCC is an industry-led initiative to provide information and tools aimed at attracting, training, and developing properly skilled workers.

TCC has an impressive set of goals and objectives, not all of which are aimed at the individual worker. They include:

- "The TechCareer Compass is to be a voluntary industry-driven effort to establish and maintain a uniform set of jobs, skill standards, training, and certifications to prepare workers for the rapidly changing information and communication technology environment.
- The TechCareer Compass will provide free public access to basic information and communication technology job-related information, but may generate revenue from a variety of premium services.
- The content will be aligned to Department of Labor Skill Standard projects, in particular a current U.S. Government initiative being coordinated by the information and communication technology industry to establish a baseline set of skill standards for the industry.
- The TechCareer Compass will provide tools to manage career growth at the individual and company levels, and will be updated with new job and skills content every 18 months to two years.
- The structured use of TechCareer Compass will in turn attract and keep workers in the information and communication technology industry, and narrow the gap between the workforce skills of today and the evolving information and communication technology industry skill needs of the future." (Lahey & Manzow, 2003)

But the real beneficiaries of the implementation of TCC are incumbent and potential information and communication technology workers. They benefit in numerous ways.

- "They can explore career development paths within the industry.
- They can compare different jobs across the industry.
- They can plan training and certification needs.
- They can locate training providers.
- They can view detailed job descriptions and skills needed for various jobs.

- They can identify which jobs do not require degrees, if appropriate.
- They can determine which jobs best fit their personality.
- They can perform skill gap assessments." (Lahey & Manzow, 2003)

The network of support groups surrounding incumbent and potential workers in the ICT industry also can benefit from using TCC. TCC is written for non-technical people so they are able to use it quite successfully. These people may include: spouses, parents, guidance counselors, human resource professionals, and other types of career counselors.

- "They can market information and communication technology careers to jobseekers.
- They can compare posted job openings to TechCareer Compass standards via alternate job titles.
- They can examine career paths so that career exploration is a simpler task.
- They can discuss technical and non-technical skill and knowledge requirements by job.
- They can suggest training and education requirements by job.
- They can highlight positions not requiring degrees to relevant candidates.
- They can recommend certifications that will provide candidates with a competitive edge." (Lahey & Manzow, 2003)

Learning institutions also benefit in several important areas from the use of TCC.

- "The TechCareer Compass defines a baseline set of skill-based learning objectives that helps identify curriculum development opportunities and upgrade requirements in existing technology programs.
- The TechCareer Compass job definitions will help in the development of training schedules.
- The TechCareer Compass will provide a valuable tool to help training providers to aide students in creating their own career roadmaps.
- The TechCareer Compass provides real-world examples that can be incorporated into demonstrations in training classes.
- Courseware providers can now add real-world information on industry careers to their materials that map directly to industry-endorsed standards.

- The learning institution may market their courses via the TechCareer Compass website to a targeted geographic population of people interested in growing their information and communication technology." (Lahey & Manzow, 2003)

The benefits to the industry from the implementation of TCC were stated earlier.

- "The TechCareer Compass attracts properly skilled workers to fill open positions in the industry resulting in a boost in productivity. That expands the industry's growth potential.
- The industry assumes a leadership role in developing skills standards, thus solving their own worker supply and skill mismatch issues.
- Several information and communication technology industry members are also leading providers of training and certification. So as demand for these services expands through exposure on TechCareer Compass, so will revenues.
- The TechCareer Compass allows businesses to assist their employees in managing their high-technology careers.
- The TechCareer Compass serves as a guideline for employers helping develop career paths for technology employees.
- The TechCareer Compass will provide a link between jobs and local training providers that can best service a specific employer's needs.
- The TechCareer Compass is also a benefit as a human resource tool for smaller businesses, since the TechCareer Compass website offers information needed to support the creation of job descriptions, hiring guidelines, individual development plans, promotion criteria, and skill gap assessments." (Lahey & Manzow, 2003)

Several prominent members of the ICT industry developed the TechCareer Compass. These included Cisco, CompuCom, IBM, Intel, and Microsoft. They implemented their solution through affiliation with their representative trade association, CompTIA. CompTIA, the Computing Technology Industry Association, spearheaded the volunteer effort to scope out the project; design the system; develop the website; collect, massage, and validate the content; establish the ongoing maintenance process; and then host and manage the finished product. But, subject matter experts from the aforementioned companies did the hard work, using information from jobs within their own organizations and by reviewing previously written standards from numerous regulatory bodies around the globe.

The TechCareer Compass website was launched in May 2002. It was quickly apparent that the solution worked extremely well. This meant that the product needed to have a large, objective review board to oversee its continued growth. So, in the summer of 2002, CompTIA implemented a Workforce Investment Advisory Board (WIAB). It acted as an oversight committee reviewing direction for all initiatives in the Workforce Development area of the association. One of the committee's largest roles was direction setting for the TCC product. The WIAB expanded input to TCC beyond the ICT industry. They sponsored inclusion of members of the training and academic communities, as well as governmental agencies in the labor and education arenas.

CompTIA and its member firms were actively involved in establishing a single set of nationally accepted skill standards for the ICT industry. As part of this effort, the ICT industry provided the national skill standards free in the public domain. The TCC website was the portal for access to the national skill standards.

TCC is the premiere skills portfolio and career development tool for the ICT industry. TCC has a friendly front end that provides access to a priceless warehouse of credible skill information and value-added tools. TCC is heavily marketed to students, counselors, job-changers, educators, and training centers. The incumbent audience is also targeted through advertisements in trade publications and certification preparation manuals.

Persons leading groups of ICT workers, such as readers of this book, should encourage their employees to utilize this resource to evaluate and maintain their skills portfolio. The TechCareer Compass is a good tool to discuss skill development issues and career plans. Visit http://tcc.comptia.org to see the variety of resources TCC offers. It is a website you and your employees will bookmark and use regularly.

Conclusion

When contemplating the fast-paced world of ICT, an analogy that naturally springs to mind is the Indianapolis 500 race. Cars whizzing past the stands at speeds in excess of 200 miles per hour is normal. I remember little of the race; it was a good thing an animated version was shown on large video screens. Otherwise, I would have been totally lost. I never actually saw the race. All I had time to see was a blur of color as the cars passed right in front of me.

How appropriate for our discussion, when you realize that the word *career* used as a verb means *to go at top speed* (Webster, 1981). Pritchett (1997) states, "In today's world, careering comes down to a race against change...a personal contest to see if we can grow as fast as the challenges we face in our work. Our schooling needs to move at full speed, and this calls for a strategy of 'learning in motion'" (pp. 23-24). As ICT professionals the constant battle is to be in the thick of the race, while at the same time retaining the ability to step back and observe the video screen. We need to keep moving ahead at full speed, while taking a little time to look at the bigger picture to see that we have our career goals on right track.

Endnote

1 CompTIA is formally known as the Computing Technology Industry Association. It is the information and communications technology industry's largest trade organization.

References

Knowles, M. (1990). *The adult learner: A neglected species.* Houston, TX: Gulf Publishing.

Lahey, E., & Manzow, T. (2003). *TechCareer Compass.* Oak Brook Terrace, IL: CompTIA.

Pritchett, P. (1997). *Fast growth: A career acceleration strategy.* Dallas, TX: Pritchett & Associates, Inc.

Smith, K. (2002). The Organization Man. *St. James Encyclopedia of Pop Culture.* Accessed July 23, 2003, from: http://www.findarticles.com/g1epc/tov/2419100921/p1/article.jhtml.

Webster, A.M. (1981). *Webster's New Collegiate Dictionary*. Springfield, IL: G&C Merriam Company.

Whyte, W.H. (2002). *The Organization Man*. Philadelphia, PA: University of Pennsylvania Press.

Chapter V

Optimizing IT Skills Management Initiatives

Ken Strauss
Bookman Testing Services, USA

Abstract

This chapter identifies the essential information required in effective IT skills management initiatives. It argues that foremost among this information is in-depth insight into an individual's specific areas of strength/weakness. In a logical step-by-step discussion, the chapter builds upon a simple assessment to finally arrive at the complexities of an assessment required to deliver this detailed insight for effective skills management programs. It then goes on to discuss reporting and analysis of detailed assessment results to maximize the benefits of skill assessments in hiring, training, and overall skills management programs.

Introduction

As technology continues to advance at an ever-increasing pace, more organizations will come to recognize the importance of IT skills management programs. It will become evident that a corporation's success will depend on the success of its information technology initiatives. Yet, the new rules of corporate success brought on by the rapid advancement of technology will dictate that IT initiatives depend not so much on the hardware and/or software technology selected, but more on the skills of the individuals responsible for implementing the systems and applications.

As technologies get more complex, requiring more knowledge, better skills, and specialization, it will become more difficult to find qualified IT professionals. Successful organizations will recognize the critical importance of effectively managing the skills of their current IT professionals. They will also recognize that the first step in managing those IT skills is to have a detailed, objective, and accurate inventory of the skills of their current staff, as well as the skills required for their future projects. With the proper evaluation of detailed IT skills, organizations will be able to save time, money, and optimize their hiring, training, project staffing, and career development initiatives.

Long before today's massive IT departments existed, industrial psychologists were assessing employee soft skills by treating each personality trait as a unique measurable attribute. In the 1990s, as corporate and industrial leaders recognized IT's critical importance to overall corporate success, attention began to turn towards assessing IT technical skills. Following the experience in assessing soft-skills, it was only natural to treat each technology as a singular unique attribute. However, this brought about a false start to IT skills management, as the real power behind an IT technical assessment lies in the evaluation of the many detailed skill sub-topics comprising the scope of a given technology. Analysis at this detailed sub-topic level harnesses the full power of IT skills assessment and opens the door to dynamic and effective skill management systems.

Most learning management systems (LMSs) and/or skills management systems treat IT skills like they do soft-skills—assigning a number on a scale representing the individual's success in achieving that particular soft-skill (i.e., 'works well as a team player' or 'shows initiative'). This treatment of each soft-skill as a unique attribute to be numerically evaluated was passed down to IT skill assessments. Each IT technology (i.e., Cobol, Oracle, Network Administration, etc.) was treated as a single attribute to be numerically evaluated. Thus an individual's IT skill profile would contain a series of numerical ratings corresponding to his/her skill level in various technologies (e.g., 5 in Oracle Programming, 4 in Powerbuilder, and 2 in Windows Programming).

The problem inherent in treating a given IT technology, such as Oracle, as a single skill to be assessed is that, unlike soft-skills, hard-skills in technologies are comprised of many different areas of knowledge. A professional working in a given technology may have very senior skills in certain aspects of the technology that he uses often on his current project, and almost no knowledge in other sub-topics of the same technology that he has not used in his current or prior projects.

This multi-skill aspect of an IT technology requires that a truly valuable assessment tool in that technology incorporates a more detailed analysis than can be determined from a single score. An assessment that analyzes skills at the detailed sub-topic level can provide the insight needed by the skills management program to optimize many IT functions including:

Project Staffing—Why build project teams in which every team member has the same weakness? With sub-topic assessments you can build teams with synergistic and complementary skills.

IT Skill Gap Analysis—Aggregate individual results to gain unparallel insight into the proficiency of your organization in a given technology. Determine the specific areas that need to be built up through hiring, training, or transfer within the enterprise.

Training—Why include topics in the curriculum in which the class already is proficient? Use sub-topic assessments to customize course content to the specific needs of the class. Trim a course from five days down to two days!

Hiring—If a determination has been made that the skill gaps cannot be closed internally, focus your candidate search on those individuals who have the specific skills to plug the skill gaps in your organization.

Unfortunately, objective and reliable skill assessment at such a detailed sub-topic level is not easy. Determining proficiency in any single topic can require asking the test taker many questions to obtain the required amount of feedback. Multiplying this number of questions over all the important sub-topics within a given technology results in an assessment process that can last for several hours (if not days!). Many of the commercially available assessments avoid this time issue by simply ignoring sub-topic analysis entirely. The resulting analysis provided by these assessments is typically a single number representing the individual's overall proficiency in the technology. Such assessments will not be a significantly useful tool in effective skills management.

Some assessments will claim to provide the needed sub-topic analysis, but their testing methodology limits their analysis to 'relative' scoring as opposed to 'absolute' scoring. Relative scoring would imply that an individual is strong in a particular sub-topic relative to his/her proficiency in other sub-topics within the technology. A 'relative' skill analysis such as this can actually undermine the success of skills management initiatives. To illustrate this point, imagine you are the manager of a baseball team that needs a quality first baseman. You ask a friend for help and he suggests that you try Bob at first base. "First base is Bob's strongest position." You play Bob at first base and he can't even catch the ball. You turn to your friend and say, "I thought you said first base was his best position?" "It is," he replies. "You should see how badly he plays third base!"

The above scenario illustrates the problems of 'relative' skill analysis. Now consider this scenario playing out in the IT department's search for a lead Java programmer on a critical project. A relative assessment of skills might imply a candidate is strong in Java; yet what it could be saying is that this candidate's Java skills are stronger than his Cobol skills, but in reality both skills are weak. It should be clear that relative skills assessment could have disastrous effects on the success of skills management initiatives.

With the success of skills management programs dependent upon the quality and detail of the incorporated skills assessment, and given the difficulty involved in assessing detailed sub-topic skills, it is evident that the choice of an assessment tool is one of the critical first steps in establishing an effective skills management program. This chapter will first discuss the characteristics required of an IT skill assessment vehicle to reliably and objectively provide the level of detail required for effective skills management. It will then cover the effective application and analysis of the detailed assessments in a skills management program.

Objectively and Reliably Determining Sub-Topic Skills

To fully realize the true value of sub-topic assessment in effective skills management, one only need review the types of feedback that can be provided by a skill assessment tool. We will begin with the simplest type of feedback—the number of questions answered correctly. Consider the assessment results of a C++ exam shown below.

C++ Assessment Results
Test Taker: John Smith; Total Questions: 45; Correct: 30; Incorrect: 15

Clearly the above feedback leaves a lot to be desired. Among its drawbacks is a failure to provide insight into the degree of skill indicated. Is 30 correct answers a bad score or a good score? What is the average score?

To some extent, additional insight into the quality of a score can be obtained from a percentile. A percentile will identify where a given score falls among the scores of all test takers. For example, if a score of 80 (on a scale of 1-100) is associated with a percentile of 65, it means that the score of 80 was higher than 65% of all scores. Consider our improved result as shown below:

C++ Assessment Results
Test Taker: John Smith; Score: 80; Percentile: 65

The percentile provides valuable insight into the skill level of the test taker. The score of 80, while above average (50th percentile), is not quite indicative of a truly senior individual. A percentile of, say, 90 would identify the test taker as in the top 10% of all test takers.

While the percentile provides additional insight into the test taker's skill/knowledge, it is still not the level of feedback needed for effective skills management. The above result does not indicate the true level of skill. Is 80 indicative of a senior-level individual or an entry-level individual? The percentile can provide some indication of the true skill level, but it will vary according to the technology being tested. For example, the Cobol language has been a programming staple for nearly 40 years. Those professionals who work in the Cobol language have had a great deal of time to develop their expertise. Accordingly, a score of 80 on a Cobol assessment (which may be indicative of a very senior individual) may only correlate to a percentile of 50! On the other end of the spectrum, consider a brand new technology, which has only been available for use for a few months. The industry professionals have not yet had the time to develop a great deal of expertise in this latest technology. A score of 45 on an assessment in such an emerging technology might be in the 90th percentile!

While the scaled score and percentile combination offer more insight than the scaled score alone, they still lack an absolute measure of skill. Consider the assessment result shown below (Figure 1).

Figure 1

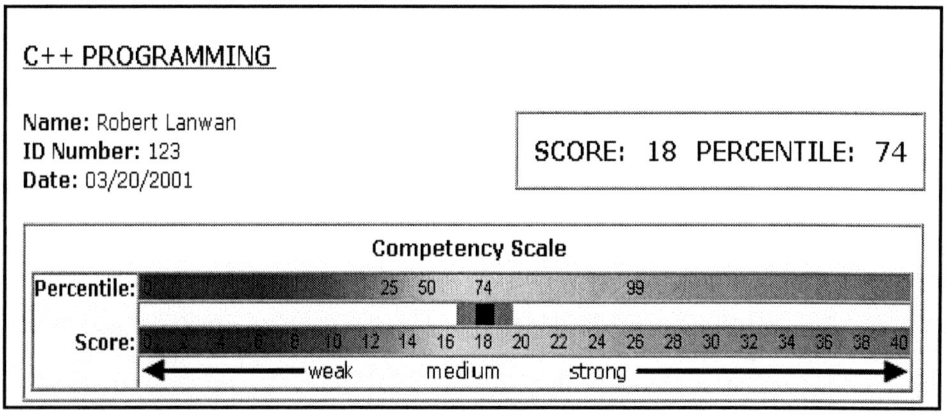

Courtesy of TeckChek

The above result not only shows a scaled score of 18 (on a scale of 1-40) and the associated percentile of 74, but also indicates that this score of 18 is a medium-level score. In other words 74% of the professionals who have taken this assessment score at a medium or lower level of knowledge. Thus 26% of test takers demonstrate knowledge above a medium level. This insight might inform a recruiter, looking to hire a senior-level individual, that they might have trouble locating viable senior candidates and perhaps should consider the candidate with a medium score. This would be indicative of a relatively new technology in which the IT industry has not yet had the opportunity to develop a great deal of expertise. Compare this assessment result to the one shown in Figure 2 in a mature technology such as Cobol II.

Figure 2

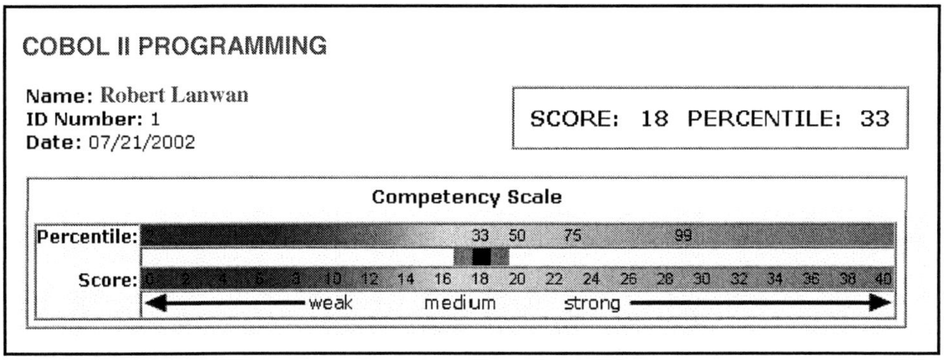

Courtesy of TeckChek

In the mature technology of Cobol II, the score of 18, while still indicating a medium level of knowledge, is in the 33rd percentile. This means that 67% of the test takers scored above the medium level. Thus, the recruiter looking to hire a senior-level Cobol II programmer might pass on the medium-level candidate with the knowledge that he/she most likely will be able to locate a candidate with the desired senior-level skill.

Is this then the complete assessment result we seek? No. It still lacks the detailed insight required of an effective skills management tool. To see how we can improve the value of an assessment, consider the C++ result in Figure 3.

This result (Figure 3) not only provides the insights of a score and percentile, but also provides the detailed sub-topic evaluation required for IT skills management. With these sub-topic evaluations for the entire IT staff, one can customize individual and group training, identify enterprise-wide skill gaps, target hiring to fill the skill gaps, ensure the availability of specific skill sets needed within the organization, and build project teams with synergistic and complementary skills.

In short, detailed sub-topic assessments will enable the IT organization to optimize the management of the current skills of employees as well as those of prospective employees.

The issue now is to identify the proper assessment tool that is structured to provide this level of reliable, more objective analysis.

Figure 3

C++ PROGRAMMING - Complete

Name: Robert Lanwan
ID Number: 123
Date: 03/20/2001

SCORE: 18 PERCENTILE: 74

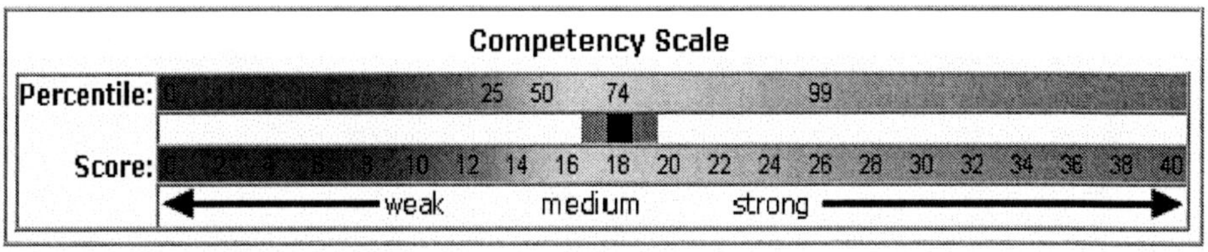

Topics showing Strength
Robert has demonstrated particular strength in the following topics within the technology, and would be a strong candidate for projects requiring expertise in these areas:

Access Control
Special Member Functions
Inheritance and Virtual Functions
Advanced Templates

Topics showing Weakness
Robert has demonstrated a very low level of proficiency in the following topics within the technology. Care should be taken when considering Robert for projects requiring skill in these specific areas:

Multiple Inheritance and Runtime Type Identification
Basic Templates
Exception Handling
Namespaces and Memory Management
Standard Template Library

Other Topics Evaluated
Robert has demonstrated neither exceptionally high or exceptionally low levels of proficiency in the following topics:

C++ Language Syntax
Types and Declarations
Expressions and Statements
Operator and Function Overloading
Standard Strings, Iostreams, and Localization
C++ Classes
Object-Oriented Programming

Courtesy of TeckChek

Finding the Right Skill Evaluation Tool

Certification vs. Assessment

The first step in locating the proper assessment tool is to recognize the difference between certification and assessment tools. Certification tools offer an official certification, degree, or other badge of merit to indicate that the test taker has scored at or above a predetermined level. Most certifications are forms of pass/fail exam that often do not indicate the extent to which the individual exceeded the certification level or fell short of it. They also do not typically provide the detailed sub-topic analysis required for IT skills management programs. Certifications are used by the test taker to establish his/her credentials. In essence, a certification exam is a marketing tool for the individual test taker.

Assessments, on the other hand, typically do not provide a pass/fail level, but are designed to provide a detailed analysis of the test taker's proficiency in a given IT technology. Most assessments will provide percentile scores showing where the test taker ranks among all test takers. These percentiles provide insight into the test taker's relative level of proficiency among the larger test population. Some of the higher quality assessments will even provide specific scores/percentiles in different areas such as "book knowledge" and "practical experience" to offer further insight into the test taker's proficiency. The best assessment tools for skills management programs are those that identify sub-topic proficiencies. It is this detailed sub-topic evaluation that distinguishes the assessment product as a critical component of a successful skills management initiative. *While a certification exam is a marketing tool for the individual test taker, a skills assessment is a fundamental skills management tool for corporate use.* In fact, to ensure the integrity of the assessment results, a good assessment tool will not be available in the open market to the individual IT professional, but will only be available to corporations for use with current employees or employment candidates.

Adaptive Questioning

Determining sub-topic proficiencies requires significantly more feedback (numbers of test questions) from the test taker than would a simple assessment of overall knowledge in a given technology. Each sub-topic must be assessed. This means sub-topic assessments could require hundreds of questions depending upon the number of sub-topics being evaluated. It is apparent that the traditional method of static testing (tests with fixed questions) may not be practical in determining sub-topic skills.

In the early twentieth century, Alfred Binet created an IQ test in which the questions were selected, by the test interviewer, as the test proceeded. Specific question selection rules were applied by the interviewer to select the most appropriate questions for the test taker based upon their prior answers. In this manner the test was designed to 'adapt' to the knowledge level of the test taker. However, it took over half a century for the advent of computers to capitalize on advantages of adaptive testing and make it a commonly used methodology.

In adaptive testing the questions are not fixed, but are determined as the test progresses based upon the prior answers given by the test taker. The more correct the prior answer is, the more difficult the next question; conversely, the less correct the prior answer is, the easier the next question will be. In this manner the test 'adapts' to the demonstrated knowledge of the test taker. Thus, stronger test takers will receive harder questions, while less knowledgeable test takers will receive easier questions, effectively eliminating questions that are pre-determined to be too easy or too hard for the test taker.

Adaptive testing can be compared to a high jump. If the jumper can clear a height of 5 feet, then the bar is raised to 7 feet. If he is unable to jump over the seven-foot bar, then the bar is lowered to 6 feet. If he jumps over the six-foot bar, then it is raised to 6.5 feet. The bar continues to be adjusted in increasingly smaller increments until the maximum height that can be cleared is determined. In this manner, an adaptive test determines the maximum level of knowledge demonstrated by the test taker.

Obviously, this method of questioning would prohibit the score from being a simple function of the number of correct answers; that would not be fair to those candidates receiving the harder questions. Instead, an adaptive test will assign a 'weight of difficulty' to each question, much like a "degree of difficulty" is assigned to every dive in a diving contest. The more difficult the dive (or the test question), the more credit is given for its successful completion and the less credit is lost for failing the dive (or test question). Losing credit for failing to answer a question correctly is the same as the bar being lowered when a jump is unsuccessful. How much credit is gained or lost is a function of both the difficulty of the question and the extent to which the question was answered correctly or incorrectly (some wrong answers can demonstrate more partial knowledge than other wrong answers and will not lose as much credit if selected).

What is the benefit of adaptive testing? There is a security benefit (test takers do not receive the same questions) as well as a test reliability component, in that prior exposure to the test questions—resulting in correct answers the second time the test is taken—will only produce more difficult follow-up questions than were received the first time. However, the major benefit of adaptive testing is that it greatly reduces the number of required questions (and thus test time) by eliminating questions that are determined to be too hard or too easy for the test taker based upon their prior answers.

For example, if a test taker has just successfully answered a question on Einstein's Theory of Relativity, it makes no sense to ask a follow-up question: "How much is 2 + 2?" Similarly, if a question to identify the current president of the United States is answered incorrectly, there is no value in asking a follow-up question to identify the 11th vice president. In both cases, success on the follow-up question can be accurately predicted without even asking the question. In this manner (eliminating questions before they are asked), adaptive testing can provide the required feedback in far fewer questions. This makes adaptive testing the perfect solution to the large amount of feedback required for sub-topic assessment.

Adapting Sub-Topics

Traditional adaptive methods are just one step towards the solution of attaining assessments at the sub-topic level. To better understand this, we need to examine a scenario in which a test subject has been broken down into 16 sub-topics. Suppose a test taker is an expert in sub-topic X, but is fairly weak in the other 15 sub-topics due to lack of exposure to them. As the topic X expert takes the test, his incorrect responses to the majority of questions outside of his specific area of expertise would cause the adaptive testing engine to select easier and easier questions.

Even though he might answer the questions in sub-topic X correctly, they will always be easy questions, and he will never have the opportunity to demonstrate his superior knowledge of sub-topic X with difficult questions.

The clear solution is to use the adaptive method independently within each sub-topic. In this manner, knowledge in one sub-topic would not impact the difficulty level of questions in another sub-topic, thereby enabling a reliable and independent assessment in each sub-topic. Adapting the test independently within the sub-topics is a fundamental and critical component of any attempt to provide detailed sub-topic assessment in a reasonable timeframe. Unfortunately, most IT assessments, with a few notable exceptions, do not employ their adaptive methods independently within sub-topics, making them imperfect tools for skills management programs.

Multiple Correct Answers

In summary, it is apparent that due to practical time limits, an assessment must employ adaptive methodology to reduce the number of required questions on the test. Further, the test should adapt independently within sub-topics to provide the reliable sub-topic detail assessment required for optimizing the skills management process. But is this the final solution for a skills assessment in an effective IT skills management program? Not quite.

Although adapting within sub-topics will reduce the number of questions required in each sub-topic, a great deal of detailed feedback is still needed to make a determination of the test taker's knowledge in each sub-topic. How many questions would such an analysis require in each sub-topic? Five? Six? Ten? In a technology that has been broken down into 16 sub-topics, this could easily result in a test of more than 100 questions!

The problem is that each question is providing binary feedback—it was answered either correctly or incorrectly. It does not provide enough insight (to what extent is the answer correct or incorrect) to optimally determine the level of the next question. If a high jumper can clear a bar at 5 feet, how high do you place the bar for the next jump? If you had more information than simple binary feedback (cleared or failed to clear the previous height), you would be able to make a more optimal placement of the bar for the next jump. If, for example, you knew the jumper had actually cleared the five-foot bar by three feet, you might place the bar for the next jump at 7 or 8 feet, rather than a smaller increase to 6 feet. This insight into how much the jumper cleared or failed to clear the bar helps to determine the optimal placement of the bar for the next jump, and thus reduces the number of required jumps to determine the maximum level the jumper can attain. By the same reasoning, greater insight into just how correct or incorrect an answer is can help to determine a more optimal level of difficulty for the next question and thus reduce the number of required questions.

The issue then is how to get more insight out of the answer to a given question. At first glance this might seem to be a futile task. After all, an answer is either correct or incorrect. But not all incorrect answers are equally incorrect! Some wrong answers can be completely off the mark, while others can at least demonstrate some partial knowledge. Even among the correct answers, some can demonstrate more insight and knowledge than other correct answers. Each answer should be provided a weight, which indicates the extent to which it is correct or incorrect. The weight associated to the selected answer can then be used to determine a more appropriate level of difficulty for the follow-up question.

Weighted answers are a common component of adaptive testing. However, the real leap in maximizing the value and the feedback derived from a question is for the question to allow for more than one correct answer. Consider a test in which each question can have up to three correct answers; the test taker is not told how many correct answers there are, but is instructed to select all the correct answers he or she finds, up to a maximum of three. Credit is gained for each correct answer selected; credit is lost for each incorrect answer selected. And credit is also lost for each correct answer *not* selected! How much credit is gained or lost by each answer is determined by how correct or incorrect the answer is.

By presenting five possible answers and allowing the selection of up to three of them, the mathematicians among us will recognize that there are 25 possible answer combinations. Each one of those combinations demonstrates a different level of knowledge. Each combination has a different amount of credit (positive or negative) depending upon the answers it comprises, and each combination leads to a different level of follow-up question within the adaptive algorithm. Twenty-five distinct answer combinations allow the test taker to pinpoint his/her exact level of knowledge posed by the question. This precision will allow for the selection of a more optimal difficulty level for the follow-up question. This concept is best grasped by seeing an example. Consider the following question on U.S. geography:

Which of the following are states in the United States?

A. Texas
B. Paris
C. California
D. Jupiter
E. Washington, DC

Let's review just five of the possible 25 answer combinations and see how they provide different levels of insight into the respondent's knowledge on this question.

1. **Texas, California—**This is the correct answer. Respondent receives the maximum credit and the most difficult follow-up question.
2. **Texas—**Credit is given for selecting Texas, but some credit is lost for failing to select California. The follow-up question will not be as difficult.
3. **Jupiter—**Respondent has no clue about U.S. geography and is most likely guessing. This response will lose significant credit and result in a very easy follow-up question.
4. **Jupiter; Paris; Washington, DC—**This is the worst of the 25 possible responses. Credit is lost for selecting Paris and Washington; a lot of credit is lost for selecting Jupiter, and credit is also lost for failing to select Texas and California. This will result in the easiest possible follow-up question.
5. **Texas; Washington, DC—**This combination would provide more credit than Texas and Paris, because although Washington, DC, is not correct (it is a district and not a state), it does demonstrate some partial understanding of U.S. geography, more so than Paris would.

The above example should demonstrate the extent to which the test taker is provided the opportunity to pinpoint his/her exact understanding of the subject questioned. This level of detail, when combined with the efficiencies of adaptive testing, maximizes the feedback obtained from the test taker and provides the detailed insight into sub-topic proficiency that is required for effective skills management.

Let us summarize what we have covered to this point:

1. Successful IT initiatives will depend upon the effective management of IT human resources.
2. Effective management of IT human resources will require detailed insight into sub-topic skills.
3. Due to time and resource constraints, a practical assessment that can deliver objective and reliable sub-topic skill assessments should employ:
   a. Adaptive questioning methodology
   b. Adapting independently within sub-topics
   c. Weighted questions

d. Weighted answers
e. Multiple correct answers

Now that we have identified what to look for in an assessment tool that can be of value in a skills management program, the next step is to review what to do with the information provided by the assessment tool. Exactly how does a skills management program utilize the sub-topic assessments to optimize its hiring, training, and IT development efforts?

Optimizing Skills Management

Now that the criteria for selecting an appropriate assessment tool have been identified, the assessment tool has been acquired, and all the employees have been assessed in the appropriate technology, how is the detailed data provided by the assessment results used in skills management? How do we effectively use this detailed insight into the sub-topic skills of employees to improve hiring, team building, training, and to increase the overall success of IT initiatives?

First, the assessment results must be placed into a database that makes them accessible, searchable, and provides for aggregation and reporting. Some organizations will build their own in-house applications, while others might purchase off-the-shelf skills management systems. The better assessment products will provide their own database with tools for searching, aggregation, and analysis. Whichever option the organization chooses, once the database is established and populated with sub-topic skill assessments, the real skills management can begin.

The simplest use of this information is to provide the individual with objective insight into his/her sub-topics of strength and weakness. This insight can help guide further training for the individual. In fact, some assessment tools, such as TeckChek, will provide a facility to map the assessment sub-topics to the training curriculum of an organization or third-party training vendor (see Figure 4). This allows the individual to quickly obtain a learning prescription, which directs him/her to specific modules in the curriculum to address their specific weaknesses. A custom training prescription based upon a detailed assessment of sub-topic skills can save a great deal of time and money in the upgrading of employee skills.

Figure 4

Training Prescription Robert Lanwan Based upon assessment results in C++				
Sub-Topic	**Vendor**	**Course Title**	**Module #**	**URL**
Inheritance and Virtual Functions	XYZ Training Co.	Advanced C++ Programming	1,3	http://xyz.com
Memory Mgmt	XYZ Training Co.	Advanced C++ Programming	6	http://xyz.com
	TrainOnline	C++ Programming	4,7	http://trainonline.com
Special Member Functions	XYZ Training Co.	Introduction to C++	9,10	http://xyz.com

While custom training prescriptions are a valuable product of detailed sub-topic evaluations, the real impact on IT initiatives is the information the assessments provide through aggregation. By combining the strengths/weaknesses of a designated group of individuals, several IT-related functions (hiring, training, team building, etc.) can be significantly enhanced and optimized.

Figure 5

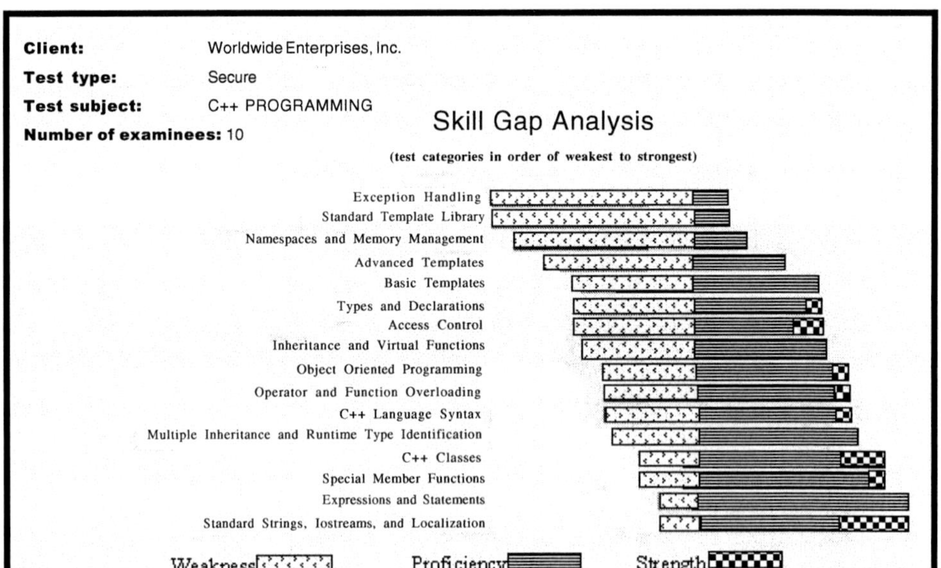

Courtesy of TeckChek

This means the assessment tool must have, or you need to create, an aggregation report. These reports are often referred to as skill gap analysis. Consider the skill gap analysis chart shown in Figure 5.

Figure 5 visually displays the aggregate proficiency of the group in each sub-topic of the tested technology (C++). Each row represents another sub-topic within C++.

The length of the (crow's feet) bar on a row represents that portion of the group that had a weakness in that sub-topic.

The length of the (horizontal lines) bar portion indicates the portion of the group that had neither a weakness nor a strength in that sub-topic.

The length of the (checkered squares) bar represents the portion of the group that had strength in that sub-topic.

To illustrate the information provided in this chart, let us examine the bottom row, Standard Strings, Iostreams, and Localization. According to the relative sizes of the bars, about 10% (crow's feet) of the group is weak in this sub-topic, approximately 50% (horizontal lines) are proficient, and 40% (checkered squares) are strong.

The insight provided by the skill gap analysis is the true catalyst in effective skills management. It will provide benefits in many human resource functions including focused hiring, team building, and custom training. First we will examine its use in **project team building**.

If the previous skill gap analysis chart (Figure 5) represents the collective skills of a proposed project team, is this a well-rounded team as currently staffed? Can a more effective team be put together? The answer depends upon the relative importance of each sub-topic to the project objectives. If the top two sub-topics, Exception Handling and Standard Template Library, are critical components of the project objective, then this proposed team might not be ideal. Approximately 90% of the team is weak in these topics (as shown in the relative length of the crows feet bar), and there is no guru on the team to provide senior-level guidance in this sub-topic (lack of a checkered bar).

There are several responses to address the weaknesses in the make-up of the proposed team. First, "what-if" analysis can be done to try to arrive at a more balanced and synergistic team. What if persons X and Y were replaced with persons A and B from the pool of employees? How would the proposed team look now? A second skill gap analysis would be produced for the new proposed team and evaluated to determine if the new mix of skills is more complementary and proficient in the required sub-topics. This 'what-if' analysis can be done repeatedly until a compatible team is identified or until it is obvious that certain skills are lacking in the employee pool, preventing the creation of a more effective team.

A shortcut approach to finding a more optimal team composition would be a direct **skills search** through the database of assessment results looking for an individual(s) with the appropriate skills to plug the identified skill gaps on the team. In addition to searching for the specific sub-topics required for the project, a good search facility might also allow for additional search criteria based upon the areas of analysis provided by the assessment tool. In addition to an overall score and percentile, more sophisticated assessment tools will provide scores for additional criteria including work speed, book knowledge, practical experience, and other parameters that may be measured by the assessment. These additional parameters allow searches to be more focused in their hunt for appropriate team members. For example, a high work speed score may be desirable for individuals who will be working on a time-critical project.

Consider the search (Figure 6) for a candidate for the hypothetical project team. The project manager has decided to search for someone to fill the skill gap in Standard Template Library on the proposed team. The project manager wants a mid-level person (overall percentile above 60). Since this person will be the project team guru in this subtopic, it is desirable to find someone who has solid experience in this sub-topic, not someone who has obtained their knowledge through reading or training. Therefore, one of the search criteria is that the candidate be over the 80th percentile in practical experience. (Note: higher quality assessments will distinguish book knowledge from proficiency gained through practical experience.) Since this is a time-critical project, the ideal candidate will have demonstrated an ability to think and resolve issues quickly. Therefore, another search criteria is that the individual be above the 60th percentile in work speed.

Naturally the search requires that the candidate have a strength in the target sub-topic of Standard Template Library. However, the project manager has also suggested that knowledge in Advanced Templates would be a plus for a team member. This does not mean that the individual must necessarily have a strength in Advanced Templates, but it does imply that the individual should not have a weakness in the sub-topic.

Figure 6

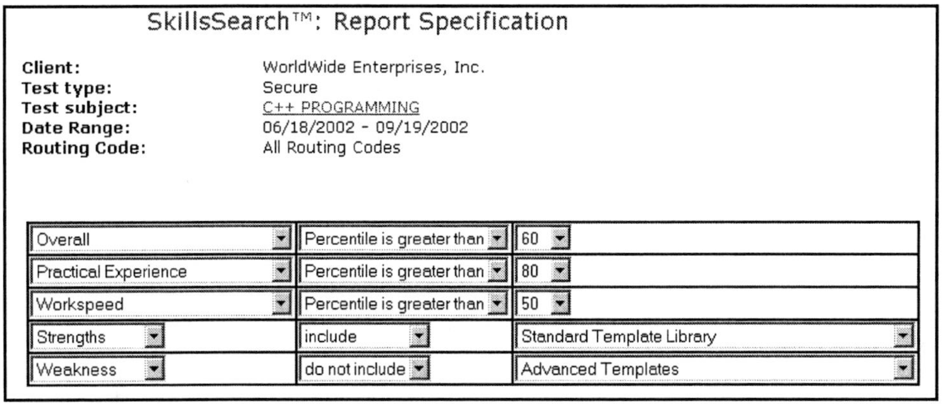
SkillsSearch™: Report Specification

Client:	WorldWide Enterprises, Inc.
Test type:	Secure
Test subject:	C++ PROGRAMMING
Date Range:	06/18/2002 - 09/19/2002
Routing Code:	All Routing Codes

Overall	Percentile is greater than	60
Practical Experience	Percentile is greater than	80
Workspeed	Percentile is greater than	50
Strengths	include	Standard Template Library
Weakness	do not include	Advanced Templates

Courtesy of TeckChek

All of the previous criteria have been supplied in the search in Figure 6.

Individuals who are identified in the above search can then be added to the proposed team and a new skill gap analysis produced. Since the individuals identified in the search will also have additional strengths and/or weaknesses that were not necessarily part of the search criteria, some of them may be better fits than others into the overall project team composition. By trying various team combinations, the optimal team for the specific project can be determined.

If a search through the enterprise fails to turn up candidates with the appropriate target sub-topic skill, skills training to develop those skills can be one solution. The value of sub-topic assessment in group training is to reduce the time and cost of the training. Using sub-topic assessments, the training need not involve the entire technology, but can focus on the training modules dealing with those sub-topics in which the group has demonstrated a collective weakness. This provides a huge savings of training time and budget by eliminating superfluous curriculum while concentrating on the desired skills.

To optimize **Custom Training Content**, a skill gap analysis report is produced representing the aggregated skills of the student body (Figure 7). This information is provided to the instructor who can then customize the curriculum to the needs of that specific group of students. Consider the skill gap analysis report in Figure 7.

Figure 7

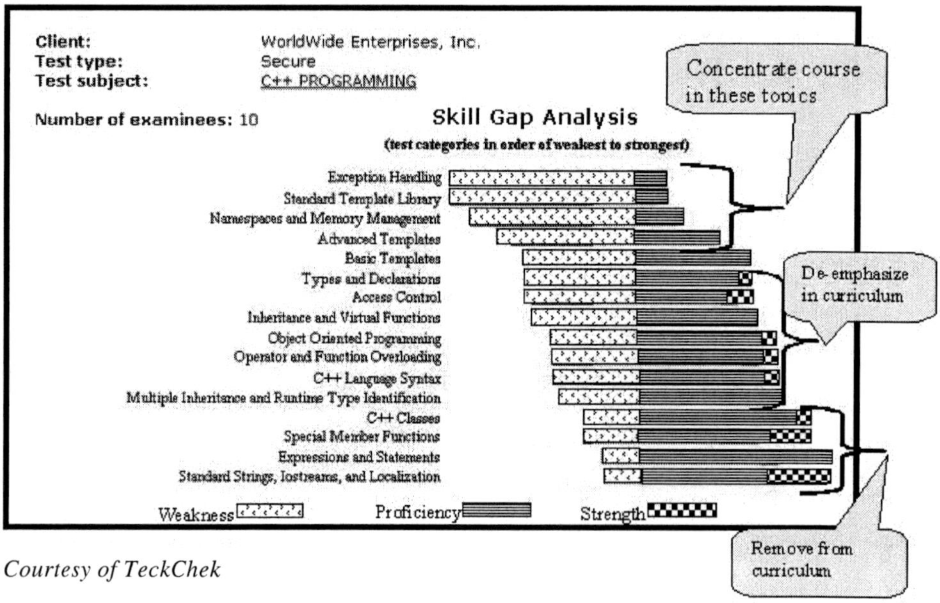

Courtesy of TeckChek

Upon reviewing this chart the instructor might choose to entirely eliminate the bottom four topics from the curriculum because over 80% of the class is already proficient in them. Instead, the course would concentrate on the top four topics for which 80% of the class has shown a weakness. This type of custom-focused training can help to significantly reduce class time as well as the cost of classroom training.

CASE STUDY

In 2000, a major resort/hotel chain wanted to improve the knowledge of its Windows 95 Help Desk team. The team consisted of 20 employees. The training vendor offered a five-day course, which was delivered in their classroom for $300 per student per day. Thus, retooling the skills of the entire department would have cost $30,000. One issue was the hotel's concern that not all team members be in training at the same time so that the Help Desk would not be closed.

The hotel first gave each team member a detailed sub-topic assessment in Windows 95. The overall assessment results were used to break the class into two groups: a group of more senior members and a group of the more junior members. A skills gap analysis using the sub-topic assessments was performed for each group. The skills gap report was then given to the vendor so the vendor could eliminate from the curriculum those topics that were unnecessary for each group. The reduced curriculum resulted in two custom classes that each covered four (4) half days. By training the juniors in the morning and the seniors in the afternoon, the entire department completed their targeted training in just four days, with each employee spending two person-days in training. The total cost was reduced to $12,000 for the 40 person-days of training and a $2,000 customization fee. This was all accomplished while maintaining 50% staffing of the Help Desk at all times.

The value of sub-topic assessment is also evident in the hiring process. Unable to locate the appropriate sub-topic skills in the employee population or provide training to develop those skills, the HR department can be alerted to look for employment candidates with a strength in the desired skills. By extending the sub-topic assessment process to employment candidates, a new level of depth is brought to the **Hiring Process** to optimize the match between job candidates and project needs. By having candidates take the assessment, not only can qualified candidates be objectively identified with enterprise-wide standards, but also candidates with appropriate skills can be found to fit into the exact needs of projects. In fact, expanding the skill gap analysis from project team to all employees will provide insight into enterprise-wide skill gaps. This insight can then be translated into more efficient and productive selection of new employees.

CASE STUDY

A major communications firm was undertaking a critical project for its Billing department. The principle technology being used in the project was Oracle. Accordingly, all employees who were to be on the project team were assessed in Oracle sub-topics. The results of the subsequent skill gap analysis indicated that the group was weak in the sub-topic PL/SQL packages. The project manager indicated that this was a fairly crucial aspect of Oracle relative to their project requirements. The HR department was instructed to begin a search for a new IT employee with Oracle experience and specifically with expertise in PL/SQL packages.

In response to its job offering, the HR department received more than 100 resumes. A short Oracle assessment was used as a screening tool to narrow the field of candidates down to the top 20% of scorers on this short assessment. The 20 candidates with the highest scores then proceeded to the next step in the hiring process, which included a background review, reference check, introductory interview, and full Oracle sub-topic assessment. The sub-topic assessment identified three of the candidates as having superior expertise in PL/SQL packages. While these three candidates were then given an in-depth technical interview, the remaining 17 candidates and their assessment results were stored in the candidate database for consideration in future opportunities.

One of the three candidates was selected for hire and was placed on the Oracle project team, where his areas of expertise helped to round out the team's Oracle knowledge base. The sub-topic assessment had not only identified the skill gaps of the project team, but had helped the organization to successfully plug those gaps through targeted hiring.

If the skill assessment tool allows for the grouping of candidate test results, then additional analysis can be done through group comparisons. Consider Figure 8, which represents a comparison between assessments taken pre-training and post-training for the same group of students. This assessment tool provides scores in a range of 1-40 with this particular analysis showing a higher distribution of scores for the post-training assessment, thus confirming the successful transfer of knowledge achieved by the training.

Figure 8

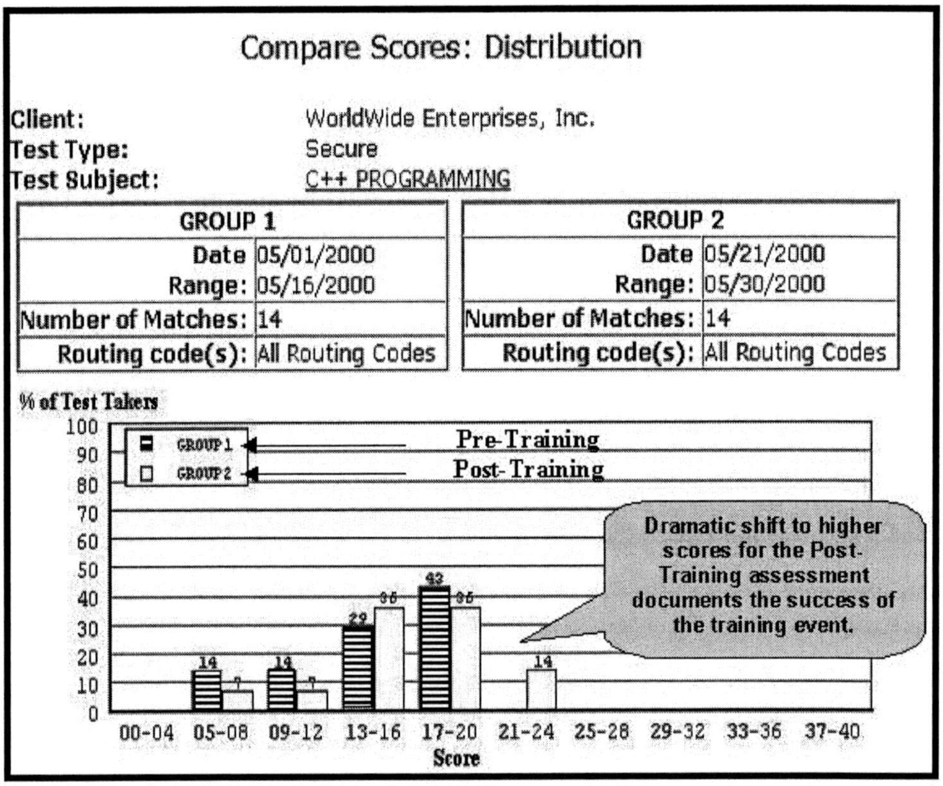

Courtesy of TeckChek

This type of comparative analysis can serve many functions. In addition to its use comparing pre-training and post-training knowledge, it can also be used in the hiring process, comparing the scores of candidates found at a job fair versus candidates who responded to an ad in the paper. Such an analysis can help an organization make better use of its recruiting expense.

This chapter has shown examples of how skill analysis can benefit IT initiatives in several ways. The key component to successful implementation of these benefits is assessing skills at the detail sub-topic level. With such detailed feedback available, creative HR managers will be able to find even more applications to improve the overall efficiency of IT skills management.

Conclusion

As virtually all industries progress towards a future that is driven by technology, a corporation's success will in large part depend upon the success of its IT initiatives. As software to drive that technology becomes more complex, the success of those IT initiatives will depend less on the selected hardware and software and more upon the skills of the people who implement the initiatives.

The most successful companies will be those which have gained the ability to effectively manage their IT skills. In their drive to succeed, more and more companies will begin to implement skills management initiatives incorporating skills inventory databases. Populating the skills database with objective skill assessments will be critical to the effectiveness of any skills management process. Thus the selection of a reliable objective assessment tool will play a vital role in the skills management process and ultimately in the overall success of IT initiatives. To optimize the skills management function, the selected assessment tool, for IT skills in particular, must provide insight into detailed sub-topic skills. It is these insights into sub-topic skills that will determine the practical value of the skills management process. Sub-topic skills will enhance many of the skill management functions, including training, hiring, skill gap analysis, and team building. Those assessment products that can provide these insights will become the cornerstone of successful IT skills management programs.

Chapter VI

Government Involvement in Skills Issues

Elizabeth Lahey
Elizabeth Lahey and Associates, USA

Abstract

Technology products and services make up approximately one-third of the U.S. economy. The statistics are similar around the globe. Governments are concerned because this industry sector significantly impacts employment and productivity rates. The birth of the information age and the criticality of knowledge workers had great potential. To date, however, the benefits are not fully realized. The rate of change in the industry has instead created a significant gap between the needs of employers and the skills of the workforce. While technology professionals cannot find jobs, employers claim they cannot hire workers with necessary skills portfolios. Government agencies are taking action to coordinate state, national, and international projects to bridge this skill gap. One project currently underway in the United States is the development of national skill standards for the information and communications technology (ICT) industry sector. It is funded by the Department of Labor.

Introduction

It is important to explore governmental skill development efforts because government wants to stimulate cooperation across companies, educational institutions, and support agencies, all of which have a vested interest in the end product, skill standards. Government legislation is a major tool because it can provide funding to create and promote national acceptance and global endorsement for developing skill standards. In the information and communications technology (ICT) industry sector, government coalitions can create skill standards that reflect extraordinary levels of rigor.[1] Individual companies could never hope to create such a set of skill standards, no matter how well researched, developed, or marketed. Skill standards that are accepted by ICT stakeholders facilitate skills planning and coordination at all levels. The country that implements such a schema has an inherent advantage in the global economy.

ICT is one of the most significant economic industry sectors in the world. Nations across the globe are scampering to make sure that they do not get left behind in the technology race. Knowing the skills necessary to update and support their employee base is vital to this effort. Governments are therefore deeply interested in identifying, maintaining, and disseminating an accurate set of skill standards they can share with their potential worker population. To have any chance of competing in a global economy, technology skills are essential to the success of even the smallest nations. In an information-based economy, size is irrelevant.

This chapter describes skill standards—not skill portfolios—because good skill standards facilitate the development and use of skill portfolios. Since creating and promoting skill standards is important to governments, I begin by explaining what is meant by the phrase "skill standards." Once this terminology is established, it will be easy to understand why governments are particularly interested in skill standards for the ICT industry sector. Statistics are presented to illustrate the impact of this sector on the overall national and world economies.

The information and communications technology industries have evolved over almost 50 years. Some may question why skill standards do not already exist for this sector. Others may wonder why governments are interested in developing and promoting skill standards at this point in the sector's history. This discussion is an overview of the ICT industry sector's impact on world labor markets using statistics from the United States. Finally, this chapter details a current project to illustrate the significant governmental involvement in skill standards efforts.

In summary the objectives of this chapter are to:

1. Define skill standards.
2. Present statistics on the significance of the ICT industry sector to the United States economy.
3. Discuss two relevant factors behind rapid change in the ICT industry sector.
4. Review the impact of the ICT industry sector change on the United States labor market.
5. Explore the United States ICT Skill Standards Project in detail.

Definition of Skill Standards

Before going into detail about why governments care about the development and support of skill standards, it is important to make clear exactly what is meant by the term, skill standards. Later we will use this information to explore how government, industry, learning institutions, and support groups use skill standards to clarify ICT skill needs.

A skill standard is simply a description of work activities that must be performed, how well the work activities must be performed, and the levels of associated knowledge and skills required for the work activities to be performed successfully. See Figure 1 for a visual representation of a skill standard.

There are two components to a work activity: the first describes the work itself and the second describes the worker. The work piece has three parts. The first is critical work functions (CWFs). Critical work functions are high-level tasks that must be performed by a person in the specified work activity. A typical worker will perform four to seven critical work functions on a regular basis. A given individual or company may perform additional functions outside the umbrella of critical work functions. But to be included as part of a skill standard, the work functions must be critical and therefore performed by every person and every company that does the work. Work functions not meeting the criteria

Figure 1: The Skill Standard

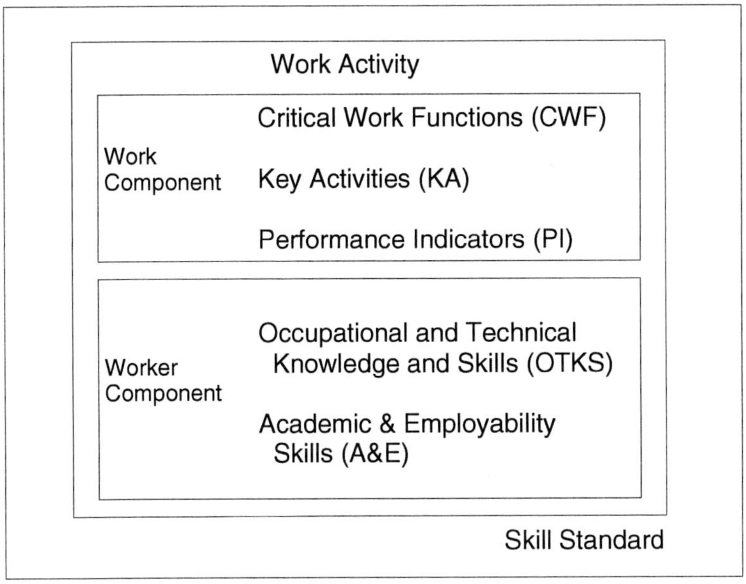

are not standard and are excluded. As an aside, a group of critical work functions differentiates one worker's role from another worker's role. Employers combine critical work functions to create jobs and job descriptions. Some examples clarify the level at which critical work functions are designed. They include: writes computer code, monitors databases, or repairs network devices.

The second part of the work component for a work activity is called key activities (KAs). Five to eight KAs further define each critical work function. The critical work function "writes code" may include tasks such as: reviews program specifications, develops program logic flows and types program code.

The final part of the work component for a work activity is performance indicators (PIs). Every critical work function has a set of PIs that tell if work is being done successfully or not. Examples for "writes code" may include: flow chart documented, code operates as expected, and code passes unit tests.

The other component of the work activity is the worker portion. The worker portion of a work activity has two parts. The first is the occupational and technical knowledge and skills (OTKSs) needed to complete the work, and the second is the basic academic and employability (A&E) skills required to do the work. Examples of these would include knowing computer start-up procedures (OTKSs) and being able to reset the computer's time after reading a clock (A&E). Figure 1 thus shows how all the components and parts fit together to create one skill standard.

Moving up the skill "food chain," each category of work (known as a job concentration), usually contains between four and eight work activities. Thus, to determine if a person is performing adequately in a specific job concentration, the employer must look at the results of multiple work activities.

Job concentrations are logical groupings of work. Actual job positions within any organization may overlap one or more job concentrations. Job concentrations and actual jobs are closely related, although not the same. The job positions are bastardized versions of job concentrations because employers need to fill voids in their existing employee skill sets that may overlap job concentrations. Employers may even combine job concentrations to minimize the number of total employees needed by the firm.

ICT Statistics

Now, with a general understanding of skill standards, we return to the ICT industry sector and explore its importance. The industry sector's impact on the economy, and therefore on national labor markets, is significant. The ICT industry sector's effect on the American worker will make it clear why the United States Government cares about skill standards.

ICT ranks in the top two fastest growing and largest industrial sectors in the United States economy, swollen by an estimated 230,000 new jobs between 1996 and 1999. Over six million workers are currently employed in the industry sector (Kennard, 2000). The growth in overall employment by this industry sector is expected to continue. The effect on the United States economy has been just as significant. Since 1995, the ICT industry sector has accounted for one-third of the real output growth in the United States economy, based upon numbers from the United States Bureau of Labor Statistics.

The growth in the size of the industry sector and the effect on the United States economy of the ICT industry sector is only outpaced by the rate of change within the industry sector itself. The number and diversity of new products and services, the rise and fall of competitors, the introduction and obsolescence of technologies, and the fall from exorbitant to rock bottom prices within months are all frequent occurrences. Today, a six-month old computer is outdated. Mergers and acquisitions such as AOL and Time-Warner seem to be odd, then seem momentarily brilliant, and then seemingly fall apart. These are all examples of ICT's changing nature.

Information and communications technology is also starting to integrate itself more effectively with more traditional industries and vice versa. This trend will continue and become more global. The industry sector is redefining itself and attempting to become a part of the mainstream consumer market in the world's economy.

Two Factors Behind the Change

Two major factors drive changes in the ICT industry sector. Both of these are, in turn, causing important changes in the labor market. Since they impact the labor markets, they also affect workers. This is where governments begin to express concern and a desire to intervene. But first, we will look at the two factors impacting change in the ICT industry sector and how they affect labor markets.

The first factor that impacts the ICT industry sector is **technology** itself. Technology is advancing at high velocity. This can be measured in two ways: the cost of technology is declining on a steep slope, and the power of technology is expanding exponentially. Moore's Law, *the power of computing will double every six months*, has proven remarkably accurate.

Most observers agree that the greatest technological change of recent memory is the Internet with its underlying infrastructure. Most of us who communicate through our email everyday forget that the thing we know as the Internet was only in labs and universities 10 years ago. When the power of the Internet is combined with wide varieties of information through digitization—voice, video, and data—the possibilities become endless. When information is transmitted from one location to another over a common global network, results are profound. This change not only impacts the ICT industry sector, but it impacts every other industry sector that utilizes ICT as well.

The global Internet network has also revolutionized computers. No longer is a personal computer a remote island. Today, it is intricately connected to vast networks of other computers all over the globe. By connecting to the Internet, the personal computer has become simply one type of gadget that can meet a variety of users' information needs. In the past, people had a telephone, a pager, an electronic organizer, a fax machine, a laptop computer, and a calculator. They may also have had a variety of other specialty devices for such things as gaming or global positioning. But each of these gadgets provided a single, distinct function. Today, ICT companies are designing information appliances that package a set of these functions into one device, connecting to the Internet. At the same time, these multi-function information appliances are becoming more specialized to meet the information and communication needs of users. The range of technological choices is more often a matter of price and personal taste (one for jogging, one for business travel, etc.) than a limitation of the appliance. Thus we see how enormous networking capacity via the Internet and digital information availability in numerous forms have fueled even more technological advances that allow people greater access to an expanding volume of global knowledge in an ever-shrinking world economy.

The second major factor impacting change in the ICT industry sector is **government policy**. Telecommunications legislation in 1996 broke down the barriers to competition in local and long-distance telephone services. This allowed firms into the communications industry from such diverse backgrounds as the traditional telephone company to the cable, satellite, and Internet industries. In 1996, the FCC auctioned the airwaves to these various firms. The allocation process greatly expanded the capacity for wireless transmission, and helped fuel and supports the exploding demand for wireless services. The FCC had apportioned and assigned control for the use of transmission space to communicate with the world. Wireless subscriptions in the United States grew from 13 million in 1993 to over 76 million in 1999 and were projected to increase to 149 million in 2003. Expressed differently, one in 10 people had a wireless phone in 1993, and six in 10 were expected to have a wireless phone in 2003 (Kennard, 2000).

To summarize, technological and governmental policy forces together help explain why the ICT industry sector is growing and changing so rapidly. Changes in government policy, increased Internet network capacity, and the digitization of information have fostered convergence. The differences between computer, telephone, cable TV, Internet service provider, satellite, TV and radio broadcast, and wireless industries are blurring. This is readily seen in the plethora of multi-function computing and communication appliances that are currently available in the marketplace.

All the information that any firm creates and manages can be distributed over the Internet to any entity desired. Once, AT&T had the only extensive network and it carried only analog voice signals. Today, there are many nationwide and global networks. They all offer multiple services, including telephony, Internet access, paging, television, and other information services. The consumer can now shop based upon the company's value proposition, which is the sum total of what a given company provides the consumer through their network's capacity.

This increased network capacity that competitors offer in the communications market is one reason for the steep drop in the cost of services. The increased capacity also allows the supplier to provide consumers more services. An example of this is the use of phone lines for voicemail access and for access to the Internet. These are multiple uses for the same network capacity. This change has shifted the value that a company offers a customer from the network itself to the content delivered over the network. This then becomes the company's total value proposition to the consumer. Some ICT companies have reacted to this shift in value by acquiring or merging with content providers. For example, Cablevision bought Radio City Music Hall, and AOL merged with Time/Warner to expand their content offerings.

ICT Changes Impact on the Labor Market and Government Response

How does all this change affect the labor market? The traditional premise was that government becomes concerned and involved once changes in an industry sector begin to have significant impact on the labor market. When workers are difficult to place in jobs because of incorrect job skills, then government wants to identify the right skill sets. It wants to keep entry-level workers off unemployment and welfare rolls. It wants to make sure women and minorities are adequately represented in the workforce mix. It wants to be certain the funding being provided to career and transitional job training programs are properly preparing people for positions that will provide them a decent salary and an opportunity to live the American dream. And it wants to make sure the industries that form the backbone of America's economic power base in technology do not suffer from a shortage of properly skilled workers.

The following is a quote from the project that the information and communications technology industry sector conducted with federal government support to establish a baseline set of skill standards for the ICT industry sector. We will look at this project in detail throughout this chapter. But let's start by reading a layman's description of the reason the effort was undertaken (Squires, 2002, pp. 4-5):

> "Despite the increasing importance of content to the ICT industry, the critical enabling technology is still the network. Personal computers, servers, routers, transmission media, and the software that is used to operate them, comprise networks. Technicians, programmers, and other frontline workers and first-line supervisors, for whom the skill standards will be created, build, expand, troubleshoot, and maintain the software and hardware that comprises networks.
>
> The many changes in the ICT industry have changed the technician's job and the skills and knowledge required to perform it. For example, previously, a cable TV technician simply installed cable television service by connecting a single coaxial cable into a simple, single function box that connected to a television. Today, an ICT company offers telephony, wireless, Internet access, and cable television service. The technician in this company must know all of these services, and the software and technologies that accompany them.
>
> ICT companies that offer multiple services have not succeeded in acquiring or creating a workforce of technicians who are able to install, troubleshoot, and maintain the multiple services offered by the evolving ICT companies. They dispatch, at great cost, multiple technicians to accomplish the service call that involves multiple services and technologies.
>
> Future technicians need more skills and different skills than technicians of the past did. A customer contact or installation is more complex today. It involves the connection of a more complex transmission medium into a multi-function box. The multi-function box provides Internet access, telephone service, television, and other information

services, and the technician must troubleshoot all of these services including the operating system and networking that makes these services possible. Skill standards can play a critical role in defining what those skills are and establishing certification programs to ensure ICT companies have the skilled labor force they need to succeed.

The skill standards will provide many benefits to the multi-service ICT companies of the future including:

- Meet the critical need for qualified technicians to support multiple-service ICT companies.
- Improve the hiring and evaluation processes for employers.
- Establish professional development path for employees to keep their skills current and to expand their skills over time.
- Allow the educational institutions to coordinate their curriculums more effectively.
- Guide the training investment choices of business.
- Allow parents and community organizations to participate better in decisions regarding educational priorities and local needs.
- Advance opportunities for minorities and women.
- Create portable certifications for a vast number of technicians in ICT.
- Create a pool of potential candidates to meet the rapid growth in the ICT industry."

In 1994 with legislation called the National Skill Standards Act, Congress created an organization under the Department of Labor to focus efforts around the development and marketing of skill standards for the United States workforce. The mission of the National Skill Standards Board (NSSB) was to support the development of a national, world-class system of voluntary skill standards to enhance the productivity and raise the living standards of the United States workforce.

NSSB established a 24-member board of directors with a 15-person office managed by an executive director. It was located in Washington, DC, near its parent agency, the Department of Labor. NSSB's first assignment was to determine how to address the skill standard challenge. It chose to tackle its legislative mandate by using a number of Voluntary Partnerships, comprised of business, education, and labor. Each Voluntary Partnership governed the development of skill standards in its specific industry sector aided by technical experts for statistical measurement and skill standards development.

The next issue addressed was the composition of the Voluntary Partnerships. NSSB needed a well-balanced combination of key stakeholders surrounding each industry sector if the skill standards were to get the proper validation, support, and usage needed to guarantee their success. Each industry sector might well have a slightly different configuration, so the key was to find large, well-networked stakeholders that played significant roles in each industry sector to speed accomplishment of these objectives. In general though, the Voluntary Partnerships would include business leaders, educators, labor leaders, state officials, and special interest groups.

The final planning decision that the NSSB had to make was defining the scope of their mandate. They chose to limit their work to establishing skill standards for baseline or entry-level jobs. The NSSB further determined that the skill standards would be validated using certification testing to prove that individuals who claimed to have acquired the skills had in fact attained the skills.

Since legislation directed that the skill standards efforts were to be voluntary, the NSSB approached various industry sectors that they believed would be prime candidates for this type of activity. One of the significant obstacles that any interested industry sector faced was its ability to establish the Voluntary Partnership arrangement necessary to manage and direct the multi-year effort.

Recruiting the large number of frontline worker resources for focus groups and surveys would be another major issue any industry sector would face. That means the industry sector had to either wield a great deal of control over the workforce's daily routine or the industry sector was so negatively affected that it was willing to overcome whatever obstacles were in the path of success. Two industry sectors accepted the challenge; one fell into each category. In the first category was manufacturing. This became the pilot skill standards project. With the help of the unions bringing together literally thousands of frontline workers, it proved to be a relatively smooth process.

The second was our industry sector, the ICT industry sector. The skill gap mismatch between employer needs and the skills of the applicants was so severe that the risk for undertaking the endeavor was well worth the reward.

The Information and Communication Skill Standards Project

The details of the ICT Skill Standards Project follow. It began in 2001 and continues today. This is persuasive evidence of the importance the government and ICT industry sector place upon making sure business, education, and workers agree on what accurate, current, and updated skills are.

CompTIA, the Computing Technology Industry Association, is acting as the project manager and is the leader of the ICT Voluntary Partnership. Its project partners include ITAA (Information Technology Association of America), NWCET (Northwest Center for Emerging Technologies), a team of technical experts, and the Department of Labor (NSSB).

The ICT Voluntary Partnership has a growing number of members. The business representation is intended to account for over 40% of the ICT jobs in the industry sector. Current members include names such as Microsoft, Intel, U.S. West, Cisco, IBM, Verizon, EDS, Compucom, AT&T, Siemens, Xerox, HP, and Novell. Representatives solicited from the education, training, labor, and civic organizations include Prosoft Training, New Horizons, ElementK, Smartforce, NetG, Thompson Courseware, Prometric, VUE, IT Career Consortium, Technology Workforce Coalition, Urban League, EDC, NWCET, AACC, CREDA, CWA, TAAA, NSF, League of Innovations, SEI, ICCP, IEEE, and others.

The detailed work plan has three stages of development activities, followed by a mass validation survey. The work plan was based upon initial summary research conducted by a team of experts. The research question was how to organize the ICT industry sector jobs into job concentrations for the purpose of grouping the skill standards interview activities. The NSSB's expert review panel, as well as the ICT Voluntary Partnership, approved the initial research strategy.

The following assumptions formed the foundation for the proposed ICT Skill Standards research (Squires, 2002, pp. 7-8):

> "**A.** The NSSB selected the information and communication technology population technician for the development of skill standards in this sector. Programmers with four-year college degrees are not to be included in the skill standards research. While these directives are

clear, they do not provide a detailed definition for technician nor do they address the question of what to do with programmers who have less than a four-year college degree or no college education at all.

The term technician is very broad. For the purposes of the skill standards research, frontline workers through first-level supervisors in ICT with less than a four-year degree will be considered 'technicians.' This excludes engineers, systems analysts, software engineers, and most programmers.

The NSSB selected ICT technicians as the target job for developing skill standards and certification. Technicians were chosen because they meet the criteria established by the NSSB—the technician job is not a profession, it does not require a four-year college degree, and it is not a management position. In addition, technicians are a critical job cluster in the ICT industry that is growing rapidly and will benefit from skill standards and certification. The industry will benefit from skill standards because there is a current and projected shortage of technicians, and skill standards will provide a blueprint that educational institutions can use to develop job-related training programs. The increase in training programs will make it possible for more people to become technicians. Moreover, certification programs are common in this industry, and a generic certification is likely to be well received.

Technicians are frontline workers who work with the ICT technology—hardware and software—that engineers design. They install, troubleshoot, program, monitor, maintain, update, repair, replace, and operate IT and telecommunications technology such as computers, routers, file servers, PBXs, computer programs, databases, telephone systems, and microwave equipment. While each sub-industry has its own type of technician, the research will identify the common work and skills in each concentration. And while technicians may or may not have four-year college degrees, they do not typically have a four-year college degree in engineering or computer science.

The vast majority of supervisors of technicians are former technicians. In addition to managerial skills, supervisors have the same skills and knowledge as technicians and are often required to step in and work as a technician.

B. Programmers with less than a four-year college degree in this sector will be included in this research. According to a 1998 DOL study, 32% of programmers have less than a four-year college degree. Many are self-taught or have certificates from Novell, Microsoft, or a community college, vocational-technical institute, or other educational institution.

The nature of programmer work has changed. The development of 'case tools' has automated a great deal of programming work. Managers make distinctions between high- and low-level programming work. The person who performs the higher-level work with a four-year college degree in computer science is a programmer or software engineer. These are the programmers who the NSSB excluded from the skill standards research. The two-year technical school graduate or the person with an MSCD certificate (Microsoft Certified Solutions Developer) performs the lower-level programming. These workers should not be excluded from the research. They administer to networks, troubleshoot equipment, and software, and provide help desk services, to name a few of the types of work they perform.

The skill standards research will provide greater clarity regarding the work performed by programmers, and in particular, junior programmers. From initial research and discussions with thought leaders, it appears that junior programmers do not do the initial design and development of larger software applications. They work on existing code to modify, update, and maintain it. Junior programmers perform some programming for proprietary languages that are part of PBXs, routers, file server administration, etc. Approximately 35% of programmers do not have a computer science degree, but were self-taught or obtained two-year technical school degrees.

C. For a number of years, the ICT industries were unable to fill skilled positions. These industries developed vendor-specific certifications, which required the gathering of job analysis, training needs analysis, and competency data. Industry members informed this project that, while they are not interested in sending subject matter experts to provide information they have already gathered, they are quite willing to share this information for the development of skill standards, which meet NSSB requirements.

> **D.** One set of skill standards will be developed for frontline workers through first-line supervisors. Distinction between these two groups will not be made in the standards, since in ICT, first-line supervisors are usually individuals who do frontline work, but who may also perform some team leadership responsibilities."

The standards committee conducted the ICT Skill Standards Project in three distinct stages. The first stage was an industry and literature review. This effort began late in the summer of 2001. NSSB assigned the project a team of experts which would collect all the known industry materials on job analysis, training analysis, and skill analysis data, as well as recruit a group of senior subject matter experts (SMEs) from the ICT industry sector to summarize its findings into previously agreed-upon skill standards formats. The objective of the initial stage was to establish a preliminary set of critical work functions (CWFs), key activities (KAs), and performance indicators (PIs), and identify gaps.

Once the SMEs had completed the initial draft skill standards, the second stage began. The objective was to have Winter 2002 focus groups analyze and verify the initial draft critical work functions, key activities, and performance indicators, and to fill in any missing gaps. In addition to reviewing the SMEs' work from the prior autumn, the focus groups were challenged to create a first draft of the taxonomy for occupational and technical knowledge and skills (OTKSs) and to develop an initial list of OTKSs for each category on the taxonomy. The target population for the focus groups was no longer SMEs, but frontline workers themselves who matched an elaborate matrix of economic and demographic criteria that represented the ICT industry sector and its workers in the United States.

The final stage of the project will conduct a focus session with industrial and occupational psychologists using sample work activities developed in Stages One and Two. Through their review of this material, these experts would then be able to utilize their expertise to develop the academic & employability (A&E) knowledge and skills.

While the A&E phase was progressing using Industrial and Occupational Psychologist expertise, an extensive national validation survey is undertaken, to confirm the accuracy of the CWF, KA, PI, and OTKS findings. The national survey would require access to tens of thousands of frontline workers, supervisors, trainers, and SMEs. Their role would be to critique the work that had been underway for over a year.[2]

All of the steps in this project may seem elaborate and costly for little apparent return. The reason for such an investment of time and energy is not obvious to those unfamiliar with similar research projects. The main reason for the rigor and accuracy of the sampling and evaluation process is to ensure that these skill standards are legally defensible in an American court of law. If any company chooses to hire, promote, or fire as a result of these skill standards, the company must be in a position to know that the federal government has demonstrated due diligence to make sure that the standards are in fact accurate representations of the entire economy. The entire industry sector and the entire minority population must be properly captured in every sample. The statistics must be gathered from companies across a representative sample of various sizes and locations among different primary and non-primary ICT employers. The diversity of the individuals involved must be validated. The result is ICT skill standards in which every user of these standards can feel confident.

The initial job concentration structure developed and approved by NSSB and the ICT Voluntary Partnership is shown in the diagram on page 142. The job concentrations describe work that is performed by technicians in a wide range of industries and reflects the rapidly evolving nature of work, including the move toward digital services, and the merging of industries, including telephony, cable, satellite, system integrators, software developers, Internet service providers, wireless, broadcast radio, and TV.

The identified sub-industries within the ICT industry sector, along with industry sectors outside of the ICT industry sector *which utilize high numbers of ICT workers*, form the foundation for the identification of primary and non-primary target companies for the selection matrix to be used in the formulation of focus groups in Stage Two and the mass validation survey. A research objective is to include participants who represent a cross-section of all these factors, as well as human diversity concerns.

The definition and verification of the skill standards followed a content-oriented approach. This type of approach requires that the persons providing the expertise must have first-hand knowledge of the work to be performed. Thus their skills are current and relevant to the contemporary work environment. Validation of skill standards involves a thorough understanding of the work process. To evaluate the validity of the standards, they must be written in the context of the participant. They should be a meaningful and accurate description of the important work functions, key activities, knowledge, and skill requirements identified for the proposed job concentrations. The focus on

Concentration	**Description**
Networking Operations	Development and maintenance of the wired, wireless, or satellite network. Includes Novell, LAN, phone networks, wireless networks, and satellite networks. Use cable, fiber optics, wireless and/or satellite communications to connect users. May work in central offices, data centers, and other central locations that manage networking "hub" centers. Monitor network performance, traffic and transmission quality, supervise switching, and troubleshoot software and hardware. Document network configuration, and execute backup plans and procedures. Adding users, maintaining security. Install upgrades. *Industries: All segments of this sector and all sectors in the economy.*
Programming	Writing and debugging code as directed by supervisor, Software engineers and/or systems analysts. Analyze, design, develop, adapt, test, and maintain computer and Internet-based applications. Use development tools and programming languages in creating and testing the software. Includes software for computer operations, networks, databases, the Internet, and consumers such as HTML, Visual Basic, XML, and high-level languages. *Industries: All segments of this sector and all sectors in the economy.*
Internet Operations and Maintenance	Use Web page development software to create or change Web pages, set up server software and hardware, manage the server, and support disaster recovery. *Industries: All segments of this sector and all sectors in the economy.*
Database Development and Administration	Design forms databases so users can create data queries and interpret results; manage growth of the database; keep data secure and create security procedures; implement backup and recovery processes; maintain system security and reliability. *Industries: All segments of this sector and all sectors in the economy.*
Field Operations	Operations and maintenance of field equipment including cell sites, satellite dishes, phone lines, head ends, etc. Primarily reflects telecommunications, but will include all aspects of telecom. Ensure the field network equipment functions properly. Maintain and troubleshoot facilities including cell sites, satellite dishes, phone lines, customer PBX's network hubs, etc. *Industries: Phone, satellite, wireless, cable, and all sectors of the economy.*
Technical Support	Educating users and solving hardware or software operation and application problems. Deal directly with customer issues. Hardware and software installation and configuration. Includes both the help-desk and the on-site technical support. *Industries: All segments of this sector and all sectors in the economy.*

incumbent workers as the rightful subject matter experts is central to the validation process.

As one final step to ensure that the skill standards are not obsolete before they are even published, the reviewers at the end of each stage are asked to bear in mind the skills and knowledge they anticipate will be required over the next three years. This dimension of the research will allow the ICT industry sector the opportunity to complete one cycle of work before they will need to begin the process anew.

The ICT Skill Standards work plan also included a detailed sampling plan for conducting focus groups and the national validation survey. As one of the first steps in the development of these sampling plans, the measurement and sampling experts on the ICT Skill Standards Project team collected data from the Bureau of Labor Statistics and Census Bureau to obtain information about the size and characteristics of the ICT technician population.

> "Due to the rapid changes in the ICT industry, the industries and occupations tracked by the BLS and Census data are not reflective of current industries and occupations. For example, telegraph is included in the BLS occupational list and webmaster is not. These data are not adequate to establish a sampling framework to be used to determine sampling percentages for the concentrations. Therefore the data are reported but not used to determine sample sizes and proportions. The sampling strategy was guided by the BLS and Census data, but was not a scientific sample...." (Squires, 2002, p. 21)

The sampling strategy was as follows: The Stage One subject matter expert panels would use approximately 18 people total, three from each of the six job concentration areas. The qualifications to be considered a "subject matter expert" included at least five years of experience in the ICT industry sector and current work duties including responsibilities within the job concentration.

The Stage Two focus groups followed the precedent set by the pilot Manufacturing Skill Standards Project. The focus groups use 30 frontline workers and first-level supervisors for each of the six job concentrations. This equates to 180 people total, split over four geographic locations. These 180 are further differentiated by primary versus non-primary in the industry sector, the company size, sub-industry, and human diversity constraints imposed upon the research for legal defensibility purposes. The criteria for participant consideration included:

- Participants must have two years of experience in the specific concentration that they planned to represent. SMEs from Stage One of the project had determined that the learning curve for a technician was approximately 24 months to become fully functional. This suggested that a technician could achieve an acceptable level of competence after two years on the job. Therefore, the research used this standard as one of the criteria to be considered a "competent worker." There was no upper limit on the amount of experience a participant could have.
- Participants must have completed to their employer's satisfaction a probationary period. Potential focus group members should be regarded by their employers as performing all duties at a competent level, according to the standards used by that specific organization to evaluate employee performance.
- The target population is frontline workers who are at the first levels on a technician career ladder. These workers have at times been referred to as "entry-level" workers, though the term "entry-level" is not meant to imply workers who only recently entered the concentration, as workers may have had over two years of tenure in their positions. To clarify who was eligible to participate, workers must have been either: (1) non-supervisory workers at the frontline of the work, or they must have had (2) first-level supervisory responsibilities and at least one year of experience in a non-supervisory position and spend *a minimum of* 50% of their workday performing the same duties as technicians who had no supervisory responsibilities.

The Stage Three focus groups consist of industrial and occupational (IO) psychologists with expertise in the ICT area. Possible criteria include:

- At least 10 years of experience performing job analysis and building competency models.
- An MS or PhD in Industrial and Occupational Psychology or the Social Sciences/Computer Science.

We have identified here (see page 145) 17 A&E skills that will be evaluated for potential inclusion in the portfolio of ICT Skill Standards. The job of the IO

Academic Knowledge and Skills	*Employability Knowledge and Skills*	
Reading Writing Mathematics Science	Listening Speaking Using information and communications technology Gathering and analyzing information Analyzing and solving problems	Making decisions and judgments Organizing and planning Using social skills Adaptability Working in teams Leading others Building consensus Self and career development

psychology experts is to determine which are appropriate to include and at what level of complexity the 17 items are required. This stage of the project is currently in process.

Two key judgments need to be made about the academic and employability (A&E) knowledge and skills:

> "**1.** Is a particular academic and employability knowledge and skill needed to perform a given critical work function? Even though the NSSB list of academic and employability knowledge and skills is widely applicable, it is still important to find out whether these knowledge and skills are needed for the work being described by a particular set of critical work functions. Therefore, one step in the process will be to determine whether or not a given academic or employability knowledge and skill is needed to perform a particular critical work function.
>
> **2.** What complexity level is needed? Once it is established that a given academic or employability knowledge or skill is needed to perform a critical work function, it is also important to then identify the complexity level required. All ratings will be done at the level of the critical work function, and raters will rate at the overall skill level rather than the key activity level." (Squires, 2002, p. 38)

While Stage Three is still in process, the national survey has also begun. The team moved into the final verification stages of the project. We anticipate that the data is fairly clean by this point in the process, since several significant changes have occurred throughout the 18-month process. The most notable to the casual observer is the shift in job concentrations. The original six job

Old Concentrations	*New Concentrations*
Networking Operations	Network Infrastructure
Programming	Programming
Internet Operations and Maintenance	Web Development and Administration
Database Development and Administration	Database Development and Administration
Field Operations	
Technical Support	Network Devices
	Technical Writing
	Digital Media

concentrations are presented, alongside the seven that existed at the start of the mass validation survey that began in spring of 2003 (see top of page).

The mass validation survey is the most controversial sampling plan yet developed. The sheer scope of the effort is unprecedented. The debate rages between the business practitioners and the statistical purists over sampling size. The number of accurately completed surveys in an ideal situation is 24,000. This includes filling all the necessary coverage gaps for diversity, demographics, sector, and sub-industry variance, and all other related constraints required to make the skill standards legally highly defensible in a court of law. The mass validation survey is underway as this book goes to press, and it presents a challenge to the research team. Whether a compromise figure can be reached is yet to be determined. But the debate continues as to how many surveys are enough to confirm the validity of the ICT Skill Standards. The only true test will likely be the first court battle the skill standards will face. But from the detail described in this chapter, it is obvious that they have already been through a thorough and rigorous review according to some of the best analysts in the ICT industry sector. As an employer, you should feel confident that you and your people are using skill information that passes both the scrutiny of your peers and the validity of the government research specialists.

United States tax dollars paid for the ICT Skill Standards Project. The information is free for anyone's use and is accessible over the Internet in the public domain. The owner of these standards is CompTIA, the manager of the Voluntary Partnership and skill standards research project. CompTIA currently has the *draft* standards available through their TechCareer Compass (TCC) website. Once the ICT Skill Standards attain formal governmental approval, they will be updated (if needed) on the TechCareer Compass website. To access the ICT Skill Standards information and other valuable tools, go to the TechCareer Compass website at http://tcc.comptia.org.

The Department of Labor and the ICT industry sector continue their creative engagement with the challenges discussed here. The agreement that the Voluntary Partnership made with the government before the funding was approved stipulated that an ongoing process would be designed. From the very start, everyone involved realized that the crux of the problem in the ICT industry sector was the velocity of change. The project would produce little benefit if it was completed and then shelved. The only way skill standards could provide any sustainable value would be if they were updated on a continuous basis. The goal of the Voluntary Partnership is to revisit skill standards in the most volatile portions of the industry sector every 18 months. The cycle will be repeated until such time as the ICT industry sector can demonstrate that it has become stable.

Conclusion

This chapter began with discussing the importance of ICT skills to governments. Our analysis has focused exclusively on the efforts in the United States. It is important to connect back to global concerns. The United States is not in any way the only country or region funding research or training activities aimed at improving the ICT skills of its workforce. Many nations are exploring ways to take advantage of the information revolution. The Internet has made it a common phenomenon for workers in India to contract with employers in America. Governments around the world want to support their unemployed workers by providing them with marketable skills. They want their countries to benefit from the raised living standards a technology-literate society can offer.

The trend is now toward defining skill standards at the international and regional levels. There are efforts underway to unite the European, Australian, and American ICT skill standards into a single set. This will allow employers and workers portability. At the opposite extreme, state and local governments are further refining existing skill standards to meet the needs of local workers and employers. For example, in an area of chip manufacturing where a more unique skill set is required to succeed, those skills need emphasis. Yet those skills are not likely to meet a global skill standard. So those skills that were diluted at a higher level become more important in local standards. Thus, local job analysis experts define work activities in chip-related areas so that workers and employers understand skill portfolio needs based upon localized skill standards.

The information and communications technology industry sector will remain one of the most significant contributors to the world economy in the near future. Few governments can afford to neglect that potential. The effect on the labor market has long-term consequences that no government can afford to ignore. The key to a government's involvement in the ICT industry sector is knowing how to properly prepare its workers for jobs. The government needs to know where to place its training and welfare support dollars. Skill standards are one way to do this. Many government agencies around the globe are working on skill standards projects; and many are very interested in pinpointing, marketing, and updating a valid set of ICT skill standards that can be provided to their workers, and their welfare and educational support agencies. Government involvement in ICT skills standards has the benefit of higher levels of rigor, universal acceptance, and global endorsement that no individual company could ever hope to establish, no matter how well researched, developed, or marketed.

Endnotes

1. Throughout this chapter the ICT acronym is used often. The reason is that the government merges the two industries into one sector for reporting purposes. Due to increasing convergence between the information technology and communications industries, this nomenclature is now commonly accepted throughout Europe, Asia, and is gaining widespread acceptance in the United States as well. It will soon replace IT as the industry norm.
2. That survey is in process today and can be accessed at http://www.comptia.org/pressroom/get_public.asp?id=178. If you or any persons you know may qualify to participate, please consider helping in the effort to validate the ICT National Skill Standards.

References

Kennard, W.E. (2000). *Telecommunications @ the millennium; the Telecom Act turns four.* Washington, DC: Office of Plans and Policy, Federal Communications Commission.

Meares, C.A., & Sargent, J.F. (1999). *The digital workforce: Building infotech skills at the speed of innovation.* Washington, DC: U.S. Department of Commerce, Office of Technology Policy.

National Skill Standards Board. (2000). *Built to work.* Washington, DC: National Skill Standards Board.

Squires, P., & Bailey, T. (2002). *Information and communications technology (ICT) work analysis plan.* Washington, DC: National Skill Standards Board.

Chapter VII

Japanese IT-Skill Dilemma

Yoko Takeda
Yokohama National University, Japan

Abstract

Japanese companies are facing a dilemma regarding their IT skills. Although many Japanese feel the need to expand the scope of their information systems by implementing newer technologies, they are still obsessed with the "not-made-for-us syndrome." Japanese IS vendors have been unable to establish a new business model, because the integration of new and old technologies is not easy. When considering the IT skills in Japanese firms, our attention is primarily focused on the characteristics of traditional IT skills before focusing on the newly required skills, because the traditional IT skills have developed strong inertia that prevents change. We will analyze the current situation of the Japanese IT-skill dilemma and discuss methods to resolve it.

Introduction

Japanese companies are facing a dilemma regarding their IT skills. Although many Japanese feel the need to expand the scope of their information systems by implementing newer technologies, they are still obsessed with the "not-made-for-us syndrome." Japanese IS vendors have been unable to establish a new business model, because the integration of new and old technologies is not easy.

When considering the IT skills in Japanese firms, our attention is primarily focused on the characteristics of traditional IT skills before focusing on the newly required skills, because the traditional IT skills have developed strong inertia that prevents change. We will analyze the current situation of the Japanese IT-skill dilemma and discuss methods to resolve it.

This chapter consists of three parts. In the first section, "IT Skills of Japanese Companies," we will summarize the characteristics of the IT skills in Japanese companies. A characteristic of information systems in Japanese companies is that users are fixated on customized systems. The Japanese IS-vendor industry has grown in response to the needs of Japanese users to improve and expand proprietary information systems. It has gained the ability to efficiently develop customized systems through long-term relationships with IS-user companies. The main method used for acquiring IT skills in both IS-user and IS-vendor companies is in-house training, thus an external labor market and external educational institutions such as universities have not grown. The most important skill for Japanese companies is to play the role of a "coordinator" between the IS users and the IS division or IS vendors.

In the late 1990s, the protracted recession and the spread of IP technology finally required that Japanese companies change their IT skills. Since 2000, government policies have been promoting an increase in engineers across various specializations and setting the career path for senior engineers who have advanced technical expertise and diverse work experience.

In the second section, "Japanese IT-Skill Dilemma," a Japanese IT-skill dilemma is discussed. IS-user companies are still obsessed with the "not-made-for-us syndrome" and prefer customized systems. They seek a "super coordinator" who can retain the existing systems and incorporate new technology to expand operations and simultaneously maintain high performance by coordinating between IS users and IS departments/vendors. However, it is not possible for coordinators to facilitate performance improvement across a wide scope of operations. Thus, the concept of a super coordinator is merely an illusion.

In contrast, traditionally, Japanese IS vendors have built up a business model compatible with the needs of the IS-user companies requiring unique customized systems. Even when using packaged software, they have thoroughly customized it to suit the needs of customers' businesses. Since the late 1990s, IS vendors have been faced with the challenging task of fostering the skills of engineers in new areas of technology while maintaining the traditional skills.

In the third section, "Beyond Dilemma," we will discuss how we can resolve this dilemma. The means to overcome this dilemma is to attack the root cause, the lack of progress in restructuring old businesses, and creating new businesses within Japanese companies. In addition, companies should promote the involvement of top management and the leadership of senior engineers towards reforming business processes that support the implementation of IT. Meanwhile, the speed for acquiring new technology would be rapid if the necessary skills were clarified, because Japanese companies have the high potential ability of engineers and users at the bottom tier.

IT Skills of Japanese Companies

Traditional IT Skills

Characteristics of Japanese Information Systems

A characteristic of information systems in Japanese companies is that users are fixated on customized systems. The use of packaged software is limited to a small part of the whole. According to METI's SSSI,[1] which is the most extensive study on the IS-vendor industry, annual sales have reached 13.7039 trillion yen, approximately US$114 billion at $1 = 120 yen in 2001.[2] An analysis by business type shows that order-made software development services constitute 49.4%, packaged software products constitute 10.8%, and business-use packages constitute only 5.3% of the total, with almost no change in this composition ratio during 1998-2001 (Figure 1).

Figure 1: Annual Sales of the Japanese IS-Vendor Industry by Business Type (SSSI[1])

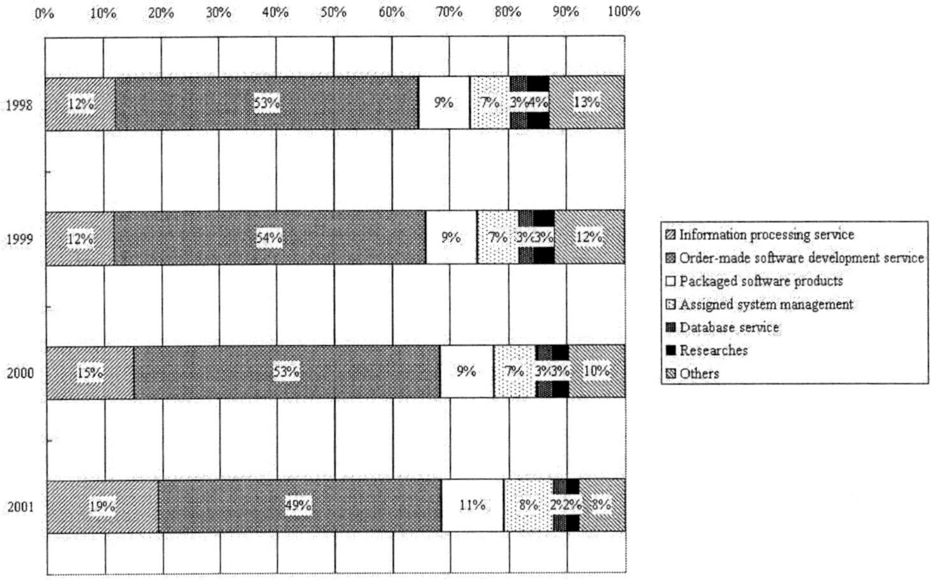

When considering the development and modification of customized systems, Japanese companies' information systems are very mature, and development productivity is high. Cusumano and Kemerer (1990) compared the system development productivity of Japanese and U.S. firms in the 1980s, and showed that the productivity of information system development in Japanese firms was 1.7 times that of U.S. firms, with 40% less faults in the year after delivery, and the code reusability was as high as 1.9 times that of their U.S. counterparts.

The drawback of the information systems in Japanese companies, which insist on using proprietary systems, is the difficulty in incorporating new technology that changes the system architecture. Many of the mainstream customized systems in Japanese firms involve modifications and expansions that have been incorporated to enable continued use of legacy systems centered on host computers, such as mainframes, that date back more than 20 years. According to the JIPDEC 2002 study,[3] host computer-based systems constitute 50.8% of the new IT investment in Japanese firms. Many of these legacy systems are applications and systems that have been developed using old programming languages such as COBOL on hardware-dependant operating systems. In contrast, there are relatively few systems that have been developed using languages such as C, C++, and JAVA on open operating systems such as

UNIX, Windows, and LINUX. In Japan, 79.1% of the companies with five or more employees and 98.4% of the companies with 300 or more employees[4] use the Internet primarily for tasks such as sharing documents, email, and groupware. However, since these older host computer-based networks use unique communication protocols, it is difficult to connect to TCP/IP networks (Tamaniu, 2003).

Compared to Japan, the focus in the United States has shifted from customized systems to commercial packaged software and system integration incorporating technology developed by external companies. In contrast to the Japanese IS-vendor industry, whose strength lies in increasing productivity within the framework of existing technology, the American IS-vendor industry is skilled at incorporating foreign innovation and is characterized by its strength in responding to changes in architecture.

The Japanese IS Vendors

The Japanese IS-vendor industry has grown in response to the needs of Japanese users to improve and expand proprietary information systems, and has gained the ability to efficiently develop customized systems through long-term relationships with their IS-user companies. Cusumano (1991) calls this type of information system development "Japan's software factories" and ascribes the high performance of Japanese IS vendors to a planned economy of scope that is implemented through the standardization of techniques, tools, management, skills, and reusability of programs.

The source of profits for IS vendors is mainly through the maintenance and operation support of existing systems than the development of new systems. According to a study by JIPDEC in 1999,[5] 59.1% of the IT-related expenditure in Japanese companies is used in the operating costs of existing systems, 16.6% is used in the maintenance costs of existing systems, whereas only 24.3% is directed toward the development of new systems. It is difficult for engineers to read codes written by other engineers. Therefore, Japanese IS vendors rarely maintain or support systems that were developed by other companies. Thus, the profits obtained from the lock-in effect are greater than those from actual development. Even when upgrading or replacing a system, more emphasis is laid on continuation of the existing system than on incorporating the latest technology; as a result, there is a high probability of the same vendor company receiving the order.

When considering the IS-user company's perspective, there is also a strong trend to employ a particular vendor to handle proprietary systems over a long term, because they tend to be apprehensive of the failure of new vendors in maintaining and supporting the existing systems. According to a study of IS-user companies conducted by JISA in 2003,[6] 86.5% of the IS-user companies responded that they would like to continue using the same vendor for the time being, 4.6% of the respondents responded that they would like to change the main vendor if possible, 1.3% responded that they would like to change a minor vendor, and 4.3 % responded that they would like to distribute work across several companies.

Training and Dissemination of IT Skills

The main method used for acquiring IT skills in both IS-user and IS-vendor companies is in-house training. Japanese companies generally have very little labor mobility, and this has led to the emphasis of education within companies. In Japan, labor shortage during the period of rapid economic growth encouraged the adoption of internal education, and this high level of internal education resulted in reduced labor mobility, forming a relationship of mutual reinforcement (Koike, 1999). Even in the IS-vendor industry, which should be subject to major changes in technology and environment, the labor turnover is not very high compared to other traditional industries, particularly in large companies, indicating a relationship of mutual reinforcement with internal education systems (Umezawa, 2000).[7]

The main in-house training method used by companies for IT engineers is on-the-job training (OJT). In a study by JITEC,[8] a comparison of all training methods revealed that OJT constituted 51.0% in IS-user companies, followed by classes with 38.6% (Figure 2). In IS-vendor companies, the quantities were reversed with 38.0% of the training being OJT and 48.1% being classes. However, the fact remains that having experienced staff who offer guidance in OJT plays an important role in the dissemination of techniques and knowledge. In a study of IS vendors by Takeda (2003), in response to a question regarding the "frequently used" methods to accumulate and disseminate techniques and knowledge in vendor companies, 32.1% mentioned "individual guidance from experienced staff," followed by "official technical materials, manuals, and databases" (24.8%); "unofficial memos, etc." (17.7%); and "training and education systems" (11.7%) (Figure 3).

Figure 2: Main In-House Training Methods Used by Companies for IT Engineers (JITEC, 2001[8])

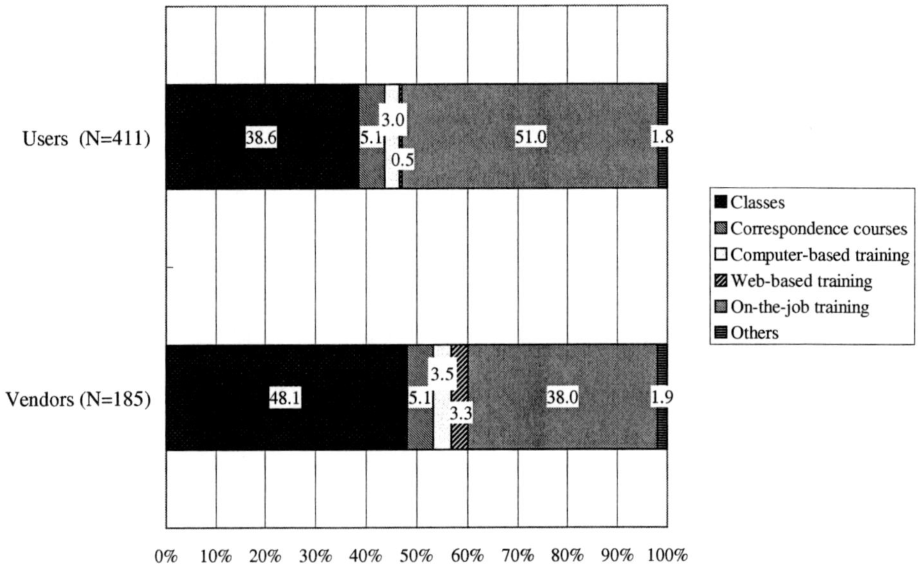

Figure 3: Methods to Accumulate and Disseminate Techniques and Knowledge in IS-Vendor Companies (Takeda, 2003) (N = 480)

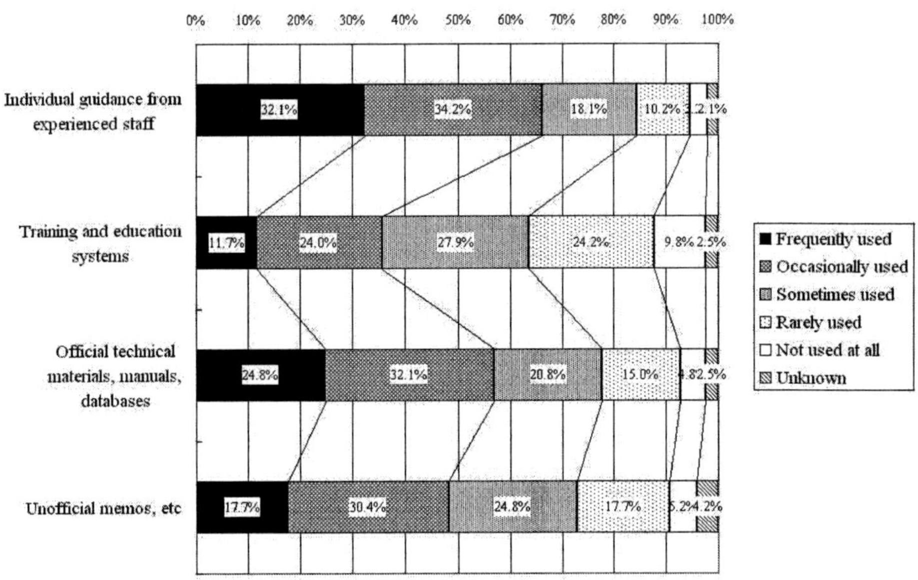

Although internal training may be the focal point, human resource development is not necessarily conducted deliberately and systematically in line with the management strategy. According to JITEC's study, in response to the question of whether the development of IT engineers reflected management strategy in IS-user companies, a majority of respondents provided negative answers, with 40.1% expressing that management strategy is "not reflected much" and 15.3% expressing that it is "not reflected." This exhibits the fact that although training may be primarily conducted internally, it is not linked to management strategy in many cases. Moreover, 64.3% of the IS-vendor companies and 67.4% of the IS-user companies responded that one of the problems in the implementation of OJT is that "guidance is not being carried out systematically." ITAA (2001) indicates that one of the problems in the United States is that the career paths of IT engineers are not shown clearly. JITEC's study highlights the same problem in Japan, with 83.7% of the IS-user companies and 54.6% of the IS-vendor companies not setting career paths for IT engineers.

Takeda (2003) studied the content of stored information and know-how in IS-vendor companies and found that while technical information constituted 33.5%, information regarding clients' business processes constituted 24.2%, information regarding clients' needs constituted 22.8%, and knowledge on how to communicate with clients and solve problems constituted 19.5%, thus showing that client-specific information and knowledge was far more prominent than purely technical information (Figure 4).

Figure 4: Content of Stored Information in IS-Vendor Company (Takeda, 2003) (N = 480)

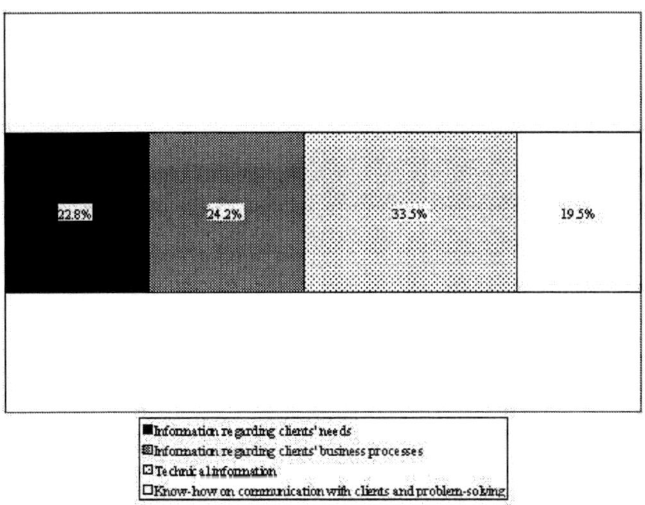

The custom of both IS-user and IS-vendor companies mainly using OJT to disseminate IT skills particular to a certain user company is consistent with the continuation and development of existing customized systems. This is characteristic of Japanese companies' information systems. At the same time, this strong trend of internally fostering IT engineers prevents the growth of an external labor market and acquisition of IT skills from external institutions, such as universities.

Acquisition of Skills from External Institutions

Academic institutions, such as universities, have not been fulfilling their role of providing education for the IT skills required by companies. In many cases, an IT-related academic background is not considered to be an issue when recruiting new technical staff, and according to a study on individual IT engineers[8] conducted by JITEC, 47.1% and 56.7% of the IT engineers working in IS-vendor and IS-user companies, respectively, responded that they had received no IT education in school.

As a part of the internal training carried out after new recruits have joined a company, it is common for a company to obtain education services from a company specializing in IT education. The programs provided by these education vendors are general and are focused on areas requiring a limited scope of knowledge. JITEC's study on education service vendors[8] shows that the most common content of IT education is on the knowledge of a particular package product (79.2%), followed by component technologies such as operating systems (68.8%), Web applications (62.5%), and programming languages (60.4%). In comparison, however, only a small proportion of this education involves the skills required to create unique systems for user companies or skills that integrate advanced knowledge of technologies and experience, such as consulting/analysis of business processes (22.9%), project management (31.3%), skills regarding interpersonal relationship (33.3%), and knowledge on business processes (27.1%).

Meanwhile, although the complete outsourcing of information systems operations by user companies is gaining considerable attention as a means to obtain external skills, it is only being implemented by a small minority. According to JISA's basic statistical survey,[9] outsourcing services constitute only 10.0% of the sales in the IS-vendor industry.

Coordinators

Traditionally, when implementing information systems, the most important role has been played by the "coordinators" who are aware of the users' needs and communicate these needs to IS vendors or the information systems division in the user company, while communicating the technical limitations and possibilities to the users and the management, and coordinating between them. The coordinators mentioned here do not hold an officially recognized post suggestive of their role, but are the personnel in IS-vendor companies and IS-user companies that effectively carry out the function of coordination. Furthermore, according to the survey on system development and IT implementation projects conducted by Takeda (2003), this role is often performed by system engineers, sales staff, and programmers in IS-vendor companies, and members of the information system departments together with diverse IT and non-IT personnel in the user departments of user companies. Therefore, it is common for numerous coordinators to work on a single project.

Coordinators are not necessarily senior engineers who are well-versed in the latest advanced technology. In many cases, IS-user companies' coordinators only need to be able to coordinate communication with IS vendors and programmers, which requires no actual technical knowledge. Even coordinators in the IS-vendor company may not require knowledge of the latest technology since most of the work is centered on the continuous development of customized systems. In JISA's 2002 survey of IS-user companies,[10] 59.9% of the respondents expressed that "familiarity with the company's business and operations" was a factor that influenced the IS-user companies' selection of IS-vendor companies, while only 43.2% listed "a high level of technical capabilities in the relevant field" as a deciding factor. More emphasis is laid on the role of coordinators with knowledge of the company's operations than on actual technical capabilities.

A coordinator also differs from a manager who has authority. In many cases, these roles are performed by staff members who are not in managerial positions, and managers who execute this role usually have little authority. Takeda (2003) shows that the involvement of managers in coordination with the partner companies was 46% for IS-vendor companies and 24% for IS-user companies in the system planning stage, and involvement during system development and IT implementation was 21% for IS-vendor companies and 18% for IS-user companies.

The skills held by coordinators mainly involve knowledge required for coordination between departments within the company or between IS users and IS vendors. Such knowledge is more difficult to document in writing for the purpose of accumulating and sharing than technical knowledge, and also tends to be more company specific and personal. As shown in Figure 3, it is more common for knowledge and know-how regarding system development and IT implementation to be disseminated individually from person to person rather than using official documents and education systems. In JISA's 2002 study of IS-vendor companies,[11] only 14.8% of the companies replied that "the company's internal system for utilizing knowledge is functional." Since there has traditionally been very little labor mobility in the management environment of Japanese companies and changes in mainframe-related technology were mild, personal skills were sufficient.

Newly Required Skills

Change in Environment and Technology

Until the 1980s, there was essentially no change in Japanese companies' information systems. Although opportunities to revise existing information systems were provided through PC-based downsizing and popularization of local area networks (LANs), systems carrying out key operations, such as production, procurement, and accounting, were handled by existing mainframe-based customized systems, marking a split between these fields.

The protracted recession that began in the 1990s and the spread of IP technology were the factors that necessitated Japanese companies to change the quality of their information systems. The most important impact of IP technology was the sudden expansion of the scope of information systems that was brought about by the open standard network connections and could be implemented with a low initial cost inside companies, between companies, and between customers and companies. The protracted recession also strengthened the pressure to restructure businesses and reduce costs within companies. Furthermore, the strong economy in the United States during the late 1990s also sent the message that Japanese companies would not be competitive on the international front unless they adopted and started using IT.

Public Policies

Japan's IT-related policies have developed rapidly since 2000. The IT Strategy Headquarters was established by the Cabinet in July 2000. The country's Basic IT Strategy[12] (e-Japan Strategy) was decided upon in November with the passing of the Basic Law on the Formation of an Advanced Information and Telecommunications Network Society (IT Basic Law). The four priority policy areas of the e-Japan Strategy have been established as follows:

1. Establishment of an ultra-high-speed network infrastructure and competition policies
2. Facilitation of electronic commerce
3. Realization of electronic government
4. Nurturing high-quality human resources

Several measures in the area of nurturing high-quality human resources in the e-Japan Strategy are related to elementary IT education targeted at schools and adults, and METI has formulated IT-skill standards as a means to establish practical IT skills required by companies (METI, 2002). The IT-skill standards clarify and systemize the abilities required for the provision of various IT-related services and aim to provide a useful dictionary for the education and training of IT professionals in both the industry and academia. In these IT-skill standards, IT services are divided into 38 specialist areas in the following 11 occupations: marketing, sales, consultant, IT architect, project management, IT specialist, application specialist, customer service, software development, operation, and education with up to seven levels of skills being set for each specialist area. For example, the occupation of an IT specialist includes the following six specialist areas: platform, system management, database, network, distributed computing, and security. It describes the proficiency of skills specific to certain specialist areas in addition to those shared among specialist areas, such as design, technical, integration management, quality management, industry specialty, leadership, communication, and negotiation. Engineers are envisioned to start with a low level of skill and have a career path that allows them to build up a high level of skill while moving through various specialist areas and occupations (Figure 5).

Figure 5: An Example of a Career Path in the IT-Skill Standards (METI, 2002)

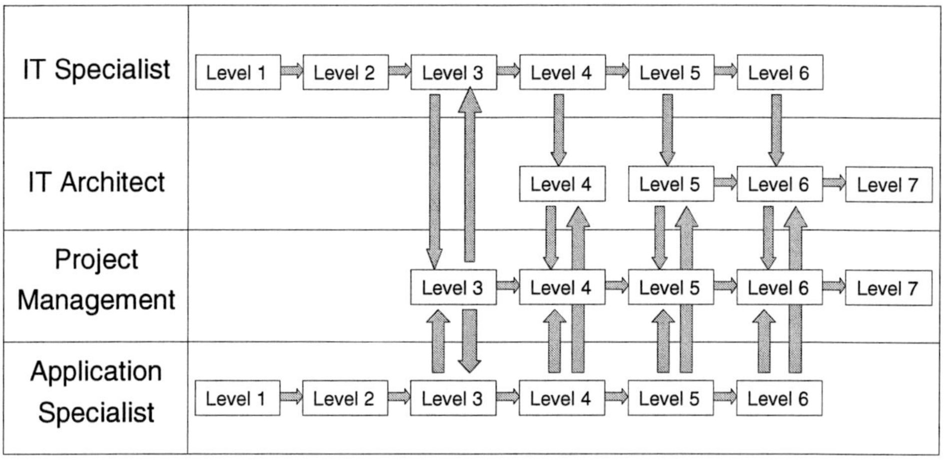

The post of information technology coordinator, requiring knowledge in both IT and management, was created for small-medium companies. The training and accreditation for obtaining the qualification is conducted by a non-profit organization, and the government subsidizes small-medium companies that use IT coordinators. As stated above, information technology in both IS-user and IS-vendor companies has been supported by staff who do not have an official designation, yet effectively play the role of a coordinator; however, small-medium companies lack such personnel. This system can be perceived as one that is created with the assumption that independent consultants will play the role of a coordinator in small-medium companies.

Furthermore, in an attempt to nurture engineers with a particularly high level of skill, local governments have cooperated with IT vendors such as Cisco Systems, Sun Microsystems, and Oracle to establish the Academy for Advanced Information Technology Professionals (AIP), which is an non-profit organization. This provides IT engineers and the planning departments of IS-user companies with systematic education in the form of lectures, practical work, workshops, and e-learning for advanced knowledge, and skills in both technology and management. Over the next five years, it is planned to nurture 3,000 advanced IT engineers, such as top-level engineers, in system development and system integration, in addition to IT managers in IS-user companies (*Nikkei Newspaper,* November 3, 2002).

These measures share the aspects of increasing the knowledge of engineers in various specialist areas that support companies' use of IT and setting the career path for senior engineers that have advanced technical expertise and diverse work experience.

IS-User and IS-Vendor Companies' Cognition

In public policy, there have been signs of a movement to improve the skills of specialist and senior engineers, but what do IS-user and IS-vendor companies perceive as necessary IT skills?

Figure 6 plots the response rates of the skills that are considered strategically most important and those considered most lacking in IS-user and IS-vendor companies. These skills can be divided into three groups.

The first group comprises skills that are viewed as being strategically important, but there is a strong sense that they are lacking. These are consulting/analysis of business processes in IS-user and IS-vendor companies and project management in vendor companies. As shown in Figure 7, the training rate in consulting/analysis of business processes is low despite its perceived importance. This leads to the observation that such skills are difficult to teach using either internal or external training. However, the training rate is relatively high for project management in IS-vendor companies, suggesting that this skill is more easily acquired than consulting/analysis.

Consulting/analysis of business processes can be interpreted as referring to a high level of knowledge that combines technical expertise, business expertise, and experience. This can be considered to correspond to the type of skill required for senior engineers as seen in the human resource development strategy of the public policy. Furthermore, the project management of IS-vendor companies also suggests that steps need to be taken to deal with the increased complexity of management within development teams when implementing such advanced systems.

The second group comprises skills whose importance is relatively high and the sense of inadequacy is relatively small. In IS-user companies, these skills include knowledge on business processes, system design, and software design/development/testing. In IS-vendor companies, the group covers system design and software design/development/testing. This group is believed to correspond to skills regarding traditional customized systems. Figure 7 suggests that most of these skills are acquired through OJT or internal training. Conventional skills are still emphasized, and it is believed that almost all these are carried out using traditional methods.

The third group comprises skills that are viewed to be low in importance, which includes skills regarding component technologies in each specialist area.[13] The skills that reflect a low sense of inadequacy are databases, operating systems, EC/ERP/SCM/CRM, programming languages, and knowledge of a particular package product. The skills that reflect a medium-high sense of inadequacy are network architecture, information security, and Web application for users. The training rate for all such skills is high, and in many cases training is conducted externally (Figure 7). The public policy aims to broaden the base of specialist engineers with extensive knowledge of component technologies. However, IS-user and IS-vendor companies lay little emphasis on such skills. In most cases, there is no perception of a severe shortage of personnel with these skills because education can be obtained from an external educator if required.

Figure 6: Skills Considered Strategically Most Important and Most Lacking for IS-User and IS-Vendor Companies (JITEC, 2001[8])

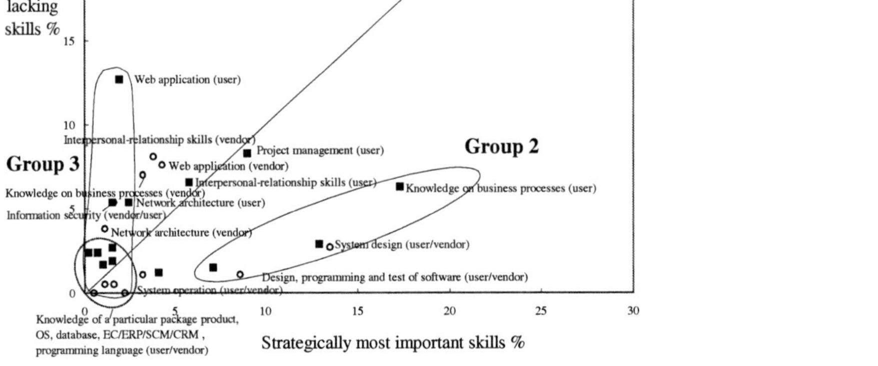

Figure 7: Internal and External Training Rates of Each Skill in Both IS-User and IS-Vendor Companies (JITEC, 2001[8])

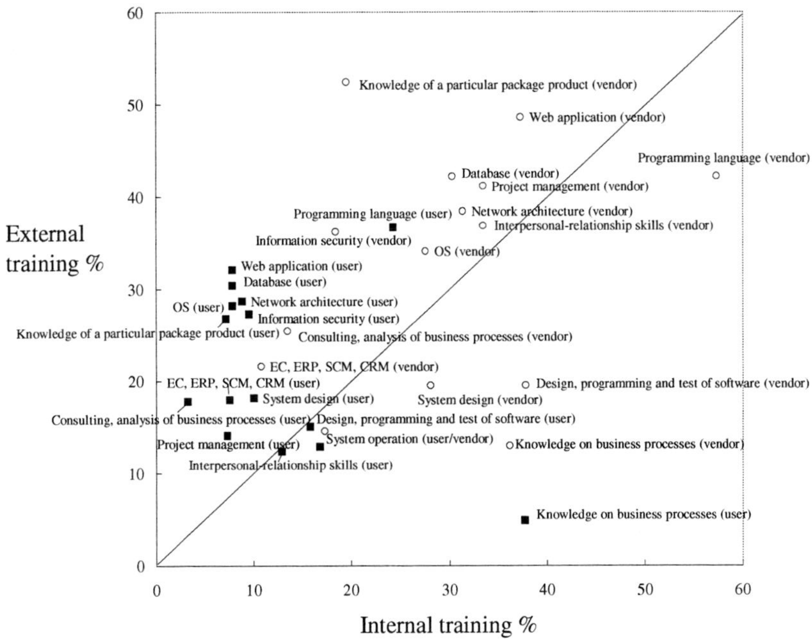

Japanese IT-Skill Dilemma

One common point that seems to be shared by IS-user companies, vendor companies, and the public policy is the awareness of the need to foster senior engineers with advanced knowledge that constitutes a combination of technical expertise and business expertise. However, the image that IS-user companies have of senior engineers seems to differ slightly from that held by IS-vendor companies and the public policy.

Figure 8 uses the data obtained in JISA's 2003 study of IS-user and IS-vendor companies[6,14] to plot the proportion of responses from IS-user companies stating that various services "will decrease in the future" or are "not required" against the proportion of responses from IS-vendor companies stating that "there will be reduced needs" or "there will be no need" for these services. IS users and IS vendors agree that there will be demand for high value-added

Figure 8: Services that Will Decrease and Will Not Be Required in the Estimation of IS-User and IS-Vendor Companies (JISA, 2003[6,14])

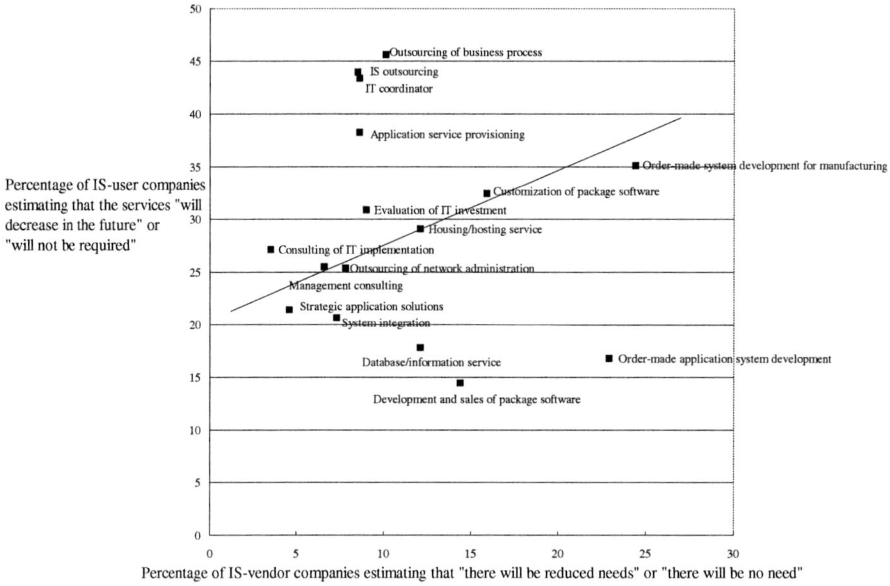

services such as system integration, consulting, and strategic application solutions. It should be noted that although IS-vendor companies rank customized system development highly among the services for which use will decrease, this is one service in which IS-user companies expect a minimal reduction in use. Customized system development is a traditional method of information system architecture that still has the greatest share of sales, as shown in Figure 1. This trend shows no signs of weakening with time. This could be interpreted to suggest that IS-user companies are demanding more advanced solutions while continuing to work under the assumption that conventional systems will be used.

Dilemma of IS-User Companies

The "Not-Made-For-Us" Syndrome

One of the reasons that IS-user companies still insist upon customized systems is due to the sunk cost represented by the existing systems. This refers not only to hardware and system development costs, but also the considerable sunk cost involved in skills regarding system operation and maintenance, and communication between IS vendors and customers.

The second reason is somewhat psychological, in that many organizations possess the view that developing a unique information system will lead to increased competitiveness of the organization. Recent IT developments have shown that even if each component technology is not unique, it is possible to sufficiently achieve differentiation through their combination, handling, and linkage with the overall company strategy. However, many Japanese companies have yet to comprehend this change in the nature of IT.

The third reason is that Japanese companies have the excellent ability to construct advanced information systems if they are within the existing limited scope of business, and there is the problem of not being able to lower present performance even if the applicable scope is expanded. This problem tends to be overlooked, but it is a major factor in Japanese companies' use of information systems.

Figure 9 shows that there is a trade-off between the expansion of the applicable operations and the performance improvement of information systems. When an attempt is made to expand the applicable scope with certain cost restraints, the quality of each system is decreased. Technological advances and improved skills shift the productivity threshold to the upper right. Normally, if the changes

Figure 9: Trade-Off Between Applicable Scope and Performance of Information Systems

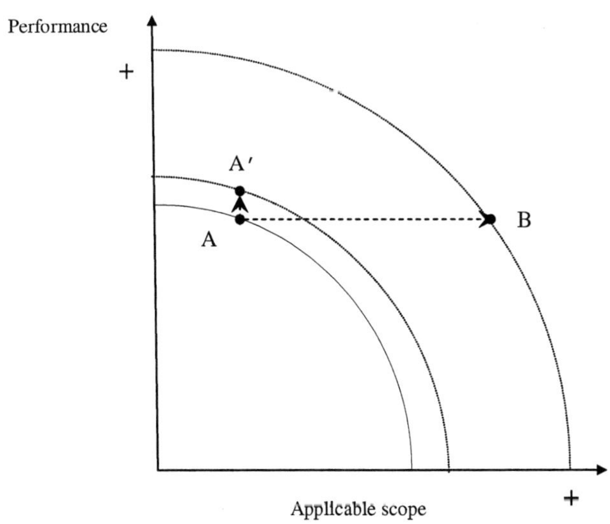

in the applicable scope of operations are small, only a small shift is required to raise performance (A→A' in Figure 9), whereas if the scope of application is expanded, a large shift (A→B) is required simply to maintain the existing performance. However, Japanese companies that tend to focus on the amount of performance improvement underestimate the shift from A to B and estimate that it is possible to handle this expansion using traditional methods.

Illusion of the Super Coordinator

It was mentioned above that the pivotal role in implementing information systems in Japanese companies has been played by coordinators instead of managers and engineers with a high level of skill. Presently, IS-user companies perceive an ideal senior engineer as a "*super coordinator,*" who is capable of coordinating difficult tasks. The super coordinator is expected to preserve existing systems and incorporate new technology to expand operations while maintaining high performance by communicating between the IS-user and IS-vendor companies or between user departments and systems departments. However, while coordinators facilitate performance improvement within a limited scope of operations (A → A'), they are not very effective in responding to a large shift such as A→B in Figure 9 with only personal efforts such as coordination. Therefore, the concept of a super coordinator is no more than an illusion. Moreover, the skills of a super coordinator are not a mere extension of the skills of a normal coordinator.

"They Would Learn Well If Necessary"

Although there are some differences in perceptions, a shortage of senior engineers is felt among the public policy, IS-user companies, and IS-vendor companies. However, while the public policy is taking active steps to foster skills in the component technologies for each specialist area, IS-user and IS-vendor companies do not sense a severe shortage of such skills. How should this disjuncture be viewed?

It is likely that the public policymakers and strategists in IS-vendor companies intend to foster engineers to prepare for a shortage of component technology engineers in each specialist area in the future. However, although IS-user companies show no resistance to incorporating new technologies if required, the Japanese economy is the result of many companies that have been unable to meet their requirements because they are still struggling to find direction in the restructuring of their business. It is possible that the management believes that specialist engineers of component technologies can be fostered, if required, by having the existing staff acquire the necessary skills. Therefore, there is presently no sign of a shortage of specialist engineers for component technologies in either IS-user companies or IS-vendor companies.

Dilemma of IS-Vendor Companies

Customization of Packaged Software

Traditionally, Japanese IS vendors built a business model in which IS-user companies required unique customized systems. As explained earlier, this model involves locking in customers with a customized system and obtaining profits in the maintenance and support phase after development has been completed.

Since the spread of the Internet in the mid-1990s, the application scope of information systems has rapidly widened. Distributed networks based on PCs and LANs and packaged software such as ERP have been widely used in systems other than traditional IT usage, such as production, procurement, and accounting tasks.

Before the mid-1990s, Japanese companies tended to extensively customize packaged software and existing technologies (Sakakibara, 1999). Even when using packaged software, IS-user companies disliked changing existing processes and tended to insist upon the unique characteristics of the company.

Customizing packaged software to suit the needs of customers' businesses was also favorable for IS vendors. Having several IS vendors handle the same packaged software meant that there was a risk that customers could easily change vendors. However, large-scale customization of packaged software prevents to the entry of competitors because it is difficult to change the system for other IS vendors. It has a lock-in effect that is nearly equivalent to building a customized system from scratch. Therefore, there was no need to move away from the traditional business model.

Limitations of the Customization Model

In such a manner, the change in the business model of IS vendors was postponed until the shock that accompanied the spread of the Internet and the protracted recession of the mid-1990s. IS-user companies need to expand the scope of IT usage while maintaining the existing performance levels under tighter cost restrictions.

IS vendors are faced with the difficult task of fostering new skills while maintaining traditional skills. IS-vendor companies understand that it is impossible to achieve these two goals simultaneously. The gap between IS-user and IS-vendor companies shown in Figure 8 demonstrates the dilemma faced by IS-vendor companies with the desire to move away from maintaining existing systems and their inability to do so.

Beyond Dilemma

Japanese IT-Skill Dilemma

Many Japanese IS-user companies are still obsessed with the "not-made-for-us syndrome," despite acknowledging the need to expand the scope of their information systems by implementing new technologies. It is not easy to maintain traditional skills while obtaining skills in the latest technology and integrate old and new technologies; as a result, the IS-vendor industry has been unable to establish a new business model. The public policy is attempting to increase the supply of engineers who are equipped to handle new technology; however, the demand is not in line with the growth in supply. This inhibits the growth of an external labor market, and development of independent consultants and outsourcing. Implementation of new technology is not advancing because of a lack of external labor market and service companies. This summarizes Japan's IT-skill dilemma.

Attack the Root Cause

The only way to overcome this dilemma is to attack the root cause of the problem—the lack of progress in restructuring old businesses and creating new businesses within Japanese companies. IT usage among Japanese companies traditionally focused on cutting costs; however, the concept of using IT to create new businesses is nonexistent. (Kokuryo & Takeda, 2003). In the March 2003 settlement of accounts, Japanese companies managed to secure increased profits on the whole; however, when viewed in detail, companies that secured profit by cutting costs without achieving growth in sales were conspicuous (Nihon Keizai Shimbun, June 1, 2003).

With respect to IT implementation, when the levels of a company are divided into top management, senior engineers, and general engineers/users, the top management faces the maximum problems. In Figure 9, an upward shift is a result of a force applied from the bottom of the organization, but a horizontal shift along the axis requires strength from the top. At present, top management in Japanese companies tends to view the implementation of IT as the traditional shift from A to A', but the shift is actually from A to B, which is impossible without the involvement of top management and integration with business strategy.

However, the information systems departments only have a small voice in Japan's IS-user companies. Furthermore, the establishment of a chief information officer (CIO) in top management to handle information systems was almost unheard of until recent years. Even in 2002, according to *CIO Magazine,*[15] only 7.6% of companies had a full-time CIO. Although 43.3% of companies have CIOs, including those that also hold other posts, only 54% of the CIOs have past IT experience, and it can be conjectured that there are many CIOs that only have responsibility over IT together with other areas and lack specialized knowledge.

The second problem is the skill set held by senior engineers. Traditionally, as emphasis has been laid on the role of senior engineers as coordinators between departments and between IS users and vendors, they lack the skills required to incorporate and use new technology. Additionally, there is also a lack of experience in coordinating interests and taking a position of leadership to implement bold reforms regarding changes in business processes that accompany the implementation of IT. They also lack the authority required to execute these measures.

Meanwhile, Japanese companies have a more homogenous and highly educated labor force than their counterparts in other countries. This suggests that general engineers and users in the bottom tier have potential ability, and the speed in acquiring new technology would be rapid if they were informed of the skills they need to acquire.

According to a survey conducted by the Japan Institute of Chief Information Officers,[16] when decision making of IT implementation is from the bottom up, innovation and overall business performance are not successful; however, cutting costs is successful. This suggests that the mechanism of decision making has to be changed at the top management level. As long as the top management in Japanese companies fails to move forward with restructuring to create businesses that produce revenues, there is a possibility that bottom-line policies will not work effectively.

Differentiation Starts Under the Pressure of Global Competition

Although the pressure of global competition becomes more severe, a majority of Japanese companies are struggling to change their business model because there is a strong inertia of their traditional business model. However, a type of differentiation has begun in the Japanese economy among a small number of companies that are performing well. The consolidated recurring profit of the top 10 companies, excluding financial institutions, has continued to grow annually, and in the fiscal year ending March 31, 2003, their profits reached 47.9% of the total profits of all listed companies (*Nikkei Financial,* April 10, 2003). It is considered that among these companies, many have succeeded in using IT to develop businesses that produce revenues, suggesting that there is a large gap between companies' ability to use IT. Using IT to develop new markets and needs and create innovations is the only way to overcome Japan's IT-skill dilemma.

Endnotes

1 SSSI (Survey of Selected Service Industries) is conducted every year by METI (Ministry of Economy, Trade, and Industry) and includes a survey of the information service industry. The information services comprise information processing service, order-made software development service, (package) software product, assigned system management, database service, and research. The number of offices within the information service industry was 7,830 in 2002. The "IS-vendor industry" referred to

in this paper is equivalent to the information service industry in SSSI. http://www.meti.go.jp/english/statistics/index.html.

2 This does not include the in-house development cost in their customer companies.

3 JIPDEC (Japan Information Processing Development Corporation) conducts a survey regarding usage of information technology among companies. The 2002 survey was conducted across 1,633 companies. http://www.jipdec.jp/kyotu_page/outline.htm.

4 White Paper of Information and Communications 2003 issued by the Ministry of Public Management, Home Affairs, Posts, and Telecommunications. http://www.soumu.go.jp/english/whitepaper/index.html.

5 The same survey as in Endnote 3 conducted in 1999 (N = 1,043).

6 JISA (Japan IT Services Industry Association) conducts a survey of large IS-user companies (N = 354 from planning departments and N = 375 from information system departments, in 2003).

7 According to the 2001 Trend of Wage, Employment, and Hours Worked of Japan, issued by the Ministry of Health, Labor, and Welfare, the annual voluntary quit rate of full-time workers in the information service and research industry that includes the IS-vendor industry was 8.4%, which was less than 10.4% for the service industry, and at approximately the same level as the rate for all other industries, which was 8.7%. The annual turnover rate in the information service and research industry was 6.6%, which was less than 10.2% for the entire services industry, and 7.9% for all other industries. http://www.mhlw.go.jp/english/database/db-l/index.html.

When a comparison is made with other countries such as the United States, the low mobility of labor in the Japanese IS-vendor industry is particularly striking. For example, the voluntary quit rate in the United States' service sector is 22.5% (Job Opening and Labor Turnover Survey, April 2002-March 2003, Bureau of Labor Statistics), surpassing the rate for Japan's service sector by more than 10%. http://www.bls.gov/jlt/home.htm.

8 JITEC (Japan Information Technology Engineers Examination Center) conducts a survey of IS-user companies, IS-vendor companies, individual IT engineers, and education vendors regarding education of information systems. The survey results were 411 IS-user companies, 185 IS-

vendor companies, 1,305 IT engineers, and 48 IS education vendors. http://www.jitec.jp/index.html.

9 JISA (Japan IT Services Industry Association)'s basic statistical survey is conducted regarding the basic financial situation and labor force of the IS vendors that belong to JISA (538 companies in 2002). The respondents of this survey tend to be larger (the average of IS-related sales = 15.79 billion yen) than that of the SSSI's respondents (the average sales = 1.75 billion yen). The survey result was 376 in 2002. http://www.jisa.or.jp/en/index.html.

10 The same survey as in Endnote 6 conducted in 2002 (N = 424 from planning departments, 449 information systems departments).

11 JISA conducts a survey of IS-vendor companies (N = 283 in 2002).

12 IT Strategic Headquarters. http://www.kantei.go.jp/foreign/policy/it/index_e.html.

13 When determining the strategically most important skill, specific component technologies were naturally at a disadvantage, there was no change in the trend of knowledge regarding component technologies, and specific package products receiving little emphasis even when the top three skills were listed.

14 The same survey as in Endnote 11 conducted in 2003 (N = 258).

15 A survey of executives and managers regarding the current status of CIOs in Japanese companies was conducted by IDG, Japan's *CIO Magazine,* in 2002 (N = 490). http://www.idg.co.jp/CIO/contents/special/special130.html.

16 The Japan Institute of Chief Information Officers conducts a survey regarding IT management (N = 175) (Utashiro, 2003).

References

Cusumano, M.A. (1991). *Japan's software factories.* Oxford University Press.

Cusumano, M.A., & Kemerer, C.F. (1990). A quantitative analysis of U.S. and Japanese practice and performance in software development. *Management Science, 36*(11), 1384-1406.

Information Technology Association of America (ITAA). (2001). *When can you start? Building better information technology skills and careers.* ITAA.

Koike, K. (1999). *Economics of workforce.* City: Toyokeizai. (in Japanese)

Kokuryo, J., & Takeda Y. (2003). Value creation on networks and corporate activities. *Proceedings of the International Symposium on Research Project 'Informatics' A06 Group,* University of Tokyo, Japan, February.

Ministry of Economy, Trade, and Industry (METI). (2002). *IT Skill Standards version 1.0.* City: METI.

Sakakibara, K. (1999). *Managing information technology: The problem of Japanese firms.* National Institute of Science and Technology Policy (NISTEP) Discussion Paper No.11 in Japanese.

Takeda Y. (2003). Communication between system providers and customers in implementation processes of information technologies. *Yokohama Journal of Technology Management Studies, 3* (in Japanese).

Tamaniu, H. (2003). *Why do Japanese firms lag behind in information systems? Proposal of legacy migration.* Japan Management Association (in Japanese).

Umezawa, T. (2000). *Human resource management of information service industry.* Minerva (in Japanese).

Utashiro, Y. (2003). Factors of IT management leveraging corporate performance. *Proceedings of the 2003 Spring Conference of Academy of Organizational Sciences,* pp. 93-96 (in Japanese).

Chapter VIII

Eliminating the Weakest Link: Leveraging Human Capital with Strategic Alliances in IT Outsourcing Supply Chains

Diana J. Wong-MingJi
Eastern Michigan University, USA

Abstract

As organizations shift from tactical to strategic approaches with IT outsourcing, their human capital portfolios of knowledge, skills, competencies, and organizational capabilities need to be reconfigured accordingly. This chapter outlines a model for constructing human capital portfolios that enable firms to strategically leverage IT outsourcing. Two organizational capabilities—rational strategic management process and connective capabilities—provide the integrating mechanisms for competencies from three sub-units that are human resource information systems (HRIS), the IS function, and supply chain management. Knowledge and skills at the individual and sub-unit level enable the development of competencies that are integrated by organizational capabilities. Given the dynamic nature of competitive contexts, managers have to reconfigure their organizations' human capital portfolio to align their firms with the external environment. In sum, creating human capital portfolios for strategic IT outsourcing supply chains requires a multi-level and multi-disciplinary approach to identify and strengthen the weakest links.

Introduction

Effective strategic IT outsourcing enables firms to operate on the cutting edge compared to too many on the bleeding edge. The trend for IT outsourcing is growing. The IT outsourcing market in North America is expected to grow from $101 billion in 2000 to $160 billion by 2005 (Gartner Inc., cited in Kaplan, 2002). The global dimension of outsourcing is even more dynamic with 3.3 million U.S. business-processing jobs predicted to move abroad by 2015 at an accelerating rate of 30-40% per year for the next five years (Agrawal & Farrell, 2003). Although outsourcing is a growing trend, not all firms experience success with it.

The purpose of this chapter is to develop a model for creating human capital portfolios to strategically leverage IT outsourcing, which systematically eliminates the weakest link of the supply chain. The model addresses multiple organizational levels because creating human capital portfolios for strategic IT outsourcing depends on interrelated knowledge, skills, competencies, and capabilities from individuals to organizational systems. At the firm level, two important organizational capabilities—rational and connective—integrate competencies from organizational sub-units. Three significant sub-units—the IS function, HRIS, and supply chain management—encompass knowledge and skills from individuals to create competencies within organizational sub-units. The model for creating human capital portfolio provides a means for managers to analyze, evaluate, and align the requisite human capital portfolio to strategically engage in IT outsourcing.

Human capital portfolios should address a range of problems that weaken connections between client firms, vendors, and contracting employees. Numerous researchers and practitioners identified various problems with IT outsourcing, some of which led to the loss of substantial investments amounting to tens or hundreds of millions of dollars. Weak links in IT outsourcing include outsourcing inappropriate activities, poor vendor selection processes, inappropriate vendor selection, unrealistic promises from vendors, inadequate written contract, ignoring human resource issues, losing control of outsourcing activity, overlooking hidden costs, absence of exit strategy from outsourcing contract, internal resistance and organizational politics between functional areas, lack of employee preparation, insufficient quality control of vendors, inadequate communication, lack of inter-firm trust and commitment, and lack of managerial competencies to manage outsourcing (Barthelemy, 2003 & 2001; Kern, Willcocks, & Heck, 2002; Klepper, 1995). Any one of the above difficulties or a combination of them can contribute to diminishing the strategic potential of IT outsourcing.

Earlier, the common wisdom prescribed outsourcing peripheral non-core activities, regardless of its size or volume, in order to be more focused and lean. This approach is a tactical use of outsourcing with the primary goal to reduce costs. However, the shift from tactical to strategic IT outsourcing is growing (Cheon, Grover, & Teng, 1995; Insinga & Werle, 2000; Kimzey & Kurokawa, 2002; Lacity & Hirschheim, 1993). McLellan, Marcolin, and Beamish (1995) found that "although the financial motivations for outsourcing are an important part of the decision, the strategic motivations appear to be increasingly more important. Outsourcing can play both a central and a support role in many strategic initiatives" (p. 318).

While IT outsourcing may help achieve financial savings of 10-40% (Kern et al., 2002), becoming strategic with IT outsourcing can build or sustain a competitive position. Strategic contributions of IT outsourcing come from: re-engineering business processes, developing new business, refocusing on core competencies, facilitating mergers and acquisitions, supporting globalization, and minimizing dysfunctional politics of IT innovations (McLellan et al., 1995). Additional benefits of strategic IT outsourcing include access to larger technology resource pools for innovations, ability for product development beyond internal resources, reduced cycle time from idea to market, and reduced development costs. Thus, a strategic approach has important implications for the IT outsourcing supply chain.

Various strategic frameworks for IT outsourcing provide guidance for managers on the complexities of outsourcing (Cronk & Sharp, 1995; De Looff, 1995;

Insinga & Werle, 2000) and the outlining of important competencies to support it (Peppard, Lambert, & Edwards, 2000). However, managers grapple with many problems related to making the necessary organizational change to align IT outsourcing with the vision and mission of their organizations. Strategic IT outsourcing depends on reconfiguring human capital portfolios to align the relevant organizational competencies and capabilities (Feeny & Wilcocks, 1998; Rockart, Earl, & Ross, 1996) along the whole supply chain from client firm to vendors to contracting employees.

A common assumption of outsourcing is that external providers supply the same or greater human capital and capabilities, but at reduced costs compared to internal sourcing. But managers often continue with business as usual when activities are outsourced without recognizing that broader organization development and change are necessary to strategically leverage IT outsourcing. When organizations initially start outsourcing, pre-existing assumptions, expectations, and practices form the basis for weakening the links between client firms, vendors, and contracting employees. The problem is further exacerbated with a focus on individual IS competence and skill sets: 'If we only have the right set of expertise with the latest IT skills.' Without engaging in organizational development and organizational change to reconfigure human capital portfolios beyond the status quo and individual perspectives, IT outsourcing will not likely achieve its strategic potential. While there is no one best configuration of human capital portfolios for all firms, considerations of some key components are necessary.

The remainder of the chapter has four sections. First, the model for creating human capital portfolios in IT outsourcing outlines two major organizational capabilities that provide integrating mechanisms to strategically leverage the potential of IT outsourcing. Second, a discussion specifies knowledge and skills from three important sub-units of HRIS, the IS function, and supply chain management that contribute to the development of competencies from individuals in sub-units. Third, managerial applications of the model for creating human capital portfolios are discussed. Last, the chapter concludes with potential applications of the model to support a strategic approach to IT outsourcing by identifying and eliminating the weakest link.

A Model for Creating Human Capital Portfolios in IT Outsourcing

In general, more rhetoric gets propagated about strategic IT outsourcing than what is actually practiced (Sanders & Premus, 2002). A critical success factor lies in developing the necessary human capital as strategic assets. Otherwise, the value of human capital can erode, be substituted, and/or superseded by higher order capabilities such as learning to learn (Collis, 1994). Functional knowledge and skills are important for fulfilling responsibilities at the individual and sub-unit level. But value creation from human capital requires an organizational and interorganizational approach. Collis (1994) explains how organizational capabilities provide strategic insights that enable managers to understand the intrinsic value of different human capital before rivals do so. The integration of competencies depends on organizational capabilities (Stalk, Evans, & Schulman, 1992). As a result, strategic IT outsourcing requires organizational capabilities that develop human capital for boundary spanning to work collaboratively across sub-units and organizations.

The model for creating human capital portfolios for strategic IT outsourcing is based on two classifications of organizational capabilities that provide the integrative mechanisms to manage the array of specialized human capital from functional areas (see Figure 1). Rational and connective organizational capabilities build upon human capital from key areas such as the IS function, human resource information systems, and supply chain management.

The rational capabilities are easily identified with the linear logic in the strategic management process of creating a vision and/or mission, identifying problems and goals, analyzing internal and external environments, designing strategy, and implementing a strategic plan. In particular, rational capabilities require organizational sub-units to provide, develop, or acquire the requisite knowledge and skills for strategic implementation. Many IT outsourcing systems are based on rational capabilities at the outset, but there are significant weaknesses in the monitoring systems, and evaluation for feedback is even weaker, if they exist at all.

Alternatively, connective organizational capabilities—organizational learning, systems integration, relational contracting, and organizational improvisation—are mechanisms that involve creative thinking and social capital to develop organization capabilities for collaborative inter-firm relationships. If organizations engage in IT outsourcing for the purpose of reducing costs, managerial

Figure 1: Creating Portfolios of Human Capital for Strategic IT Outsourcing

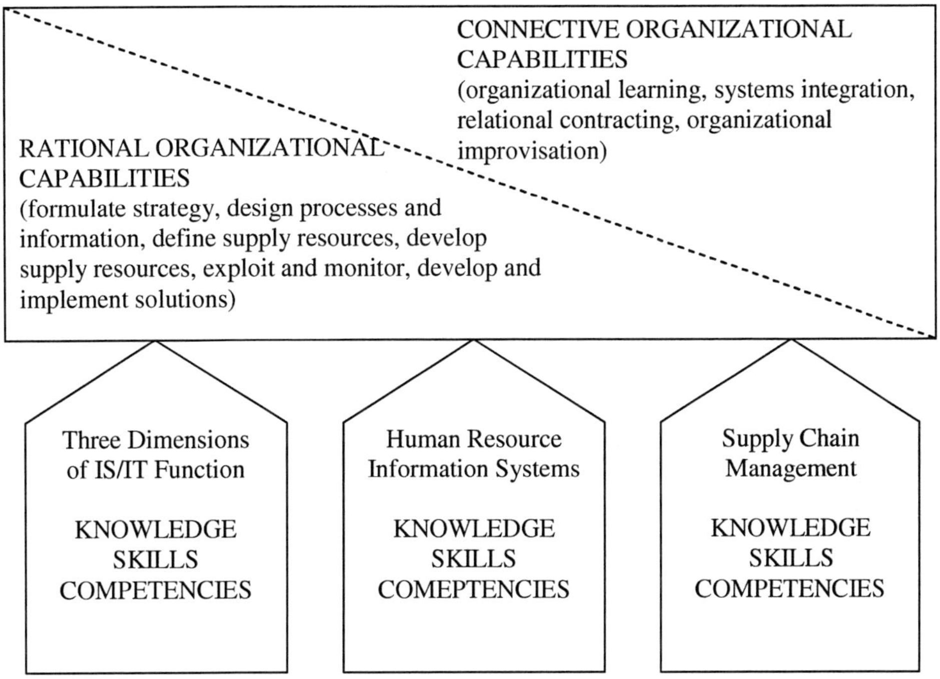

attention to connective organizational capabilities are severely limited. As a result, the lack of connective organizational capabilities leads to some of the weakest links in IT outsourcing. Compounding the difficulties is that connective organizational capabilities are much harder to capture, understand, and develop because of their intangible nature. A key point is that connective organizational capabilities are important complementary strategic assets to support the rational ones.

Rational Organizational Capabilities

Rational organizational capabilities support a strategic role for IT outsourcing. An empirical study by Peppard et al. (2000) identified six macro-competencies for generating strategic value from IT resources with a series of supporting micro-competencies. The six macro-competencies are to formulate strategy, design processes and information, exploit and monitor information use and costs, define supply resources, develop supply resources, and develop, implement, and operate solutions.

First, formulating strategy relies on the ability to evaluate strategic information and technology-based opportunities for a business strategy. Part of the process also involves defining decision-making parameters. This macro-competence builds on micro-competencies such as influencing business strategy and maximizing information resources, incorporating technological innovation in the vision, allocating necessary resources, and defining IS/IT policies to implement business strategies.

Second, the design processes and information competence translates the business strategy into specific processes and information-based requirements for action. The five related micro-competencies are prioritization, aligning information with strategy, performance improvement, information innovation, and designing business processes and operations for strategy implementation.

Third, the macro-competence of exploit and monitor is based on two micro-competencies. One is exploitation planning to identify and plan information use. Two is benefit evaluation with continuous monitoring and evaluation of costs versus benefits.

Fourth, the macro-competence of defining supply resources translates the strategic vision into long-term information supply resource requirements. Two related micro-competencies are: 1) infrastructure design of long-term supply capabilities to meet future demands, and 2) technology analysis to monitor and understand technological advances with the development of appropriate supporting infrastructure.

Fifth, the macro-competence of developing supply resources centers on creating and maintaining information. Five supporting micro-competencies for this include sourcing and evaluating supply options, developing supplier relationships, maintaining technology standards, creating and maintaining technical architecture, and developing IT technical skills.

The last macro-competence centers on developing, implementing, and operating solutions. It is supported by seven micro-competencies—defining service-level requirements, developing IS/IT application, defining information requirement, applying technological solutions, implementing systems with new work processes, continuing with security planning, and conducting change management for implementation.

In sum, the six macro-competencies at the organizational level build upon 25 micro-competencies to create strategic value from a firm's information resources. Empirical evidence supports the importance of linking IT to organizational competitive priorities in order to achieve a competitive advantage (Sanders & Premus, 2002; Willcocks & Lester, 1997). Hence, Peppard et al. (2000) developed a well-grounded framework of rational organizational capabilities for IT outsourcing.

Another set of rational capabilities focuses on seven IT management competencies at the organizational level, which comes from an empirical study by Sambamurthy and Zmud (1997). The seven major categories of IT management competencies are business deployment, external networks, line technology leadership, process adaptiveness, IT planning, IT infrastructure, and data center utility. Among the seven major categories, their framework includes 29 related specific competencies that overlap with ones identified by Peppard et al. (2000). The similarities among the rational organizational capabilities focus on developing IT resources as a strategic asset. Rational organizational capabilities enable managers to evaluate the development of human capital in relation to the goals and vision of the firm (Willcocks & Lester, 1997). At the same time, the effectiveness of rational organizational capabilities relies on support from connective organizational capabilities.

Connective Organizational Capabilities

Connective organizational capabilities refer to organizational learning, systems integration, relational contracting, and organizational improvisation to enable integration and alignment of competencies for business strategy implementation. While rational capabilities identify "what to do," connective organizational capabilities focus on 'how to do' the strategy or the means for implementation. Both sets of organizational capabilities are necessary to facilitate strategic IT outsourcing.

Connective organizational capabilities can only be treated in a cursory fashion within the limitations of this chapter. The strategic role of IT outsourcing depends on connective organizational capabilities to generate the absorptive capacity and mobilize firm resources with a holistic systems approach. Key managerial competencies that help to develop absorptive capacity in organizations include finding, testing, acquiring, and integrating technology from external sources (Kimzey & Kurokawa, 2002).

In order to generate absorptive capacity, numerous researchers address the importance of organizational learning (Argyris, 1992; Fiol & Lyles, 1985;

Raelin, 2000; Senge, 1990) from partners in strategic alliances (Hamel, 1991; Kogut, 1988; Lyles, 1988; Parkhe, 1991) and do so more competently than their rivals. Learning capabilities facilitate organizational adaptation:

> "…because learning skills are essential to flexibility, continuous improvement in quality, efficiency and speed, and to developing new applications regarding existing operations, technologies, and services." (Tracey & Smith-Doerflein, 2001, p. 100)

Related to organizational learning is the organizational capability for systems integration across the whole IT outsourcing supply chain. Systems integration begins with a governance structure that enables client firms to retain control over resources whether they are internally or externally sourced (McLellan et al., 1995).

An effective governance structure starts with a well-developed contract that evolves into trusting relationships between partner firms (Ring & Van de Ven, 1994). The critical role of trust in strategic alliances cannot be over-emphasized. An effective governance structure for IT outsourcing supply chains prevents misunderstandings because explicit discussion of issues helps to establish a strong foundation for the partnership. Also, governance structures can be a tool for conflict resolution and contribute toward establishing norms. The process for creating a governance structure is important in and of itself because the development of the partnership sets the stage for power dynamics, norm development, and team building.

Related competencies that are important for systems integration include contract writing, process management, specification development, tactfulness, buyer-supplier relationship development, and numerous others that are related, generating social capital for effective supply chains that extend to supply chain networks. During the life cycle of IT outsourcing, systems integration needs to evolve from formal governance structures toward relational contracting that is less dependent on formal legal regulation of partnership behaviors.

As a connective organizational capability, relational contracting establishes intentionally incomplete agreements for maintaining flexible developments between contracting parties. The goals and objectives are clearly articulated while plans of action are kept somewhat vague (Macneil, 1978; Milgrom & Roberts, 1992).

> "The property, products, or services jointly developed and exchanged in these transactions entail highly specific investments in ventures that cannot be fully specified or controlled by the parties in advance of their execution." (Ring & Van de Ven, 1992, p. 487)

Relational contracting builds upon a complex combination of competencies such as product knowledge, production systems, strategic supplier selection, leadership skills, social networking, supplier relations, negotiating skills, conflict resolution, problem solving, creativity, and stress management. Effective relational contracting depends heavily on these various competencies for generating trust at the interpersonal, organizational, and interorganizational levels (Zaheer & Venkatraman, 1995; Jeffries & Reed, 2000).

As organizations move down the learning curve with relational contracting, the related capabilities can be extended into additional strategic alliances. Managers may expand beyond a linear pattern of the IT outsourcing supply chain with a complex array of horizontal and diagonal strategic alliances. As a result, IT outsourcing may evolve as a network of strategic alliances. But the strength and potential of IT outsourcing supply chain networks depend upon the weakest link in a portfolio of advanced competencies for relational contracting. Furthermore, the portfolio of managerial competencies needs to diffuse organizational learning beyond the individual firm to its IT outsourcing partners.

In addition to the connective organizational capabilities of organizational learning, systems integration, and relational contracting, human capital portfolios for strategic IT outsourcing also require organizational improvisation. Although improvisational skills are highly developed in the performing arts, both IT and management researchers are slow to understand their importance for organizational effectiveness. Athletes, musicians, physicians, firefighters, and numerous other professionals hone their skills and accumulate a deep knowledge base to develop improvisational expertise because the nature of their work involves non-routine situations within the boundaries of their profession. Recently, researchers investigated how firms respond extemporaneously in the moment to unexpected events that take place outside of normal routine organizational practices (Ciborra, 1999; Miner, Basoff, & Moorman, 2001). Standard operating procedures are insufficient to address unforeseen developments, especially in situations of IT innovations. Organizational improvisation "...is the deliberate and substantive fusion of the design and execution of a novel production" (Miner et al., 2001, p. 314). When faced with surprising situations, managers make use of both thinking and behavioral responses to create a solution based upon intention, intuition, competence, and design (Ciborra, 1999). But improvisation at the organizational level goes beyond any individual. Organizational improvisation is not any collective reaction. It is based on broad organizational routines, cultures, and collective capabilities with distinct competencies.

IT outsourcing often introduces many surprises to established business practices and routines. Although organizational improvisation has a critical role to respond accordingly in such circumstances, few managers intentionally develop this organizational capability. Given constant change, managers with strong improvisational skills will likely be more effective performers. In contrast to individual improvisations, firms require improvisational capabilities across functional units at an organizational level, and across organizational boundaries in the IT outsourcing supply chain.

Research on organizational improvisation identified important associations with innovation, learning, entrepreneurship (Miner et al., 2001), organizational memory (Moorman & Miner, 1998), power (Silva, 2002), and organizational change (Orlikowski, 1996). In order to address weak links in IT outsourcing supply chains, firms need to deliberately enact three forms of organizational improvisation—behavioral, artifactual, and interpretive productions (Miner et al., 2001). As firms compete at the cutting edge of management practices, organizational improvisation reinforces the idea that the cutting edge is constantly on the move.

The four connective organizational capabilities—organizational learning, systems integration, relational contracting, and organizational improvisation—are interrelated. An empirical study indicated that organizational improvisation is special type of learning that involves real-time, short-term learning to enhance or detract from other learning processes (Miner et al., 2001). In addition, organizational learning supports the development of organizational improvisation as an explicit organizational capability, especially for innovation. Systems integration relies heavily on the ability of relational contracting across organizational boundaries in IT outsourcing. At the same time, relational contracting depends on systems integration to institutionalize and legitimate partnerships to build trust in strategic alliances. Relational contracting also involves processes of organizational learning across firm boundaries to develop effective working relationships. Hence, systems integration facilitates learning processes across the firm to develop the learning competencies. During the initial phase of norm development, organizational improvisation has an important role to play in relational contracting by enacting the partnership within the bounds of the organizational system. Developing connective organizational capabilities helps to pre-empt misunderstandings and problems that easily plague different aspects of the IT outsourcing supply chain.

The four connective organizational capabilities do not make up the complete list. Additional connective organizational capabilities such as knowledge management, organizational culture, and change management also merit elaboration. But these topics are dealt with extensively in the management and IT literature. The brief discussion of the four connective organizational capabilities outlined two capabilities that are easily recognizable from the management literature and two that are less well known, but appear on the horizon as important innovative management practices.

A key issue about connective organizational capabilities lies in its complementary relationship with rational organizational capabilities. The weakest link in many IT outsourcing supply chain partnerships is the emphasis on one set of organizational capabilities, often rational capabilities, while ignoring the critical role of the other one. Human capital portfolios for optimizing IT outsourcing have a complementary balance of rational and connective organizational capabilities to effectively integrate competencies from organizational sub-units. The following section highlights important competencies from three sub-units that provide key success factors in implementing strategic IT outsourcing.

Competencies from Key Organizational Sub-Units

Three organizational sub-units—in particular, the IS/IT function, HRIS models, and supply chain management—contribute important knowledge, skills, and competencies toward building an organization's human capital portfolio (see Table 1). Specialized knowledge and skills that are further honed by experiences, roles, and organizational processes at the sub-unit or functional level support the development of organizational competencies (McGrath, MacMillan, & Venkatraman, 1995). Thus, when organizations become more strategic with IT outsourcing, existing competencies are not necessarily replaced as much as they are reconfigured and built upon to support the firm's strategic process. The following discussion examines competencies arising from the IS/IT function.

Table 1: Knowledge, Skills, and Competencies for Tactical Approaches to IT Outsourcing

	3-D IS Functions	HRIS Models	Supply Chain Strategies
Knowledge	Hardware Software MIS Procedures	HR Knowledge Job Description Specs Performance Evaluation HR Regulation Compensation	Logistics Product Specifications Quality Manufacturing Procedures Suppliers
Skills	Technical Programming Analytical Presentation Interpersonal Project Management	Marketing Recruitment Selection Termination Negotiating/Bargaining Writing RFPs Training	Interpersonal Negotiation Conflict Resolution Process Management Teamwork Decision Making Quantitative
Competencies	Vendor Evaluation Business Evaluation Training	Contract Writing Research Competencies Expectation/Norm Development Power and Control	Strategic Thinking Buyer-Supplier Relationship Development Change Management

Three Dimensions of the IS/IT Function

De Looff (1995) provides a comprehensive, three-dimensional framework to describe the IS function for outsourcing (see Figure 2). The first dimension addresses the temporal IS activities that include planning, development, implementation, maintenance, and operation. The second dimension encompasses the IS components of personnel, procedures, personnel, data, software, and hardware. The third dimension refers to the firm's business processes supported by the IS function, which can include human resources, finance, production, etc. For example, IS may support or control the point of sales to facilitate inventory control and order replacement stock. Outsourcing IS/IT activities should account for the extent of 'what' and 'how' along each of the three dimensions. IS/IT professionals require technical, interpersonal, and business competencies to work effectively within their unit and across different organizational units and/or organizations.

Figure 2: Three Dimensions of the IS Function (De Looff, 1995, p. 283)

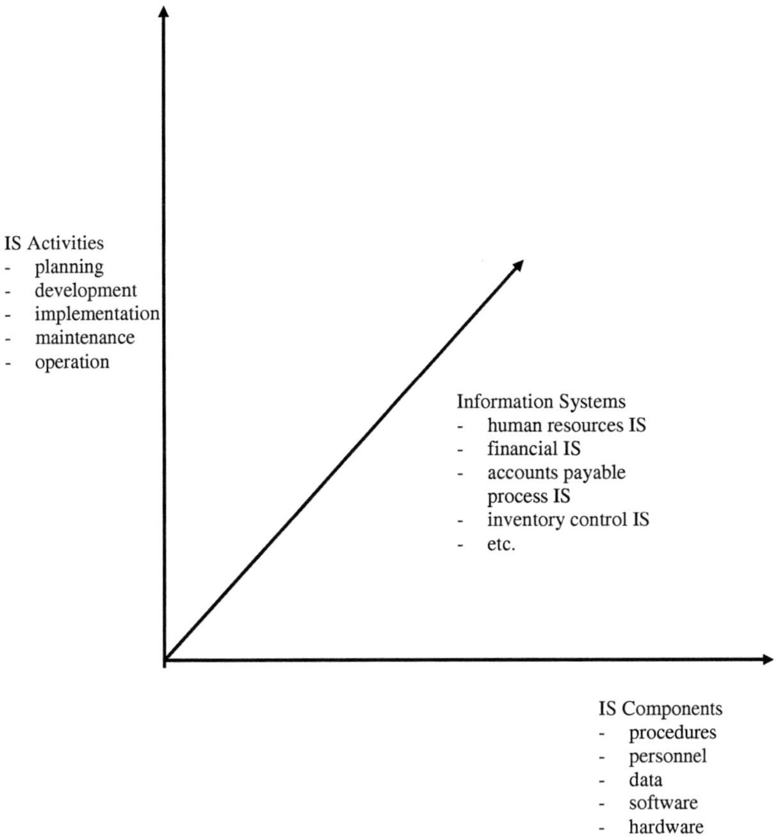

One approach for calculating the firm's value of human capital is to use a ratio of strategic benefits from skill development to the costs of developing skills (Lepak & Snell, 1999), as well as buying them from an outside vendor—i.e., IT outsourcing. IT skills in and of itself requires a set of skills such as technical abilities, analytical thinking, measurement and evaluation competencies, interpersonal communication, and presentation abilities. Criteria for assessing value relate to lowering costs and/or increasing benefits to customers of the organization. As a result, organizations should invest in generating human capital based upon expectations of future productivity (Becker, 1964; Tsang, Rumberger, & Levine, 1991) with strategic value.

While a particular perspective of human capital argues for developing and maintaining core employee skills rather than peripheral ones, empirical research findings on current trends in IT outsourcing appear to challenge this prescription (Cheon, Grover & Teng, 1995; Kimzey & Kurokawa, 2002; Storey, Quintas, Taylor, & Fowle, 2002). The shift to greater strategic leveraging of IT outsourcing involves partnering with outside vendors who are responsible for key functions such as innovations in R&D.

An implication for developing IT skills portfolios is determining an appropriate balance of human capital contributions from internal and external sources. Organizations with minimal or no outsourcing experience may want to start with low-risk tactical IS activities. As firms develop the necessary competencies to manage outsourcing, a more strategic deployment of IT outsourcing can be leveraged. Currently, there is no clear-cut prescription about outsourcing non-core activities versus core activities. The decision should be contingent on a firm's ability to move down the learning curve with IT outsourcing and organizational capabilities for learning to learn from strategic alliances partners.

Some firms have IT outsourcing models that often emerge in an ad hoc fashion over time (De Looff, 1995), while other firms make more informed and intentional decisions (Cronk & Sharp, 1995; Insinga & Werle, 2000). Sometimes particular IS activities and tasks are already outsourced at the outset when a firm engages in adapting to IT technologies. So managers have different options for IT outsourcing, and the best option is always contingent on the situation. Attention now turns to summarizing the five different HRIS models that involve different portfolios of human capital.

Five Models for Human Resource Information Systems

Human resource information system structures describe the relationships between IT outsourcing partners from client firms to vendors to contracting employees. In a study of IT outsourcing in a variety of industries, Kosnik and Wong-MingJi (2003) identified five major HRIS structural models. They are local contracting, HR centralizing, purchasing HR, primary staffing firm, and primary non-staffing vendor.

These five distinct HRIS models for IT outsourcing are described with implications for developing human capital portfolios. For organizations engaged in making decisions about IT outsourcing, there is increasing demand for a more comprehensive scope concerning the options for IT outsourcing arrangements and a means to compare the pros and cons of each one. Many organizations experienced very expensive lessons along the way as they shifted from one HRIS model to another and/or accumulated multiple models in different parts of their organization. Information regarding the pros and cons of

Figure 3: Human Resource Information Systems Supply Chain Models

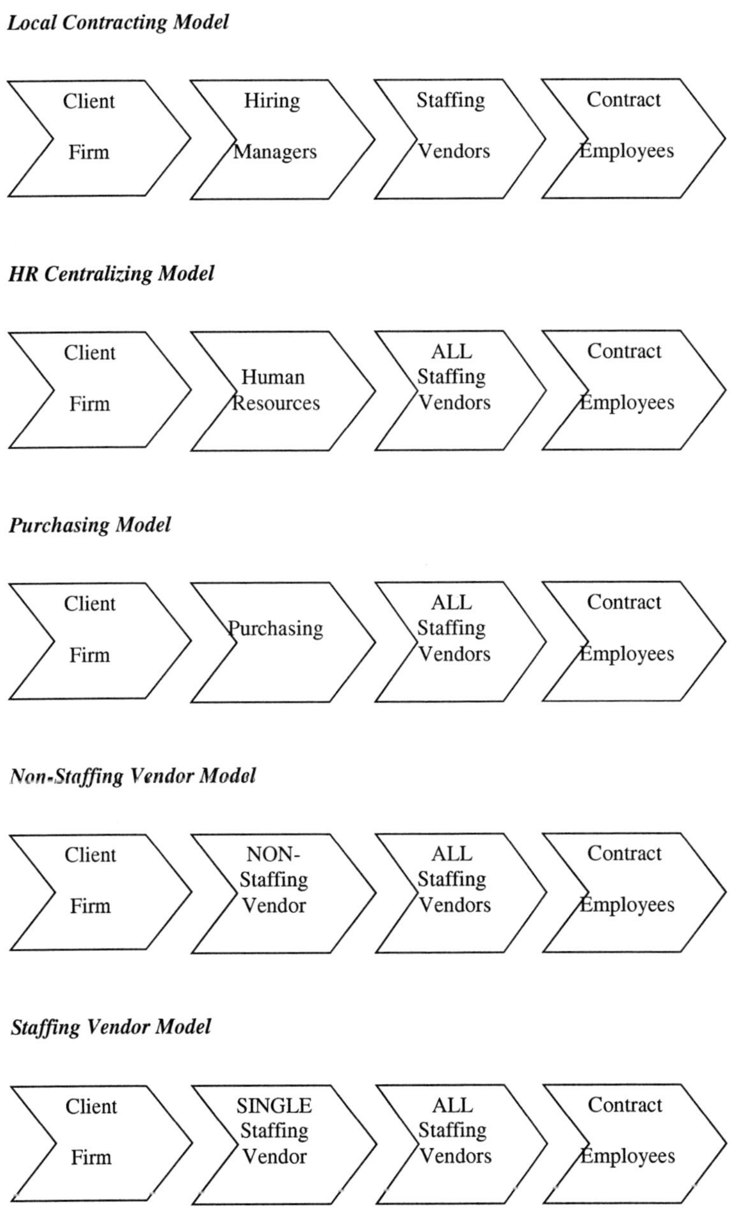

each HRIS model to support the business strategy is a critical starting point for managers to begin with in IT outsourcing decisions. The five HRIS models are briefly outlined below (see Figure 3).

Local Contracting Model

Local contracting is the traditional and most common HRIS model in which an organization obtains temporary staffing from various staffing vendors to address absentees, vacation, seasonal variations, and ad hoc projects. Individual hiring managers in a firm work with staffing vendors to make hiring decisions. Local contracting permits a high quality of service from vendors because of minimal bureaucracy, empowered hiring managers to hire qualified employees, and a relatively good alignment between specific staffing vendors and particular functional needs. However, hiring managers are distracted from their primary responsibilities in order to deal with numerous staffing vendors who are trying to increase sales. Also, the firm incurs high costs from a lack of standardization in hiring practices and procedures, subjective "quality" issues, high labor costs, and dependence on the capabilities of staffing vendors and contract employees. Furthermore, not all hiring managers have the requisite HR skills to make the best decisions related to the HR function. In sum, local contracting is the most flexible, high-quality, expensive, inefficient, and ineffective HRIS model for IT outsourcing.

HR Centralizing

HR centralizing is the standardization of hiring temporary workers by the HR department to drive down costs. Firms tend to adopt this approach when non-core employees reach a certain ratio of core employees such as 10%. The cut-off point depends on a number of variables related to the firm's competitive position and industry dynamics. The advantages of HR centralizing include more uniform hiring practices, billing rates, and pay rates. Previous hiring managers can refocus their attention on their functional responsibilities. HR professionals can develop standard criteria for a preferred vendors list. As a result, firms have greater security regarding the few staffing vendors that provide high-quality service.

Managers also need to consider the disadvantages of the HR centralizing model. Since the relationship between staffing vendors and hiring manager is severed, hiring managers experience greater frustration with more mismatches of temporary contractors to the tasks and related responsibilities. The staffing vendors often skirt around lower margins by "loading" the requests for proposals (RFPs) with cost plus factors or "category jumping" in the hiring process. Other disadvantages include additional departmental responsibilities in HR, which decrease outsourcing efficiencies. The HR centralizing approach tends to evolve into one of a "gatekeeper," which is usually tactical and administrative, rather than strategic. The responsibility creates an unwanted burden for the HR function. HR professionals often treat staffing vendors as competitors and threats to the full-time permanent workforce. This results in political conflicts and jockeying between HR and staffing vendors. In addition, gatekeepers in HR usually lack the human capital to effectively manage IT outsourcing responsibilities. Consequently, common outcomes with centralizing of HR outsourcing include some standardization with additional bureaucratic costs, but are not able to extrapolate the necessary human capital from non-core employees.

Purchasing HRIS Model

Purchasing HRIS is the allocation of managing staffing vendors to a firm's purchasing unit. Contract employees are treated in a similar fashion to purchasing other raw material inputs of a firm. The model's approach is to reduce costs by increasing efficiencies. The rationale for using purchasing professionals is to maintain control over hiring by using purchasing competencies for standardization in hiring practices, pay rates, and bill rates. Client firms often gain a better understanding of their vendors' mark-ups and margins to minimize the loadings on the RFPs. Staffing vendors usually provide higher quality and more flexible service than other HRIS models because they compete to be listed as a preferred supplier. Staffing vendors strive to include both special skills and volume staffing.

The disadvantages of a purchasing approach to HRIS stems from a rigid application of supply chain management (SCM) techniques to the hiring process, and treatment of staffing vendors and contract employees. SCM contradicts the realities of human capital idiosyncrasies. Purchasing staff often lack HR expertise. Client firms also need vendor management system software to manage the information flow. The hiring manager and staffing vendor relationship is severed. The staffing vendors treat client firms as a "source" account for low margins and send high-quality employees to other firms that provide higher margins. Also, staffing vendors tend to recruit out the higher end talent away from the client firm. Even though numerous firms use this approach, the purchasing HRIS model provides firms with low value added human capital. Alternatively, the management information systems function can be responsible for the process, which also entails similar advantages and disadvantages to the purchasing HRIS model.

Non-Staffing Vendors Model

The non-staffing vendor model has a non-staffing firm managing the complete range of staffing vendors for a client firm. When the proportion of non-core employees grows to a point where earlier HRIS models fail, firms may hire non-staffing vendor management firms to standardize the hiring process and manage their staffing vendors. In the 1980s, these firms were referred to as "managed services" firms, and later, evolved to vendor management systems (VMSs) with the integration of Web-based tools to manage the information flows. By using non-staffing vendors, firms can achieve standardization of hiring practices and bill rates, just-in-time information for vendors and client firms, single-source invoicing and paying, and a single point of contact for hiring managers. Advantages for staffing vendors include increased market share and market power when others exit the market due to low rates, decreasing errors and omissions, and reduction in contract pay rates. However, the best vendors will not work with the low pay rate, and non-staffing vendors' capabilities tend to be software firms without HR staffing service expertise.

As a result, the disadvantages of using a non-staffing vendor include severing the relationship between hiring manager and staffing vendor, a commodity approach with low touch, lower service quality, and lower competition between vendors. Generally, the human capital from contract employees from non-staffing vendors is a lower quality for lower costs, along with increased mistrust and animosity between contract employees, staffing vendors, client firms, and VMS firms.

Staffing Firm Model

Staffing firm model is based on selecting one staffing vendor to manage all the HRIS outsourcing needs. The goals are to achieve cost reductions and manage the logistics of non-core employees. The advantages of the staffing firm model for IT outsourcing include the addition of staffing expertise to the VMS level, improved economic profitability for staffing vendor, and more cooperative partnerships along the supply chain. In this model the staffing firm often assigns job orders to its own recruiters before sending them to other vendors. There is no staffing vendor competition. The contracted staffing vendor usually cannot fulfill all of a client's needs. As a result, secondary vendors are used to fill the gaps. But secondary vendors tend to send hard-to-place workers. Consequently, client firms experience higher turnover, training costs, and lower quality of service. The implications are that the quality of value added human capital from contracting employees is lower and animosity is high among the stakeholders.

The five HRIS models—local contracting, HR centralizing, purchasing HRIS, vendor management systems, and staffing firm—are different structural arrangement options for IT outsourcing. Deriving value added human capital from each one involves substantial challenges. While the structure of the first three models enables client firms to retain greater control, managers need to have the requisite knowledge and skills to effectively handle staffing vendors and contract employees. Important managerial competencies include negotiating optimal contractual terms, monitoring and assessing contract employees, developing trust with vendors, communicating evolving needs, and holding vendors accountable for poor quality service. The last two models involve lower bureaucratic costs for client organizations, but the quality of service can be a significant issue. The amount of power and control significantly shifts to the primary vendor. Managers of the client firm need highly sophisticated inter-firm relational knowledge and skills to work effectively with vendors because minimizing opportunism is critical to extrapolating the benefits and preventing uncontrolled spiraling costs.

A critical feature of all five HRIS models for IT outsourcing is the importance of creating healthy collaborative working partnerships throughout the whole supply chain—client firm, vendors, and contract employees. For IT outsourcing to shift from a tactical to a strategic mode, managers in client firms and vendor firms must develop the necessary 'soft' technologies. This requires a cognitive shift from a buyer-supplier relationship to one of strategic alliance partnership.

By drawing upon Klepper's (1995) prescription for building such collaborative strategic IT partnerships, critical human capital capabilities are as follows:

1) Client firms and vendors need shared objectives, beliefs, and values. To be an attractive IT outsourcing vendor, client firms should also look for characteristics that include complementary service capabilities, strong

financial viability, good management capabilities, and strong reputable status to weather difficult times. Managers should conduct a systematic comprehensive assessment of vendors before contractual negotiations by gathering the information from different managers in the firm that have experience with the vendor and from other vendor clients. Thus, knowledge base of measurement techniques and research skills to develop data collection instruments and conduct evaluative analysis are key human capital competencies for this initial process.

2) Communication skills are important throughout the process of IT outsourcing partnership development. Intentional development of a communication infrastructure to manage the IT outsourcing partnership helps to sustain the collaborative process in a long-term relationship. Specific communication skills center on being able to effectively bargain or negotiate and resolve conflicts. Strong communication skills support the growth of trust and commitment in IT outsourcing relationships.

3) Clarifying expectations on the part of client firms is critical, which requires a comprehensive understanding of how the pool of external technologies can support the organization's strategy. The critical human capital capability at this point is integrating all three critical components—expectations, strategy, and technological capabilities. A positive continuous cycle of expressed expectations, fulfilled expectations, trust building, and cycling back with greater expectations sustains an expanding cycle, and hence, the client-vendor relationship. As a result, growing equity and efficiency develop to characterize a healthy strategic alliance, where informal relationships begin to supplement the contractual one (Ring & Van de Ven, 1994) in the IT outsourcing supply chain. Unfulfilled expectations would disrupt the cycle and shift it toward a negative direction that may lead to the end of the IT outsourcing relationship.

4) Human capital generated from the above three items contributes to another key process for developing successful IT outsourcing supply chains—norm development. Managers in client firms and vendors depend on a common set of norms to guide actions. IT outsourcing can fail without adequate norms to create shared expectations of behaviors (Kern & Blois, 2002). Unlike the previously discussed human capital capabilities that individual managers can develop and apply, norm development is a competency that depends upon the collective parties involved in IT outsourcing relationships where organizational power and politics often influence the dynamics.

5) Exercising power and justice is a set of interrelated competencies for strategic alliances in IT outsourcing partnerships. According to Klepper (1995), the exercise of power has a just or unjust impact depending upon the balance of benefits accruing to the parties involved. How power is exercised affects the future potential for the relationship to evolve productively or fall apart often with high costs for at least one partner in the process. IT outsourcing partners can achieve mutually compatible balance by investing in relationship-specific assets such as technology development, methods, processes, standards, and firm-specific knowledge of the other partners. Judicious application of power with relationship-specific assets between the firms contributes to the growth of increasing expansion and commitment for leveraging the strategic capabilities in IT outsourcing partnerships.

In summary, the five HRIS models let managers evaluate what is the most appropriate scheme for aligning the IT outsourcing supply chain with the firm's strategy. While a greater amount of power and control reside with the client firms in the first three models (local contracting, HR centralizing, and purchasing HR) and with the vendors in the last two models (non-staffing vendors and staffing vendors), varying portfolios of human capital and skills make it possible for partners to maximize opportunities.

Strong negotiating skills are important in the firm's portfolio of human capital for all five HRIS models. Negotiating clearly developed contracts helps the firm to not only reduce costs, but also mitigate foreseeable problems. In additional, important professional skills related to HRIS include writing requests for proposals, contract writing, recruiting, selecting, hiring, training, and terminating at an organizational level between client firms and vendors as compared to the process for a permanent workforce. Some of these skills are comparable to purchasing/supply chain management competencies. The knowledge base should include job descriptions and requirements, performance evaluation, human resource regulations, and related HR knowledge. While many HR knowledge and skills are somewhat standard within the human resource function, HR professional competencies need to advance beyond the unit level to an organizational level in order to build partnerships with vendor firms. For example, job descriptions and RFPs become specs for vendors. In another instance, training should include not only developing cross-functional teams and team-building skills, but also building inter-firm teams to develop strategic alliance partnerships. Competencies from organizational development and change also have an important role in facilitating a broad perspective for strategic IT outsourcing partnerships too. The next section draws from supply chain management research to align the HRIS models with the three dimensions of the IS functions.

Supply Chain Management Strategies

Supply chain management focuses on integration to manage the flow of goods, services, and information from initial sourcing and purchasing of raw materials through to production and distribution to the end users. Given constant environmental changes, managing supply chains takes place in a context of fluctuating uncertainty. Lee (2002) built upon Fisher's (1997) demand uncertainty framework to create a 2x2 matrix from low to high supply and demand uncertainty for supply chain strategies. Firms simultaneously face uncertainty at both ends and require organizational competencies to deal with them at the same time.

Demand uncertainty refers to the predictability of functional versus innovative products. Uncertainty is relatively greater for innovative products compared to functional ones. Examples of functional products are stable goods such as basic food items, utilities, and gas, while innovative products are rapidly changing like high-end computers, fashion apparel, and video games. Supply uncertainty refers to stable versus evolving supply base and manufacturing processes. Usually mature industries have established manufacturing technologies and relatively standard products in place that may undergo only incremental change. In contrast, evolving supply processes are in early developmental stages with rapid changes.

By juxtaposing the two continuums of supply and demand uncertainties, firms can use IT capabilities and the Internet to develop supply chain strategies. Lee's (2002) framework is illustrated in Figure 4. There are no clear-cut or exact prescriptions for specific alignments between HRIS models and the supply chain strategies, only broad brush suggestions that are conducive for a logical fit.

Efficient supply chains have low demand uncertainty with functional products and low supply uncertainty with stable processes such as steel, grocery, and food. The goal is to maximize cost efficiencies by maximizing economies of scale and eliminating non-value added activities. The IT technologies should focus on efficient, accurate, and cost-effective information transmission through

Figure 4: Supply Chain Management Strategies for Supply and Demand Uncertainties (Lee, 2002, p. 108)

Supply Uncertainty	Demand Uncertainty: Low (Functional Products)	Demand Uncertainty: High (Innovative Products
Low (Stable Process)	Efficient Supply Chains	Responsive Supply Chains
High (Evolving Process)	Risk Hedging Supply Chains	Agile Supply Chain

the supply chain. IT capabilities need to support tight and seamless integration of information.

An appropriate alignment of HRIS models and the IS function can support efficient supply chains. The two HRIS models of HR centralizing and purchasing HR provide the potential for standardizing and centralizing human capital for efficient supply chains. Initially, activities of the IS functions for IT outsourcing should deal with the IS components and collaborate on the IS activities of planning, development, and implementation. The maintenance and operation IS activities need to remain in-house, as well as many of the IS systems, until such time that the IT outsourcing relationships develop into a strategic alliance partnership, at which time risk is lowered to entrust a broader array of activities to an external partner. At this point, the client firm gains some experience with various vendors to make a more informed selection.

Risk-hedging supply chains have low demand uncertainty with functional products and high supply uncertainty with evolving processes such as seasonality with some food produce or agricultural supplies. Firms can manage the supply risk by pooling and sharing resources to minimize disruptions. The critical IT role is real-time information transparency to support cost-effective trans-shipments for all firms that share in the supply risk.

IT outsourcing activities generally focused on a significant portion of IS activities such as development, implementation, maintenance, and operation, as well as many IS components, because multiple partners need to share in the financial responsibilities for risk-hedging supply chains. If most of the IS functions remain in-house with one partner, a significant imbalance of power develops, which may damage the strategic alliances. Also, Internet technology can support multiple sourcing options by establishing the necessary search support capabilities. Particular information systems targeted for outsourcing depend on each firm's overall business strategy as to what to retain as core activities versus what to leverage from external sources. To support IS activities, firms may use a combination of HRIS models within an organization to support risk-hedging supply chains, because functional areas such as productions may be completely outsourced while others such as inventory management are shared with other organizations. R&D and marketing may remain in-house.

Responsive supply chains face high demand uncertainty from innovative products and low supply uncertainty with stable processes. Firms in the computer or pop music industry must deal with such conditions. Being relatively flexible to effectively respond to changing diverse needs of customers requires capabilities for mass customization. Often the production process is set up for build-to-order. The required IT support must facilitate accurate specifications of variations in customer requirements, rapid information transfer to production facilities, and prompt delivery of the product. Underlying the process, firms require human capital to learn and stay abreast of new trends.

The most appropriate HRIS models to align with responsive supply chains are local contracting, non-staffing vendors, or staffing vendors. Fluctuations in demand with innovative products depend on a flexible workforce that provides a wide spectrum of human capital and quantity of labor. Using contract workers is related to firms with superior levels of innovation (Storey et al., 2002). IT outsourcing plays a critical strategic role in responsive supply chains by providing access to a greater pool of technology-oriented human capital. Production IS systems and most IS activities are likely candidates for outsourcing, while the storing of sensitive data regarding IS components are retained in-house with multiple security measures. However, firm size and industry characteristics would configure the particular IS functions to outsource and narrow the selection of the three HRIS models.

Agile supply chains are the most dynamic because they must deal with uncertainties from both ends of supply and demand. Evolving processes of supply and innovative products of demand create a volatile situation for managers. Advanced Internet IT capabilities can support agile supply chains. Examples of such developments can be found with firms such as Cisco, Adaptec, and Xilinx in the semiconductor and computer industry.

Agile supply chains are linked to multiple IS functions on all three dimensions—components, systems, and activities. HRIS models should be staffing vendors and non-staffing vendors depending on the particular needs in different functions. Many of the IT outsourcing relationships have to develop as strategic alliance partners along the supply chain, otherwise the client firm will not be able to draw upon the necessary flexibility for configuring a portfolio of human capital to support volatile changes coming from multiple directions.

In summary, information technologies and supply chains are integrally interconnected, where one would have a difficult time existing without the other. IT provides supply chains with the basic backbone to acquire, process, and transmit information. At the same time, development of supply chains demands more innovative systems from IT. Hence, a contingent approach with the four supply chain strategies allows managers to configure the most appropriate alignment of human capital from IT outsourcing and HRIS models for effective implementation of their business strategy. Different supply chains address varying levels of uncertainty in supply and demand conditions that firms contend with in sustaining a competitive position.

Supply chain management professionals identified important skills that contribute to increasing the strategic effectiveness of their function. Giunipero and Pearcy (2000) conducted a comprehensive review of key purchasing/supply management skill sets, which found some similarities with additional new requirements for future professionals. Their research findings indicated that skills-related strategy, process management, teamwork, decision making, behavioral, negotiating, and quantitative capabilities are important for future purchasing/supply management professionals in order to become more strategic in managing their responsibilities. The employment of these skills takes place within an organizational context with professionals from other functional areas. However, the development of particular purchasing and supply management skills and competencies for an organization depends on whether they are sourced internally or externally from vendors. The relatively new knowledge and skills sets for supply chain management overlapped with those needed by IT professionals, especially business skills, change management, and strategic thinking. Thus, within different functions, there is an increased awareness to develop competencies for strategic alignment.

Overall, research studies on the IS function, HRIS models, and supply chain management provide managers with directions for building an interdisciplinary approach, and cross-functional orientation, to create human capital portfolios for IT outsourcing. The competitive landscape is increasingly complex and goes beyond individual expertise or particular functional perspective. Value added contributions from human resources or supply chain management professionals depend upon their strategic alignment with other functions in an organization because many of their skills cannot be strategically deployed in isolation. Hence, some organizations use cross-functional teams to address complex strategic issues. IT outsourcing challenges certainly require such an approach. The challenge for managers in attracting, sustaining, and reconfiguring human capital from inside and outside the firm lies in being sufficiently equipped to reconfigure firm resources at a moments notice.

Managerial Approaches to Creating Human Capital Portfolios

In the future, IT outsourcing will continue to have an important role as more firms shift from a tactical approach to a strategic one. Being strategic with IT outsourcing involves a radically different managerial mindset from the highest office down throughout an organization. A more strategic role for IT outsourcing also implies that information competencies cannot remain within the purview of the IS function or with IT experts, but need to be diffused out into other parts of the organization (Peppard et al., 2000). As a result, value creation comes from aligning the firm's internal resources with the changing competitive conditions.

Given the various strategic frameworks available for IS/IT functions and IT outsourcing (Cronk & Sharp, 1995; De Looff, 1995; Willcocks & Lester, 1997), creating the appropriate human capital portfolio is critical to support the application of a strategic orientation (Peppard et al., 2000). Managers require a portfolio of human capital that includes competencies from multiple functional areas and organizational levels for organizational transformations. In order to eliminate the weakest link in IT outsourcing, the first task is to identify where the weaknesses lie in the supply chain system. The model for creating human capital portfolios for IT outsourcing provides managers with a guide to review their supply chains' alignment and balance of multi-level competencies and capabilities, and to identify where to direct firm resources for strengthening the connection.

The IS function, HRIS models, and supply chain management provide a collection of knowledge, skills, and competencies at the individual and sub-unit levels for integration by rational and connective organizational capabilities. While many authors recognize that IS/IT professionals tend to be technically proficient, competencies related to 'business,' 'interpersonal,' and 'change agent' skills are weak links in portfolios of human capital (Lee, Trauth, & Farwell, 1995; Markus & Benjamin, 1996). At the same time, management professionals often lag behind in understanding the competitive potential of IT until they embark on a journey to learn and apply new information technologies. Pressures from cost reductions are only entry points into moving down the learning curve toward strategically leveraging IT capabilities. Hence, as IS/IT professionals develop competencies to relate to an organization's business strategy, and as managers accumulate experience and insights into using new technology, the weak link from different parts of the organization can be eliminated.

Creating human capital portfolios also has important implications within the global context of IT outsourcing as firms engage in "offshoring." Global dynamics of IT outsourcing supply chains to locations such as India, China, and Ireland are certainly important in configuring a portfolio of human capital. Managers have the option to approach the situation from bottom up—with aligning fundamental basics of the IS/IT function's hardware and infrastructure, along with the requisite training of partners at multiple locations, or from top down—with finding strategic alliance partners to develop the inter-firm capabilities with the requisite organizational transformations.

Compared to domestic supply chains, managers have to globalize their organizations' human capital portfolios to function effectively in multiple geographical and cultural settings. Key factors of the model to address are connective organizational capabilities, IS activities in the IS function, the staffing and non-staffing vendors models for HRIS, and agile supply chains. All these different components have a highly tacit nature that is relatively more dependent on the ability to develop viable connections in human relationships for high performance. Without the necessary international cultural competencies to bridge the cultural differences between global organizations, strategic IT outsourcing will be substantially limited by weak links that will be detrimental to expected outcomes. Further specifications of the model for creating human capital portfolios in a global context are beyond the limits of this chapter.

Overall, developing a strong link between IT outsourcing and business strategy should advance an organization's competitive capability. If IT outsourcing contributes as a core competence to sustain a competitive advantage, top management must allocate the necessary support and resources. Additionally, Cohen and Levinthal (1990) stated that firms needed to develop 'absorptive capacity' to internalize and assimilate external knowledge, especially when organizations face special challenges arising from the outsourcing of key functions. As a result, skillful management of IT outsourcing requires firms to develop the necessary learning capabilities with managerial competencies and organizational capabilities. Without absorptive capacity to skillfully manage IT outsourcing, firms often find themselves in a quagmire of problems to the point of where the costs rapidly erode any benefits and possibly reverse the process to in-sourcing.

Conclusion

There are at least two important limitations to note about this chapter. First, the broad brush approach limits the development of detailed specifications for human capital portfolios of strategic IT outsourcing. Second, the discussion notably omitted critical human capital concerning IT outsourcing in a global context. In the future, the role of international cultural competencies as human capital in IT outsourcing warrants more attention.

Future developments on the role of human capital in strategic IT outsourcing need to examine which organizational capabilities and competencies are effective under different competitive conditions. Innovative leaders reconfigure portfolios of human capital in managing IT outsourcing to align their organization with environmental changes. Since a substantial portion of organizational capabilities for IT outsourcing is tacit in nature, accumulating experience is expected to provide a competitive edge if firms employ a learning approach. In addition, developing metrics to measure the strategic benefits derived from different organizational capabilities and competencies would enable managers to continuously monitor and revise their human capital portfolios as competition renders them obsolete.

In conclusion, this chapter discussed the development of human capital portfolios for strategic IT outsourcing supply chains that encompass knowledge, skills, competencies, and capabilities from different functional areas through various organizational levels. An interdisciplinary approach—with IS function, HRIS, and supply chain management—provides important building blocks for integration by the rational and connective organizational capabilities. Managers have a guide to analyze their existing IT outsourcing situation and focus on eliminating the weakest link. Human capital portfolios are rarely complete or perfected because of changing competitive conditions. In response, managers have to reconfigure human capital portfolios to adapt or, more powerfully, transform the rules of competition. Henceforth, human capital portfolios for strategic IT outsourcing supply chains remain as compositions of just-in-time works in progress.

References

Agrawal, V., & Farrell, D. (2003). Who wins in offshoring. *The McKinsey Quarterly: Global Directions,* (4), 1-5.

Argyris, C. (1992). *On organizational learning.* Cambridge, MA: Blackwell Publishers.

Barthelemy, J. (2001). The hidden costs of IT outsourcing. *MIT Sloan Management Review, 42*(3), 60-69.

Barthelemy, J. (2003). The seven deadly sins of outsourcing. *Academy of Management Executive, 17*(2), 87-100.

Becker, G.S. (1964). *Human capital.* New York: Columbia University Press.

Cheon, M.J., Grover, V., & Teng, J.T.C. (1995). Theoretical perspectives on the outsourcing of information systems. *Journal of Information Technology, 10,* 209-219.

Ciborra, C.U. (1999). Notes on improvisation and time in organizations. *Accounting, Management and Information Technologies, 9*(2), 77-94.

Cohen, W.M., & Levinthal, D.A. (1990). Absorptive capacity: A new perspective on learning and innovation. *Administrative Science Quarterly, 35*(1), 128-152.

Collis, D.J. (1994). How valuable are organizational capabilities? *Strategic Management Journal, 15,* 143-152.

Cronk, J., & Sharp, J. (1995). A framework for deciding what to outsource in information technology. *Journal of Information Technology, 10,* 259-267.

De Looff, L. (1995). Information systems outsourcing decision making: A framework, organizational theories and case studies. *Journal of Information Technology, 10,* 281-297.

Feeny, D., & Wilcocks, L. (1998). Core IS capabilities for exploiting IT. *Sloan Management Review, 39*(3), 1-26.

Fiol, C.M., & Lyles, M. (1985). Organizational learning. *Academy of Management Review, 10*(4), 803-13.

Fisher, M. (1997). What is the right supply chain for your product? *Harvard Business Review, 75*(2), 105-116.

Guinipero, L.C. & Pearcy, D.H. (2000). World-class purchasing skills: An empirical investigation. *The Journal of Supply Chain Management, 36*(4), 4-13.

Hamel, G. (1991). Competition for competence and inter-partner learning within international strategic alliances. -(1), 83-103.

Insinga, R.C., & Werle, M.J. (2000). Linking outsourcing to business strategy. *Academy of Management Executive, 14*(4), 58-71.

Jeffries, F.L., & Reed, R. (2000). Trust and adaptation in relational contracting. *Academy of Management Review, 25*(4), 873-892.

Kaplan, J. (2002). Outsourcing trends in uncertain times. *Business Communication Review, 32*(7), 28-32.

Kern, T., & Blois, K. (2002). Norm development in outsourcing relationships. *Journal of Information Technology, 17,* 33-42.

Kern, T., Willcocks, L.P., & van Heck, E. (2002). The winner's curse in IT outsourcing. *California Management Review, 44*(2), 47-69.

Kimzey, C.H., & Kurokawa, S. (2002). Technology outsourcing in the U.S. and Japan. *Research Technology Management, 45*(4), 36-43.

Klepper, R. (1995). The management of partnering development in I/S outsourcing. *Journal of Information Technology, 10,* 249-258.

Kogut, B. (1988). Joint ventures: Theoretical and empirical perspectives. *Strategic Management Journal, 9*(4), 319-332.

Kosnik, T., & Wong-MingJi, D.J. (2003). The romance and nightmare of HR outsourcing and workforce flexibility. *Proceedings of the International Human Resource Management Conference,* Limerick, Ireland.

Lacity, M., & Hirschhim, R. (1993). *Information systems outsourcing: Myths, metaphors, and realities.* Chichester: John Wiley & Sons.

Lee, D.M.S., Trauth, E.M., & Farwell, D. (1995). Critical skills and knowledge requirements of IS professionals: A joint academic/industry investigation. *MIS Quarterly, 19,* 313-340.

Lee, H.L. (2002). Aligning supply chain strategies with product uncertainties. *California Management Review, 44*(3), 105-119.

Lepak, D.P., & Snell, S.A. (1999). The human resource architecture: Toward a theory of human capital allocation and development. *Academy of Management Review, 24*(1), 31-48.

Lyles, M.A. (1988). Learning among joint venture sophisticated firms. *Management International Review, 28,* 85-97.

Macneil, I.R. (1978). Contracts: Adjustments of long-term economic relations under classical, neoclassical, and relational contract law. *Northwestern University Law Review, 72,* 854-905.

Markus, M.L., & Benjamin, R.I. (1996). Change agentry—the next IS frontier. *MIS Quarterly, 20,* 385-407.

McGrath, R.G., MacMillan, I.C., & Venkatraman, S. (1995). Defining and developing competence: A strategic process paradigm. *Strategic Management Journal, 16,* 251-275.

McLellan, K., Marcolin, B.L., & Beamish, P.W. (1995). Financial and strategic motivations behind IS outsourcing. *Journal of Information Technology, 10,* 299-321.

Milgrom, P., & Roberts, J. (1992). *Economics, organization, and management.* Englewood Cliffs, NJ: Prentice-Hall.

Miner, A.S., Bassoff, P., & Moorman, C. (2001). Organizational improvisation and learning: A field study. *Administrative Science Quarterly, 46*(2), 304-337.

Moorman, C., & Miner, A.S. (1998). Organizational improvisation and organizational memory. *Academy of Management Review, 23*(4), 698-723.

Orlikowski, W.J. (1996). Improvising organizational transformation over time: A situated change perspective. *Information Systems Research, 7*(1), 63-92.

Parkhe, A. (1991). Inter-firm diversity, organizational learning, and longevity in global strategic alliances. *Journal of International Business Studies, 22*(3), 579-601.

Peppard, J., Lambert, R., & Edwards, C. (2000). Whose job is it anyway? Organizational information competencies for value creation. *Information Systems Journal, 10,* 291-322.

Raelin, J.A. (2000). *Work-based learning: The new frontier of management development.* Upper Saddle River, NJ: Prentice-Hall.

Ring, P.S., & Van de Ven, A.H. (1992). Structuring cooperative relationships between organizations. *Strategic Management Journal, 13*(7), 483-498.

Ring, P.S., & Van de Ven, A.H. (1994). Development processes of cooperative interorganizational relationships. *Academy of Management Review, 19*(1), 90-118.

Rockhart, J.F., Earl, M.J., & Ross, J.W. (1996). Eight imperatives for the new IT organization. *Sloan Management Review, 38*(1), 43-55.

Sambamurthy, V., & Zmud, R.W. (1997). At the heart of success: Organization-wide management competencies. In C. Sauer, P.W. Yetton, & Associates (Eds.), *Steps to the future: Fresh thinking on the management of IT-based organizational transformation* (pp. 143-163). San Francisco: Jossey Bass.

Sanders, N.R., & Premus, R. (2002). IT applications in supply chain organizations: A link between competitive priorities and organizational benefits. *Journal of Business Logistics, 23*(1), 65-84.

Senge, P.M. (1990). *The fifth discipline: The art and practice of the learning organization.* New York: Doubleday.

Silva, L.O. (2002). Outsourcing as an improvisation: A case study in Latin America. *The Information Society, 18,* 129-138.

Stalk, G., Evans, P., & Schulman, I. (1992). Competing on capabilities: The new rules of corporate strategy. *Harvard Business Review,* (March-April), 57-69.

Storey, J., Quintas, P., Taylor, P., & Fowle, W. (2002). Flexible employment contracts and their implications for product and process innovation. *International Journal of Human Resource Management, 13*(1), 1-18.

Tracey, M., & Smith-Doerflein, K.A. (2001). Supply chain management: What training professionals need to know. *Industrial and Commercial Training, 33*(3), 99-103.

Tsang, M.C., Rumberger, R.W., & Levine, H.M. (1991). The impact of surplus schooling on worker productivity. *Industrial Relations, 30*(2), 209-228.

Willcocks, L.P., & Lester, S. (1997). In search of information technology productivity: Assessment issues. *Journal of Operational Research Society, 48,* 1082-1094.

Zaheer, A., & Venkatraman, N. (1995). Relational governance as an interorganizational strategy: An empirical test of the role of trust in economic exchange. *Strategic Management Journal, 16*(3), 373-392.

Chapter IX

An Exploration of the Value of Information Systems Certification: The Perspective of the Human Resource Professional*

John E. Anderson
East Carolina University, USA

Kevin Barrett
Dixie State College, USA

Paul H. Schwager
East Carolina University, USA

Abstract

Realizing that human resource (HR) professionals are often the gatekeepers to employment in organizations, this exploratory study examines the perceptions of HR professionals in relation to education, experience, and information system (IS) certification. Survey results were obtained from approximately 100 HR professionals who are members of local chapters of the Society for Human Resource Management (SHRM) in North Carolina. We conclude that education, certification, and experience are imperfect substitutes for each other. In addition, there seems to be a joint or halo effect conferred upon a balanced candidate. HR professionals are also willing to associate substantial positive organizational benefits with certification, specifically: enhanced IT staff credibility, competitive advantage, level of service, consistency of service provided. HR professionals also associate substantial employee benefits with certifications, specifically: enhanced credibility, preparation for new position within the current organization, compensation, mobility, preparing for other certification tests, and meeting a job requirement.

Introduction

Because the current information technology (IT) environment is characterized by rapid dynamic change, evolution of current technologies, and creation of new technologies, the skills portfolios of IT professionals are under constant pressure to develop in parallel. An important way to develop the IT skills portfolio is certification. While the perspectives of IT professionals and IT managers have been studied in the past (CompTIA, 2001), there has been no research on the perspective of human resource (HR) professionals toward IT certification.

The perspective of the HR professional is important. As the initial gatekeepers through which potential employees must pass to attain interviews with IT managers, the certification perceptions of HR professionals are worthy of study in and of themselves. In addition, the perceptions of HR professionals may have important implications for information systems (IS) curricula.

Background

A profession exists when its members are required to obtain requisite training, complete a certification process underpinned with rigorous standards, engage in continuing education, abide by a code of ethics, and submit to sanctions, including loss of certification for malpractice or unprofessional behavior. Although routinely referred to as a profession, the IT field lacks explicit, generally accepted standards for requisite training and certification, a code of ethics, and sanctions for unprofessional behavior (Linderman & Schiano, 2001). While "profession" advocates carry out the painstaking process of consensus building, businesses' support of and individuals' quest for IT certification proceed at a fevered pace and rival the popularity of certification programs in professions such as Accounting, Architecture, Engineering, Financial Planning, Human Resources, Law, Medicine, Military, and so forth. While there is admittedly a lack of generally accepted IT certification standards, the staying power of IT certification is an important "profession"-like expression. Indeed, the popularity of certifications such as A+, CCNA, CNA, Network+, MCSE, and MOUS (Ray & McCoy, 2000; Noack, 2001) implies that there is a market for the knowledge base and skills associated with those certifications, and strongly hints that the Academe is not the only place that requisite training and continuing education can be acquired.

While some argue that certification is a fad, others argue that certification is here to stay and will increase in importance because certification: provides an independent assessment of a professional's knowledge, raises professional stature, increases the knowledge base of both the individual and the organization in which the holder works, may provide an alternative to obtaining a graduate degree, may give job applicants an edge, can act as a knowledge refresher, and may aid employers in narrowing the applicant pool to manageable numbers (Cohen, 2001).

Certification's current popularity is attested to by a number of recent events:

1) major Technical-Certification-Expo-2000 and 2002 conferences,
2) designation of March 2000 as Certification Month by 32 United States state governors,
3) the availability of over 400 business certifications, and
4) the increasing frequency of employment ads specifying specific certification preferences attest to certification's popularity.

According to Adelman (2001), as of the year 2000, about 1.65 million individuals had earned 2.5 million IT certifications worldwide. Quasi-professions that lack certification are even being enticed to introduce certification to capitalize on commonly cited benefits (Leonard, 2002):

1) obtain further professional education and development,
2) move to a higher level of professional expertise,
3) improve career opportunities, and
4) enhance credibility by demonstrating mastery of a relevant body of knowledge (Barry, 2001; Library Administration and Management Association, 2002).

There also appears to be a growing international interest and participation in U.S.-based certification programs (Barber & Brackner, 2001). As the economy evolves, new opportunities arise outside of traditional service areas that motivate the need for new certifications to address the often-complex issues associated with emerging markets (AICPA, 2000; Braun, Mauldin, & Fischer, 2001; Freir, 2001; Gerbitz & Salea, 2001). Unfortunately, in some cases, certification proliferation causes confusion for consumers who are unfamiliar with a particular certification and the level of its prestige (Braun et al., 2001; Kraus, 1999). To some extent, this confusion syndrome is moderated, as a given specialization domain matures and convergence is achieved as to which certifications provide the greatest utility to individuals and organizations.

Several studies have explored the value of certification to certified professionals and to the business managers that employee certified professionals (AICPA, 2000; Barber & Brackner, 2001; Barry, 2001; CompTIA, 2001; Freir, 2001; Hrisak, 2001; Ray & McCoy, 2000; Schroeder & Reichardt, 2001). Professionals earn certifications to improve and assess skills, enhance credibility, improve compensation, increase productivity, open up new career opportunities, and measure training effectiveness. Seventy-six percent of certified professionals actually realized their certification-benefits expectations (CompTIA, 2001). Business managers cite improved credibility, employee productivity, higher level and consistency of service, competitive advantage, and ability to attract and retain highly qualified staff as the key benefits of certification. Ninety-two percent of business managers actually realized all or nearly all of their certification-benefits expectations (Ray & McCoy, 2000). While these earlier studies certainly reflect positively on certification, they overlook the value of certification to HR professionals. HR professionals are generally involved in all phases of the hiring process. They are often involved in approving position advertisements, screening resumes, and doing initial interviewing (Mondy, Noe, & Premeaux 1999). IT certifications are often indicated in position advertisements, as well as resumes and the interview process. With recruitment and selection as basic HR functions, the HR professional is often the first barrier that an IT professional will encounter in pursuing employment with a particular organization. As the initial gatekeepers to employment, HR professionals' perceptions of IT certification is worthy of study in and of themselves. In addition, those perceptions may have important implications for IS curricula.

Despite the fact that certifications have historically had a negative impact on their salaries, many academics have nonetheless obtained certification to augment their skills. The quest for certification has recently been legitimized and indeed given a compelling mandate by the American Assembly of Collegiate Schools of Business' recommendation for greater interaction between academicians and practitioners (Marcis & Bland, 2001). There is, however, considerable debate as to whether certification has a place in the IS curriculum of four-year educational institutions. One side of the debate employs a generalist argument to make the case for excluding certification from IS curriculums. The generalist argument asserts that the primary mission of most four-year colleges and universities focuses on the development of students' critical thinking and analytical skills, and their appreciation for the arts, diverse cultures, foreign languages, the scientific method, and the history and politics of their own and other societies, not community-college-oriented, workforce-development training of vendor-specific certification (Brookshire, 2001). The other side of the debate uses a value argument to make the case for inclusion of certification in IS curriculums. The value argument focuses on the student, employer, and education institution benefits associated with specific student and professor certification in four major areas: hardware (A+, vendor-neutral), software (MOUS, vendor-specific, Microsoft Office User Specialist), networks (Network+, vendor-neutral), and systems design and analysis (MCP-Microsoft-Certified Professional, MCSD-Microsoft-Certified Solution Developer, and MCSE-Microsoft-Certified Systems Engineer, all vendor-specific). Benefits to students and employers correspond closely to those noted above in connection with IT professionals and IT managers. From an institutional perspective, certification provides an assessment tool for evaluating course and program content and student competencies, and may contribute to a program's visibility and respect (Ray & McCoy, 2000).

The Value of Certification

Smith and Nagle define value as "the objective worth to a customer of satisfying the benefits they seek from a product or service. It's the potential level to which willingness to pay (WTP) can be raised, and revenue captured…." They argue that while WTP is useful as a concrete value measure, the level and antecedents of value must be understood to set prices that reflect the real value of a product or service. The first objective of measuring value is to define the value creation system and the four or five value drivers that account for the majority of the value created for customers (2002).

This study is an initial exploratory attempt to understand the value creation system and value drivers of IS certification on HR professionals' hiring decisions.

Problem and Purpose

While the perspectives of IT professionals and IT managers have been studied in the past, there has been no research on the perspective of the HR professionals toward IT certification. The purpose of the present study is to explore the perspective of the HR professional toward IT certification. The following objectives were motivated from the literature review and formulated to accomplish the purpose of this study:

1. Determine the value of IT certification to HR professionals relative to formal education and experience in the hiring decision for IT professionals.
2. Determine the organizational benefits of a certified IT staff from the perspective of HR professionals.
3. Determine the employee benefits of IT certification from the perspective of HR professionals.
4. Determine the relative credibility of IT certification as compared to other certifications in business and industry from the perspective of HR professionals.
5. Determine whether HR professionals prefer theory-based education or application-based education, and whether certification should be part of an information systems curriculum.

Methodology

Due to the exploratory nature of this study, the perceptions of HR professionals were solicited with a survey instrument (see Appendix A) that was given to members from local chapters of the Society for Human Resource Management (SHRM) in North Carolina. Parts of this survey reflect the design of portions of the CompTIA survey so that the data generated by HR professionals can be compared to data generated by IT managers and certified professionals (CompTIA, 2001).

Presentation and Discussion

Surveys were collect by the presidents of six local North Carolina SHRM chapters at a monthly meeting. Based on the indications of the presidents and the researchers' presence at several of these meetings, it is estimated that the response rate is in excess of 30%. From these meetings, 101 usable responses were obtained from SHRM members. In this section, demographic data will first be presented. The results will then be presented in order of the research questions answered.

Table 1: Descriptive Statistics for Demographic Data

	Statistic				
Demographics	N	M	SD	Min.	Max.
Number of full-time employees currently in organization	93	4,178.89	15,249.92	4	85,000
Years served as a HR professional	95	12.13	8.35	0	33
Years served in a HR management position	94	8.64	8.10	0	32

Demographics

To determine organizational and respondent characteristics, respondents were asked to disclose the number of years served as an HR professional and as an HR manager, the number of full-time employees in their organization, and their organizational affiliations. Table 1 shows that the average HR professional has served as an HR professional for about 12 years and as an HR manager for about 9 years, and currently works in a medium-sized organization (the range values and standard deviation suggest significant skewing is distorting the average employee's data). Figure 1 reveals that approximately 73% of the HR professionals (i.e., all but "others") participating in this study are in managerial positions and thus intimately involved in the hiring of new personnel (for ease of reference, all respondents are now referred to as HR professionals). This finding strengthens the meaningfulness of the HR perceptions that underpin the subsequent analysis of each of this study's five objectives.

Figure 1: Job Title

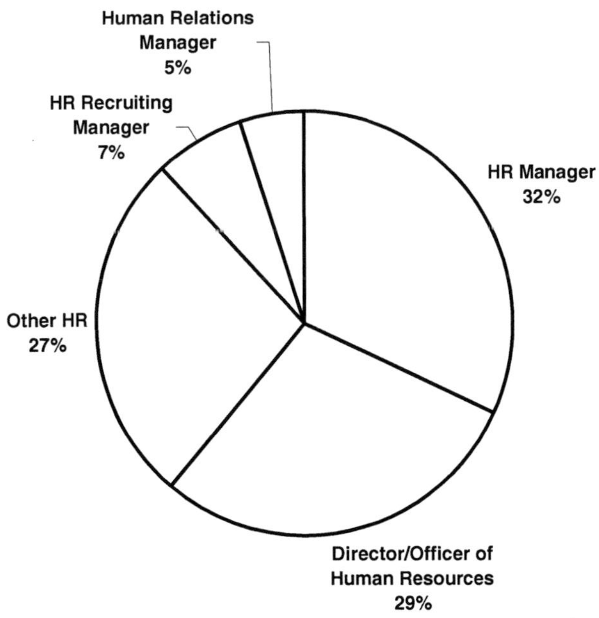

Discussion of Research Objectives

Objective 1: Determine the value of IT certification to the HR professional relative to formal education and experience in the hiring decision for an IT professional.

Objective 1 was measured by a set of three scenario questions. Respondents were asked to indicate the relative percentage weights (summing to 100%) that they would assign to education, certification, and experience when making a hiring decision in each of the following scenario contexts (the scenario ordering has been changed relative to the survey to facilitate discussion):

1) "*Scenario 1:* Candidate has no degree but several years of experience."
2) "*Scenario 2:* Candidate has an Associates Degree from a Community College/Vo-Tech."
3) "*Scenario 3:* Candidate has a Bachelor's Degree from a University."

As shown in Figure 2, HR professionals, on average, place about 16% of the relative weight of their hiring decisions for no-degree candidates on education, apparently establishing the lack of a degree as something that has to be

Figure 2: Relative Weights Used by HR Manager in Hiring Decision for Hiring an IS Professional

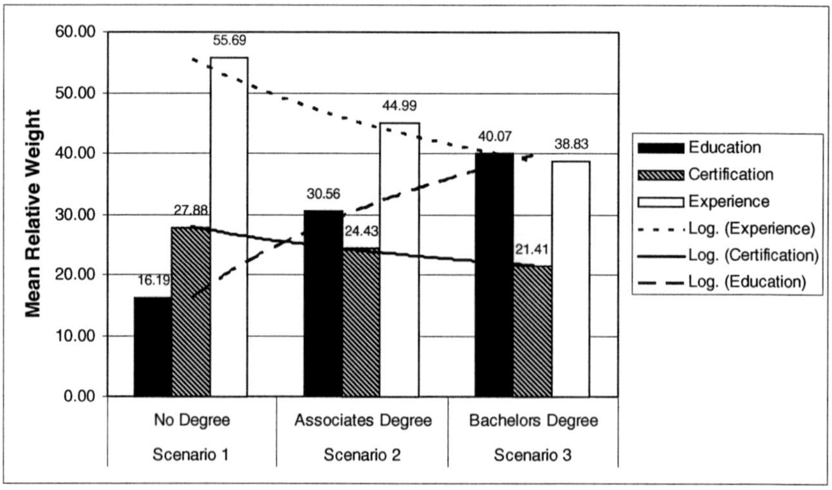

explained, compensated for, or replaced by significant experience and meaningful certification. In moving to the case of candidates with an Associates Degree, HR professionals nearly doubled the relative weight associated with education. Clearly, having some sort of degree establishes an important milestone in the minds of HR professionals faced with a hiring decision. Please note that the increase in the relative weight of education is subsidized largely by a decreasing emphasis on work experience. As a practical matter, this study does not allow us to say how much experience places an Associates Degree candidate on par with the "many years of experience" of the no-degree candidate. However, it appears that relevant experience is highly valued and that it takes relatively less experience to place an Associates Degree candidate on par with a no-degree candidate.

In the case of a Bachelor's Degree candidate, HR professionals strike an interesting balance between education and experience, and draw nearly equally upon certification and experience to strike that balance. The continued strong presence of each of these components suggests that they are imperfect substitutes for each other. That is, each component exerts its own positive influence on the perception formation of HR professionals. The log curves indicate that each tradeoff component experiences diminishing marginal returns in moving from the no-degree scenario to the Bachelor's Degree scenario, suggesting the obvious outcome of the desirability of the balanced candidate. That is, there appears to be a joint or halo effect associated with having all three components adequately represented. Given the progression of educational achievement from no degree to a four-year Bachelor's Degree, it appears that adequate education means a four-year degree. Unfortunately, however, this study does not allow us to define what adequate is for purposes of how much or what type of "in-field" work experience, or how many or which certifications.

We note the relative flatness of the certification curve, the flattest of the three curves. Although the weight given to certification does diminish as education level increases, it is slight when compared to the decreased weight given to experience. Education and experience may be substitutes for each other to a point. The flat certification curve suggests that certification is a unique part of the hiring mix not substitutable by education or experience. The flat certification curve further suggests that certification is the least vulnerable to diminishing marginal returns and thus the best investment alternative, given a Bachelor's Degree and adequate relevant experience, for becoming a more desirable, balanced job candidate.

Although more research is needed, the education-certification-experience dimensions may operationalize as theoretical breadth, technical depth, and practical application.

Objective 2: Determine the organizational benefits of a certified IT staff from the perspective of the HR professional.

Objective 2 was measured by a set of nine benefit factors drawn from the survey used in CompTIA's 2001 Training and Certification Study (CompTIA, 2001). A 10th factor, ethical conduct, was added on an experimental basis to see to what extent HR professionals perceive that certification enhances ethical behavior, and thus the extent to which IS can be perceived as being more of a profession. Figure 3 discloses those factors along with HR professionals' corresponding perceptions. In general, HR professionals felt that certification provides their organizations with at least "some benefit" for each of the factors. HR professionals also perceived substantial (substantial was selected as a modifier to communicate the notion that all of the findings are noticeably beyond the "some benefit, i.e., "5" demarcation) organizational certification benefits arising from enhanced IT staff credibility (5.61); enhanced competitive advantage (5.24); level of service (5.23); consistency of service provided (5.22);

Figure 3: HR's Perceived Organizational Benefits of Certified Staff

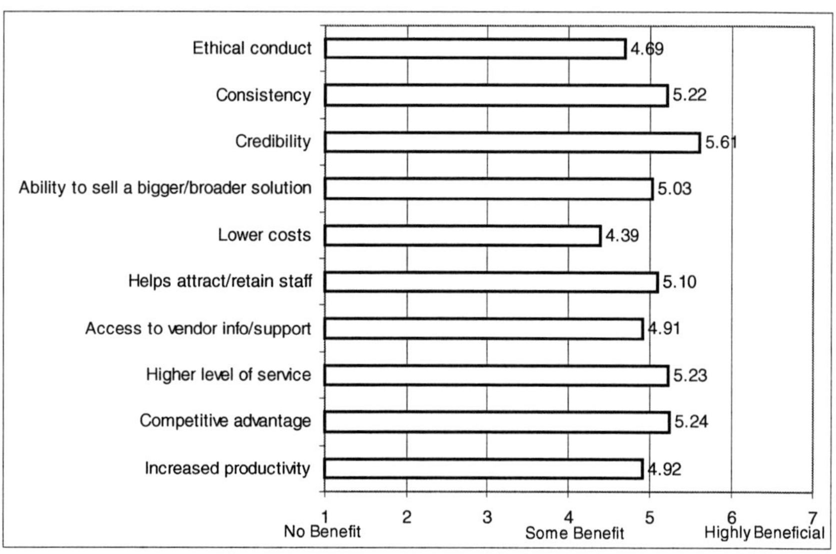

higher, improved ability to attract and retain staff (5.10); and ability to sell bigger/broader solution (5.03). With regard to ethical conduct, a "benefit" score of 4.69 suggests that HR professionals perceive certification as offering some benefit in regards to employee ethical conduct. It may be that HR professionals perceive that certification activates adherence to an implicit code of ethics and thus accommodates the perception that the IS profession takes on more "profession-like" characteristics. Explicit certification-related sanctions for unethical behavior would likely strengthen these ethical-conduct findings.

Objective 3: Determine the employee benefits of IT certification from the perspective of the HR professional.

Objective 3 was measured by a set of nine benefit factors drawn from CompTIA's 2001 Training and Certification Study (CompTIA, 2001). Figure 4 discloses those factors along with HR professionals' corresponding perceptions. In general, HR professionals felt that certification would provide their employees with at least "some benefit" for each of the factors. HR professionals also perceived substantial (as previously operationalized) employee certification benefits arising from their enhanced credibility (5.65), preparation for new position within the current organization (5.51), compensation (5.36), mobility

Figure 4: HR's perceived employee benefits of certification

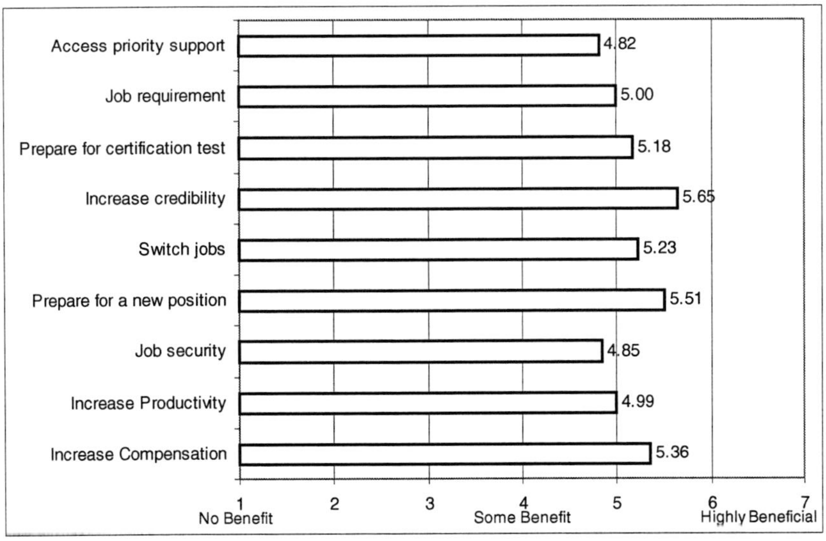

(5.23), preparing for other certification tests (5.18), and meeting a job requirement (5.00).

Objective 4: Determine the relative credibility of IT certification as compared to other certifications in business and industry from the perspective of the HR professional.

Objective 4 was examined with three questions that compared the credibility of IT certification to Accounting, Human Resource, and other industry certifications (e.g., CFP, Series 7, APICS, etc.). Figure 5 reveals that HR professionals view IT certification as having slightly more credibility than those from "other" industry certifications and their own HR certifications, and roughly equal credibility with the Accounting profession's CPA certification. This finding is consistent with the findings associated with prior objectives, reflects HR professionals' perceptions that certification helps organizations (if certified employees stay) and employees that certify, and thus makes a meaningful contribution to the perception that information systems is a profession.

Figure 5: IS Certification Credibility, Compared to Other Certifications

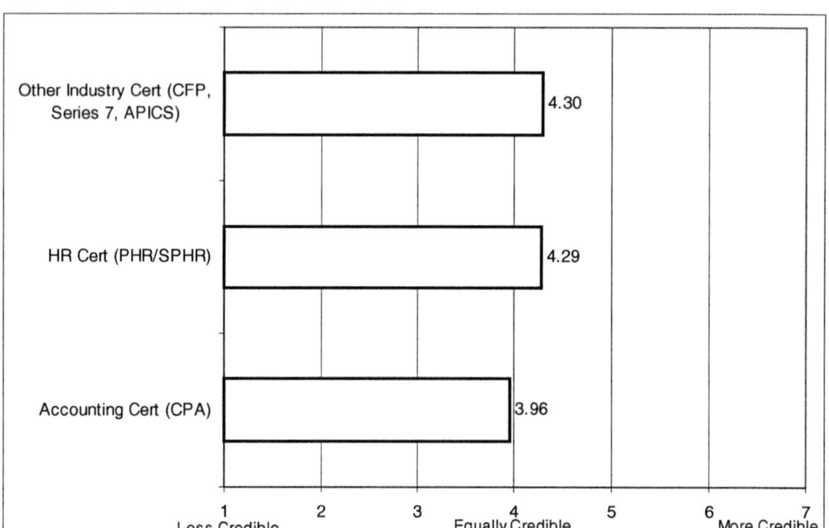

Objective 5: Determine whether HR professionals prefer theory-based education or application-based education, and whether certification should be part of an IS curriculum.

Objective 5 was evaluated by asking respondents to state the extent to which they agreed with two statements:

1) "A Bachelor's Degree curriculum in Information Systems that produces breadth of knowledge (i.e., a theoretical foundation) is more valuable than a Bachelor's curriculum that produces depth of knowledge (i.e., technical or applied skills)."
2) "Certification courses should be part of the Bachelor's Degree curriculum."

As noted in Figure 6, HR professionals were very nearly neutral (i.e., 4.15) with regard to Question 1, suggesting that there ought to be a balance between theoretical and technical and applied components in IS curriculums. With regard to Question 2, HR professionals' 5.18 metric (i.e., somewhat agree) seems to indicate that certification may be a meaningful way of introducing depth to the curriculum and thus striking that balance.

Figure 6: Certification in a Four-Year Degree Program

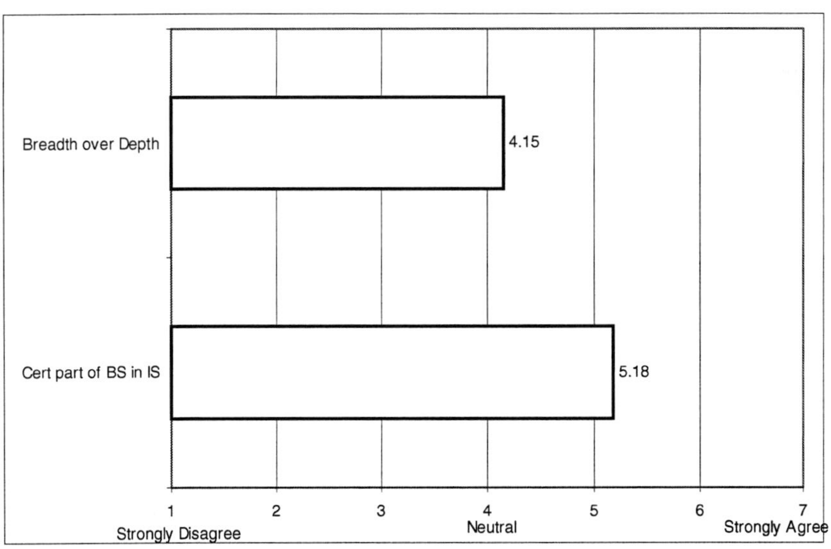

Conclusion

This exploratory study yields a number of interesting insights into HR professionals' information systems certification perceptions and the implications those perceptions have for IS curriculums. Based on the findings of this study, we can conclude that certification, education, and experience are imperfect substitutes for each other. Thus, each component exerts its own unique, positive influence on HR professionals' perception formation. In addition, there seems to be a joint or halo effect conferred upon a balanced candidate. The relative weights of the three dimensions in an HR professional's hiring decision for a job candidate with a Bachelor's Degree seems to be 40% education, 20% certification, and 40% experience, with education and experience receiving approximately equal weights, and certification receiving half of the weight of education or experience. In light of their neutrality towards the task of declaring either a theory-based or a technical/application-based IS curriculum most desirable, HR professionals seem to be suggesting that there ought to be a balance between theoretical and technical and applied components in IS curriculums.

We can also conclude that HR professionals are willing to associate substantial positive organizational benefits with certification, specifically: enhanced IT staff credibility, competitive advantage, level of service, and consistency of service provided. HR professionals also associate substantial employee benefits with certifications, specifically: enhanced credibility, preparation for new position within the current organization, compensation, mobility, preparing for other certification tests, and meeting a job requirement. Finally, HR professionals view IT certification as having about the same level of credibility as certifications from other business service areas.

Future Research

Exploratory research is valuable as a preliminary procedure for construct definition and hypothesis development. This study, as an initial exploratory attempt to understand the value creation system and value drivers of IS certification on HR professionals' hiring decisions, has found value as the first step in constructing the conceptual framework for future research on the value

Figure 7: Framework for Future Research

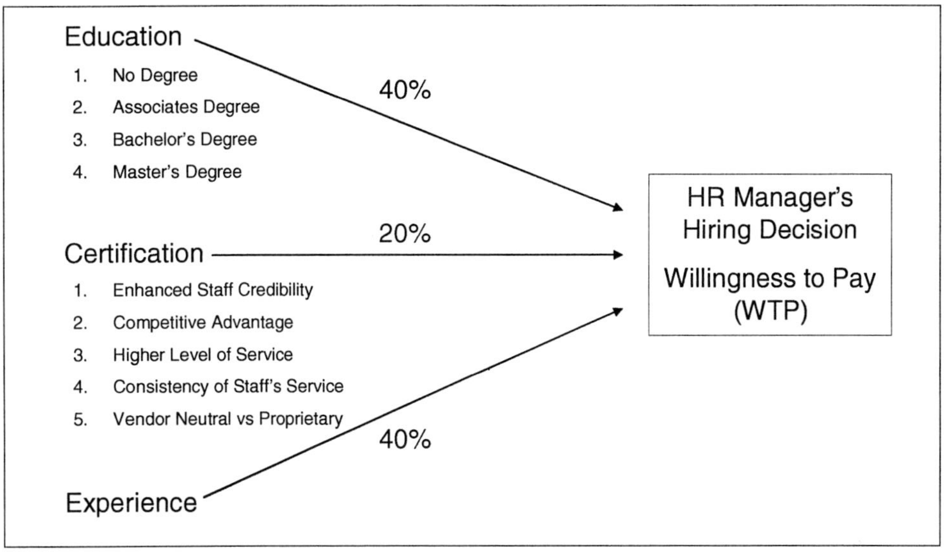

of IS certifications. A next step is to develop and test hypotheses using a measurable construct such as customer willingness to pursue (WTP), as seen in Figure 7. The use of willingness to pursue, in place of the willingness to pay construct, is used in this model because of the HR professional's gatekeeper role in the process. Once the HR professional has determined the merits of the individual applicant, the applicant will be pursued via other organizational means.

Additional research possibilities include looking as the influence of a Master's Degree and internships upon the value of IS certification, the influence of outsourcing either the HR or the IS function on the value of certification, and the influence of HR professional education in reference to the differing levels and type of IS certifications on the value of certification.

Endnote

* *An early draft of this chapter was presented at the Americas Conference on Information Systems, AMCIS, Dallas, Texas, August 2002.*

References

Adelman, C. (2001). The medieval guild in cyberclothes: International dimensions of industry certification in information technology. *Tertiary Education and Management, 7*(3), 277-292.

AICPA (2000). IT credential to help CPAs make business sense out of technology. *Journal of Accountancy*, (July), 95-98.

Barber, R.L., & Brackner, J.W. (2001). Certification. *Strategic Finance*, (September) 71-72.

Barry, J.N. (2001). Certification, is it worth the price? *Library Journal*, (February), 96.

Braun, R., Mauldin, S., & Fischer, M.A. (2001). The CFE designation in perspective. *The CPA Journal*, (April), 42-48.

Brookshire, R.G. (2001). Information technology certification: Is this your mission? *Information and Technology, Learning, and Performance Journal, 18*(2), 1-2.

Cohen, D. (2001). Is certification in your future? *HR Magazine*, (June), 296.

CompTIA. (2001, November 15). *2001 Training & Certification Study*. Available online at: http://www.comptia.org.

Freir, K.D. (2001). Certification corner: Certification statistics and demographics. *Cost Engineering*, *43*(8), 13.

Gerbitz, K., & Salea, R.S. Market research: Data suggest demand for global business credential skills. *Journal of Accountancy*, (September), 65-66.

Hrisak, D.M. (2001). Global challenges call for more CMAs and CFMs. *Strategic Finance*, (June), 46-49.

Kraus, W.E. (1999). Certification improvement thanks to peer review. *Cost Engineering*, *41*(4), 22-24.

Leonard, B. (2002). A brief history of HRCI. *HR Magazine,* (March 14). Available online at: http://www.hrci.org/about/history.html.

Library Administration and Management Association. (2002, March 12). *Certified Public Library Administrator (CPLA) Certification Program Overview*. Available online at: http://www.pla.org/projects/certification/certification.html.

Linderman, J.L., & Schiano, W.T. (2001). Information ethics in a responsibility vacuum. *The Data Base for Advances in Information Systems*, *32*(1), 70-74.

Mondy, R.W., Noe, R.M., & Premeaux, S.R. (1999). *Human resource management* (4th ed.). Upper Saddle River, NJ: Prentice-Hall.

Marcis, J.G., & Bland, E.M. (2001). The value of professional certifications in academe. *Atlantic Economic Journal*, *29*(1), 116.

Noack, D. (2001). Certification mystification. *Link-Up*, *18*(5), 17.

Ray, C.M., & McCoy, R. (2000). Why certification in information systems? *Information and Technology, Learning, and Performance Journal*, *18*(1), 1-2.

Schroeder, D.L., & Reichardt, E. (2001). IMA 2000 salary guide. *Strategic Finance*, (June), 24-37.

Smith, G., & Nagle, T. (2002). How much are customers willing to pay? *Marketing Research*, (Winter), 20-25.

Appendix A: The Survey

Information Systems Certification

S U R V E Y

This survey is part of a study concerning the benefits of information systems (IS) certification and the implications those benefits have for curriculum design. Please respond to all applicable questions. ***Your individual responses will be completely anonymous, treated confidentially, and used in summary form only***. Thank you for your support.

Balancing Trade-offs in the Hiring of an Information Systems Professional

For questions 1 through 3, please indicate the relative weights that you would use to make a hiring decision for an IS professional:

1. Scenario 1: Candidate has an Associates Degree from a Community College/Vo-Tech

   Education _____% + **Certification** _____% + **Experience** _____% = **100%**

2. Scenario 2: Candidate has a Bachelor's Degree from a University

   Education _____% + **Certification** _____% + **Experience** _____% = **100%**

3. Scenario 3: Candidate has no degree but several years of experience.

   Education _____% + **Certification** _____% + **Experience** _____% = **100%**

Organizational Benefits of Certified Staff

For questions 1 through 10, please indicate the extent to which you feel each of the designated items is an **organizational** benefit of certification using the following scale:

	No Benefit		Some Benefit			Highly Beneficial	
1. Increased productivity/tasks completed quicker.	1	2	3	4	5	6	7
2. Competitive advantage.	1	2	3	4	5	6	7
3. Higher level of service.	1	2	3	4	5	6	7
4. Access to vendor information/support.	1	2	3	4	5	6	7
5. Helps attract/retain staff.	1	2	3	4	5	6	7
6. Lower costs.	1	2	3	4	5	6	7
7. Ability to sell a bigger/broader solution.	1	2	3	4	5	6	7
8. Credibility.	1	2	3	4	5	6	7
9. Consistency.	1	2	3	4	5	6	7
10. Ethical conduct.	1	2	3	4	5	6	7

Employee Benefits of Certification

For questions 1 through 9, please indicate the extent to which you feel each of the designated items is an **employee** benefit of certification using the following scale:

	No Benefit		Some Benefit			Highly Beneficial	
1. Increase compensation.	1	2	3	4	5	6	7
2. Increase productivity.	1	2	3	4	5	6	7
3. Job security.	1	2	3	4	5	6	7
4. Prepare for a new position/responsibility.	1	2	3	4	5	6	7
5. Switch jobs.	1	2	3	4	5	6	7
6. Increase credibility.	1	2	3	4	5	6	7
7. Prepare for certification test.	1	2	3	4	5	6	7
8. Job requirement	1	2	3	4	5	6	7
9. Access priority support.	1	2	3	4	5	6	7

Certification Credibility

For questions 1 through 3, please indicate the extent to which you feel information systems certification has comparable credibility to the designated certifications using the following scale:

	Less Credible			Equally Credible			More Credible
1. Accounting certifications: ex. CPA (Certified Public Accountant).	1	2	3	4	5	6	7
2. HR certifications: ex. PHR/SPHR (Senior/Professional in Human Resources).	1	2	3	4	5	6	7
3. Other industry certifications (CFP, Series 7, APICS, etc.).	1	2	3	4	5	6	7

Certification in a Four-Year Degree Program

For questions 1 and 2, please indicate the extent to which you are in agreement with the indicated proposition using the following scale:

	Strongly Disagree			Neutral			Strongly Agree
1. Certification courses should be part of the Bachelor's Degree curriculum in Information Systems	1	2	3	4	5	6	7
2. A Bachelor's Degree curriculum in Information Systems that produces breadth of knowledge (i.e., a theoretical foundation) is more valuable than a Bachelor's curriculum that produces depth of knowledge (i.e., technical or applied skills)	1	2	3	4	5	6	7

Comments

Please provide any comments that you feel would be helpful to this study.

Background Information

1. How many years have you served as a human resources professional?
   __________Years
2. How many years have you served in a human resources management position? __________Years
3. What is your current job title?______________________________
4. How many full-time employees currently work in your organization?
   __________Employees
5. Which of the following best describes your organization's primary business activity?

☐ Agriculture/Mining/Construction	☐ Information Systems	☐ Trade & Retail	☐ Transportation & Public Util
☐ Nondurable Manufacturing	☐ Government	☐ Health Care	☐ Other __________
☐ Durable Manufacturing	☐ Finance, Insurance, Real Estate	☐ Services	

Thank You for your time and assistance!	☐ Please check the box if you would like a summary of this study and then fill out the personal information table below.
Personal Information (**please fill this section out only if you would like a summary of this study**):	
Name:	
Address:	

Chapter X

Extreme Interviewing to Find Team Oriented Programmers*

Clement James Goebel, III
Menlo Innovations LLC, USA

Richard Sheridan
Menlo Innovations LLC, USA

Thomas Meloche
Menlo Institute LLC, USA

Abstract

Many software development hires fail to add significantly to the team's overall productivity. The typical response is to increase the number of interviews and prepare an examination of sophisticated technical questions for the candidates. But what if your most important hiring goal was to find new technical employees with good teaming skills? One organization decided to create an immersion interview experience that provided candidates with the opportunity to demonstrate their teaming skills.

Introduction

Hiring new employees is a challenging task. Most managers recognize the importance of identifying the candidate's technical skills, but fail to effectively screen for the soft skills that will allow them to successfully function as an effective member of the team. Even talented individuals with the proper skills might not be a good fit if they have a difficult time fitting into the company culture. Worse, hiring a permanent employee for a specific technical skill alone is likely a mistake. If an employee is hired solely for his or her deep knowledge of C++, what happens if the company later decides to focus on Java? The employee is almost always retained, but was selected primarily for a skill set that is now irrelevant. How would you change your interview process if you felt that teamwork was as important, or more important, than any specific technical skill? This chapter describes how one company changed its interview process after deciding that soft skills such as collaboration and teamwork were even more important than expertise with a particular technology or development tool.

The Need

In 1999, the executive management team of Interface Systems Inc. decided to improve their software development capability. Specifically, they wanted to put in place a process that would provide a more predictive planning capability. This improved planning also needed to accommodate rapidly changing requirements, because Interface Systems was entering into emerging markets where the definition of a successful product was constantly evolving. Executive management also recognized that in order to succeed, they needed more than a new set of forms and reports, they needed to fundamentally change the way in which the technical team went about its business, and likewise they needed to change the team's culture. Improving project-planning skills while creating an improved corporate culture were both accomplished, in large part, by fully adopting the practices of *extreme programming.*

When Interface Systems later decided to add new developers to the team, great care was taken to devise an interviewing process that would communicate the corporate culture to the candidates while at the same time allowing the candidates to demonstrate their teamwork skills.

Key Practices of Extreme Programming

For developers who have not been exposed to the practices of extreme programming, the culture shock can be profound. In an extreme programming environment, collaboration is increased by having all of the developers work in one room without any barriers such as cube walls to separate them. This collaboration is further enhanced by another practice called paired-programming, in which a pair of programmers sits together in front of one computer, working together. As work is completed on a project, the individuals frequently change partners to form new pairs. This rotation of partners helps promote continuous dissemination of knowledge throughout the team while discouraging routines from developing within a particular pair that may result in negative behaviors (Thompson, 2000, p. 105).

In addition to close collaboration, extreme programming strictly schedules developer activities. These developer activities are defined by reviewing the user-definable behaviors of the software system. Then, effective project management requires decomposing of the overall project outcomes into smaller tasks that typically represent no more than a few days of effort (Project Management Institute, 2000, p. 59). In extreme programming, each of these small tasks is described on an index card, known as a *story card* (see Appendix A for examples). These story cards are used to create a schedule that quickly completes a working but incomplete system and then incrementally adds functionality. Developers work on the tasks in the exact order that they are scheduled (Beck, 2000, p. 85). This is important because the software development schedule in extreme programming is driven by delivering the maximum amount of business value as early as possible, unlike the standard software development plan which is focused on making the developers feel efficient. For many programmers, this level of project scheduling rigor initially appears to be micro-management. However, most teams soon appreciate how the well-coordinated efforts produce tangible results at regular intervals throughout a project, typically resulting in praise from both managers and customers alike.

A Hiring Mandate

As the team at Interface Systems gained competence in using the extreme programming practices, management developed greater confidence in the accuracy of the team's estimates. The team's improved ability to predict software schedules, along with an expanding list of new features driven by the needs of an emerging market, led the executives to conclude that they needed a way to double the productive output of the team. This conclusion prompted executive management to expand the development team from 12 developers to 24 as quickly as possible. Normally, the hiring process of reviewing resumes, interviewing candidates, and negotiating offers could easily take a month for each successful hire. In this case the goal was to hire 12 developers, and to have them all on board and contributing in less than 90 days.

Key Challenges

Doubling the size of the existing development team was not meant to merely increase body count, but instead needed to quickly increase the team's productive output. New team members needed to understand the team's product and technology tools, but more importantly they needed to be comfortable adopting the extreme programming practices and collaborative teamwork that had become central to the team's efforts.

These software development processes, as adopted, required that new team members value a high level of interaction with other team members. It was also important to select candidates that would embrace the goals of the process instead of merely moving through the steps of the process on their way to a paycheck. While teamwork is a term that most job applicants are familiar with, most of them have spent the majority of their careers being rewarded for individual achievement or effort. Central to Interfaces' new philosophy was the greater value placed on team achievement rather than individual efficiency. So therefore it was vital to *communicate* to prospective new hires that all team members were expected to subordinate individual goals to team goals, and more importantly for the interview process, *observe* an applicants' behavior when faced with this challenge.

Team Participation in the Hiring Process

Because the existing team would be working very closely with new hires, using practices such as paired-programming, their participation was central to the selection effort. The management team also felt that by having the existing team select the candidates, the existing team members would have a stronger stake in helping the new hires assimilate into the team environment.

While recognizing the need for team participation, the management team was concerned that unguided selection would have left the current team members selecting candidates based upon traditional hiring criteria such as specific technical skills. This concern is also known as the halo effect, which is "the tendency to attribute positive traits to someone with whom you have something in common. This leads to hiring people most like yourself" (Anonymous, 1992). Because the new team practices allowed talented developers to quickly add new skills to their repertoire, the need for skills-based selection was less important. Instead, the goal became to add new team members with a variety of backgrounds and skills to extend the overall experience of the team. Therefore the key selection criteria was that the candidates were interested in using the company's new practices, wanted to work closely with peers on assigned tasks, and had an ability and aptitude to learn new skills.

So that the candidates could demonstrate teamwork during the interview, the interview process was designed to represent an immersion in the team's practices. Therefore candidates would pair with other candidates and collaboratively work through exercises that mimicked the daily work done at Interface.

Candidate Pool

The first task was developing a pool of candidates. The HR manager and a contracted recruiter took on the job of finding at least four candidates for each of the 12 positions. They advertised in newspapers, attended job fairs, and solicited candidates from other recruiters and current team members. Their initial screening was focused not on technical skills, but simply on contacting the candidates and determining their ability to communicate clearly. They were instructed to look for energy, enthusiasm, and curiosity. As candidates were offered the opportunity to participate in the interview process, an HR representative described the unusual format to them over the phone. Because this search occurred during a period of almost no unemployment in the information technology industry, the process of identifying 50 candidates took six weeks.

Interview Format

Traditional interviewing happens when a candidate arrives at the appointed time and then meets with a series of potential peers and/or managers that engage in an open discussion after reviewing the candidate's resume. This interviewing process tends to provide an inconsistent interviewing experience and most likely creates biased results. Strategies that have been identified for reducing bias include: ask exactly the same questions of every candidate, limit access to resumes and other ancillary information, use multiple interviewers, and train the interviewers (Campion, Campion, & Palmer, 1997).

Several options were explored in a close collaboration between the software development management team and the human resources department. Under considerable time pressure, the following format was decided upon. All 50 candidates were invited to a first interview on a Saturday. The goal of the first interview was to identify candidates with good communication and teamwork skills. No comparisons of technical skills or experience would be done at this time; this would instead be an immersion exercise designed to allow candidates to demonstrate their teaming skills. The top candidates would be invited back for a second interview the following week, then job offers would be extended by Friday of that same week. The candidates would be interviewed and offers extended in only one week.

The interviews were constructed around a series of interactive exercises so that each candidate would have a similar and comparable experience. These interactive exercises were devised to simulate key activities in the team's new process. In this manner the candidates would become better informed about the team, while at the same time the team could gain insight into each candidate's skills and talents.

The First Interview

On Friday, the day before the first interview, 12 volunteers from the existing team were assembled to learn and practice the interviewing process. The volunteers worked through the exercises that the candidates would be asked to perform so that they would be familiar with the exercises. The team then reviewed the goal of the first interview: identification of candidates with good teamwork and interpersonal skills.

Figure 1: Seating Area

Each of the 50 candidates had been assigned to one of two groups for the Saturday interview. As they assembled, they were given name badges. They were then directed to a seating area inside of a large warehouse (Figure 1).

This warehouse was known as the Java Factory, a nickname based upon its earlier function as the warehouse where printers were assembled on an assembly line, and its new role as the open collaborative workspace of a software team working in Java. This was probably the first in a sequence of red flags that helped candidates understand that this was not a typical work environment. As the candidates assembled, they were provided with dough-nuts, coffee, and juice.

Introduction to the Java Factory

After assembling, the candidates were introduced to the company, the team, and the extreme programming practices by the VP of Product Development in a 45-minute PowerPoint presentation. In this presentation, special attention was given to the fact that programming at Interface Systems was done using paired-programming, and that formal unit testing of code was required of all programmers. Questions were answered in a short question-and-answer session, and then the HR representative provided the more traditional 15-minute presentation on company benefits. Then the VP of Product Development described how the remainder of the day would be spent in three 30-minute exercises designed to reinforce the development processes outlined in the presentation and that the evaluation on who to bring back for second interviews would be based upon demonstrated teamwork.

The First Exercise

While the candidates were seated in the large group, it was explained that they would be provided with a set of software development tasks, presented as extreme programming story cards, that they would then estimate. Each candidate would be paired with another candidate, and together they would have 20 minutes to estimate 32 story cards for a fictitious product. Each pair of candidates would be provided with a packet of pre-written story cards and a blank multiple-choice answer sheet on which they could record their estimates. Each pair would be seated with a developer from Interface Systems who could answer any of their questions. In the final stage of instructions, the candidates were reminded that they were not being evaluated as to their programming talents, but rather their ability to think critically, ask good questions, and most importantly on their ability to make their partner look good.

In order to get everyone into position for the first exercise, candidates were assigned a random number between 1 and 12, and then were asked to move to a table with that number on it. Each table then had two candidates and one interviewer, along with all of the materials required for the exercise. This exercise quickly identified individuals who were unable or unwilling to help their partners participate. It also quickly identified individuals who could help draw on the experience of their partner to make better decisions. During the 20 minutes, the room was very noisy, again providing a good demonstration of our working environment, and the energy level was high. At the end of the 20-minute period, candidates were brought back to a central seating area for instruction on the second exercise, while interviewers made quick notes about the interactions that they observed between candidates.

The Second Exercise

During the instructions for the second exercise, it was explained to the candidates that they would answer a set of questions that were similar to more traditional interviews. To further reinforce the standard practices of the Java

Factory, they would be assigned a new partner for this exercise, and they would need to work with that partner to answer the questions together as a team. Once again it was reinforced that candidates were not being evaluated on the technical merits of their answers, but instead on their ability to collaborate with their partner to synthesize a single answer that combined their experience.

Candidates were then assigned a new partner and were seated with a new interviewer. Each interviewer had the same list of questions and would look to facilitate a dialog between the candidates. Most of the questions were formatted as to require an odd number of responses to further reinforce that candidates should not simply split the workload in half.

- What are the three most effective practices that you have seen used to deliver successful software projects?
- Describe the most challenging bug that you helped someone else fix?
- What are five useful metrics in knowing when a method or subroutine is too long?

Again, after 20 minutes the candidates were once again recalled to a common seating area. At this point the candidates were served lunch. Additional volunteers from the company served pizza and other options to the candidates while answering questions about the company.

The Third Exercise

At the conclusion of lunch, the candidates were assembled for instructions regarding the third and final exercise of the day. In this exercise the candidates would be paired once again with a new partner and a new interviewer. This time the pair would fulfill the role of product manager and build a software development schedule. Each product manager pair would receive a set of story cards and be asked to organize those tasks into a three-phase release plan without exceeding a pre-established budget. The same story cards that were used in the estimating exercise were reused, but the estimates were standardized for all of the teams. Again the selection criteria for being invited back for a second interview were shared with the candidates. Those candidates that best demonstrated critical thinking and teamwork skills would be invited back for a second interview. In other words, make your partner look good and your chances improve.

In this exercise the interviewers simply answered any questions that the candidates had about the process or the intended market for the product being planned. In addition to providing a third opportunity for candidates to demonstrate their skills, this exercise—like the two prior exercises—reinforced the presentation on what daily life in the Java Factory would be like. At the end of the 20-minute session, candidates were invited to one final question-and-answer session with the VP of Product Development, and the interviewers again made notes about interaction skills they had witnessed. The candidates were thanked for their participation. The VP also offered to send a free copy of Kent Beck's "Extreme Programming Explained" to candidates who sent an email describing how the interview experience had been for them. The candidates were then sent home.

Selection of Candidates for Second Interviews

Because we ran two back-to-back sessions like this, each of the 12 interviewers had watched 12 candidates work through various exercises during the day, and three different interviewers interviewed each candidate. At the end of the day, we reviewed each of the almost 50 candidates. As each candidate was reviewed, interviewers were asked if they had any positive comments regarding the person's interaction skills. Very quickly the team was able to sort candidates into three groups: poor teamwork skills, adequate teamwork skills, and strong teamwork skills. The 15 with the strongest teamwork skills were invited back for second interviews.

At the end of the day, the management team and the HR representatives reviewed the results. Perhaps most remarkable was the ability for 12 interviewers to quickly agree on relative rankings for each of the candidates.

Second Interviews

Second interviews were scheduled during normal working hours during the week that followed the first interviews. Second interviews were also built around three activities.

The first activity was for the candidate to sit down with a pair of developers from Interface and estimate a new set of stories. The threesome would estimate the stories together at a more deliberate pace than in the first interview. The estimates would also be based upon the technology that was most familiar to the candidate. This allowed the interview team to assess the candidate's experience level without quizzing him or her on technical trivia. This was important given our concerns about interview consistency. Strictly scripting a standard set of questions would not allow us to explore each candidate's strengths, while allowing the interviewers to create their own questions on the fly causes liability concerns.

The second activity was for the candidate to sit with a different pair of developers from Interface who were actually programming. After only a couple of interviews, the team quickly learned to immediately place the candidate in front of the keyboard. This gave the candidate real-world experience with paired-programming, as well as the opportunity to watch the rest of the team working in their native habitat.

The third activity was a one-on-one meeting with the VP of Product Development. The VP would ask some of the traditional questions about the candidate's background, so that the candidate would know that we had actually received their resume. He would then further probe their experience in the interview process to date and their interest in the extreme programming practices. Those candidates that had obtained a copy of the book on their own and read it were considered promising, as well as candidates who were concerned that extreme programming did not solve all software development problems, but were still clearly compelled to learn more about the opportunity.

Figure 2: Java Factory Work Environment

The Decision Process

On Friday, after the second interviews had been completed, all of the available team members were assembled. Each candidate's name was listed on a whiteboard along with his or her relative experience level within the industry. Team members were then asked to speak up for candidates that should be added to the team.

At first the discussions reverted into which candidate had the strongest technical skill sets. The team was reminded that it was a goal to hire new team members with the broadest diversity in both skills and experience, and that the focus should be on how well the potential team members would adapt to the extreme programming practices and the team's new value set. The VP of Product Development then helped to refocus the discussion by summarizing with a new question: "Which of the candidates would you like to do paired-programming with?" At that point the ranking was quickly arrived at and the VP decided to make offers to the top eight candidates.

Seven of the eight candidates accepted positions.

Integration of New Hires into the Team

Over the next four weeks, the seven new team members arrived. New team members were immediately assigned a partner on the morning they arrived and set to work on the stories for which their partner was already responsible.

The integration of new employees into this environment is almost impossible to imagine. New employees were writing production code on their first day at work. This was true even if they had never used the development environment before and even if they had never used the Java language before. The support of paired-programming and knowing at least seven other team members from the interviewing cycle provided a strong support network. The open and collaborative environment provided visible access to role models who demonstrated that interrupting others was not only tolerated, but also was an expected behavior.

The integration of new employees was so quick and so complete that when new hires were asked to participate in a second round of hiring, only 30 days after the first, candidates could not tell the new employees from the old timers without asking.

The Results

The company hired 14 developers within two months using this process. There was only one new hire lost to attrition during the life of the team. In almost any context, the results were stunning. It was the context of the times that made the results almost unbelievable. All of the hires were completed between February and June of 2000, one of the most difficult hiring periods in the history of our industry. They also occurred in the Midwest, where the propensity to change jobs is far lower than in other regions and typically results in fewer qualified candidates. Finally, they occurred at a time when extreme programming, paired-programming, and collaborative work environments were not part of anyone's vocabulary.

Many of the candidates wrote glowing emails thanking the VP of Product Development for the opportunity to experience what for them was a unique interview. Even the receptionist and the HR representatives were amazed at how many candidates were strongly affected by the interview and made significant efforts to further communicate their desire to join the team. While the team's work was technically interesting, it was not more so than many other opportunities in the region. Clearly, this process and the development practices touched basic needs for a large number of people. We believe that the interview process effectively communicated a culture of interdependent teamwork, and that this message was communicated in a manner that allowed candidates to see how they could successfully transition into our environment if they were selected to join the team.

Unlike most hiring processes, the close collaborative nature of the extreme programming practices made integration of new hires simply a part of the normal work process, rather than an unpleasant distraction for otherwise productive employees. Perhaps the most telling example of the success was that after just six weeks, a new hire was familiar enough with the culture and skilled enough in the practices to be a mentor to new employees just joining the team. It was a joy to manage and work with such a team.

Screening for Technical Skills

At Interface Systems, new product development focused on Java and Web technologies. Most of the 14 candidates that were hired did not have any commercial experience with Java. During the estimation session in the second interview, the project elements, or story cards, were estimated based upon the technology most comfortable for the candidate. This made the candidate the de facto expert and allowed the interviewers to quickly gauge the limitations of the candidate's professional experiences. While there was a small efficiency penalty to pay for adding new developers who did not know Java's syntax or idioms, there were offsetting benefits. The team's broader set of expertise often made it easier to incorporate new technologies as quickly as the Web world continues to invent them. And the broader experience base often allowed the team to consider a problem from several different viewpoints.

Perhaps most interesting of all were the two candidates who were hired without professional software development experience, yet performed well in each of the interviews. Both were music majors who had taught themselves computer programming, and both hoped to find entry-level positions. In both cases, we believe a standard interviewing process would have screened out these candidates because of their weak and non-relevant resumes. But this interviewing process selected these two candidates over other more skilled entry-level candidates, and actually ranked them higher than more experienced candidates. Both of these new hires became valuable contributors on the team, and their technical skills grew quickly. It proved to us that the speed with which an entry-level contributor can be grown within an organization is less related to the initial level of technical knowledge that they bring to the table and more related to their ability to interact well with their peers, their desire to learn, and the accessibility of the company culture.

A Second Generation Repeats the Process

Since these events occurred, none of the authors have had the opportunity to use this interviewing format again. The human resources department considered the original experience so successful that they facilitated interviewing for another technical department—professional services—using the same process, even though the other department did not use the extreme programming practices. The professional services department provided contracted programming services to customers using traditional software development techniques. This team added six new team members using a very similar interviewing format. This hiring effort was also considered more successful than the typical serial interviews with question-and-answer formats.

The development of this process was far from rigorous. We have not attempted to demonstrate through experiments that this format is better or more predictive than others. Nor have we continued to research parallel experiences with other immersion interview techniques. Nonetheless, all three authors look forward to using this process in the future. We believe that it provided a very effective technique to identify candidates that would integrate well into a team while at the same time broadening the team's capabilities and experience base.

Managerial Implications

When some managers are introduced to extreme programming, they often marvel at the notion of two programmers working together at one keyboard. Almost without fail they ask, "What happens if a pair of programmers fight?" This is a reasonable question, because it is obvious that if two programmers are involved in an unproductive conflict, overall team effectiveness will drop. However, if two programmers are involved in a respectful and productive conflict, then useful information is being shared between the parties that will increase overall team effectiveness. So what do we do when programmers fight? If the discourse appears to be respectful and productive, then we continue working, pleased that important information is being shared between appropriate parties. If either party is failing to be respectful or the efforts fail to become productive, then we encourage peers to step in and help facilitate, or as members of the management team, we step in to help facilitate and coach the team.

After exploring the scenario of arguments within a paired-programming environment, we then always make it a point to return the favor and ask the inquirer about what happens in their environment when two programmers fight. Common answers often include building buffers between the two individuals so that the conflict has less of an impact on team performance. At this point it pays to persist in the questioning and ask how well that worked out when all of the team's work was integrated at the end of the project. Often we are treated to managers rolling their eyes and telling us war stories about how the individuals in conflict still managed to make a mess of things and how large problems came to light at the end of the project. These stories are excellent examples about confusing a lack of open debate with harmony. Isolating programmers with opposing points of view simply promotes a false harmony and often hides growing problems until it is too late to fix them.

The software development practices promoted by extreme programming make it obvious that teamwork is an essential ingredient for successful software development projects. But teams that do not use extreme programming will suffer just as much as a team using extreme programming when individual team members do not work well with their teammates. It might just not be as obvious during the early stages of the project. So the next time you are adding new team members, you need to decide if it is an adequate test of a candidate's teamwork skills to ask them if they are a team player. Or is it instead an appropriate investment of resources to devise an interview that will allow the candidate to demonstrate the skills that you value the most?

Endnote

* *An earlier version of this chapter was developed as a white paper for the Menlo Institute and was published on the Menlo Institute's website at www.MenloInstitute.com.*

References

Anonymous. (1992). Personal bias can threaten interview process. (Human resource measurements: Perspectives on testing and hiring procedures for the HR professional). *HR Magazine*, *37*(9), S04.

Beck, K. (2000). *Extreme programming explained: Embrace change.* Reading, MA: Addison-Wesley-Longman.

Beck, K., & Fowler, M. (2001). *Planning extreme programming.* Reading, MA: Addison-Wesley-Longman.

Campion, M.A., Campion, J.E., & Palmer, D.K. (1997). A review of structure in the selection interview. *Personnel Psychology, 50*(3), 655.

Project Management Institute. (2000). *A guide to the project management body of knowledge (PMBOK®)* (2000 ed.). Newtown Square, PA: Project Management Institute.

Thompson, L. (2000). *Making the team.* Upper Saddle River, NJ: Prentice-Hall.

Appendix A

Formal project management breaks projects into smaller units that can be estimated, assigned, and tested for completeness. These smaller units are called work packages (Project Management Institute, 2000, p. 209). In extreme programming, work packages are captured on index cards and called user stories (Beck & Fowler, 2001, p. 45). This appendix presents three sample story cards for a fictional project. The goal of this project is to build a website for planning weddings. Two dozen story cards for this fictional project were used for the exercises in the first interviews. At the top of each story card is the project code, "Wed," a tracking number, and a story title. A description of the desired outcome for this work package follows. At the bottom of the card are the initials of the card's author. Extreme programming does not stipulate this format, but this format is representative of how many extreme programming teams capture their user stories, or story cards.

Exhibit 1: Sample Story Card

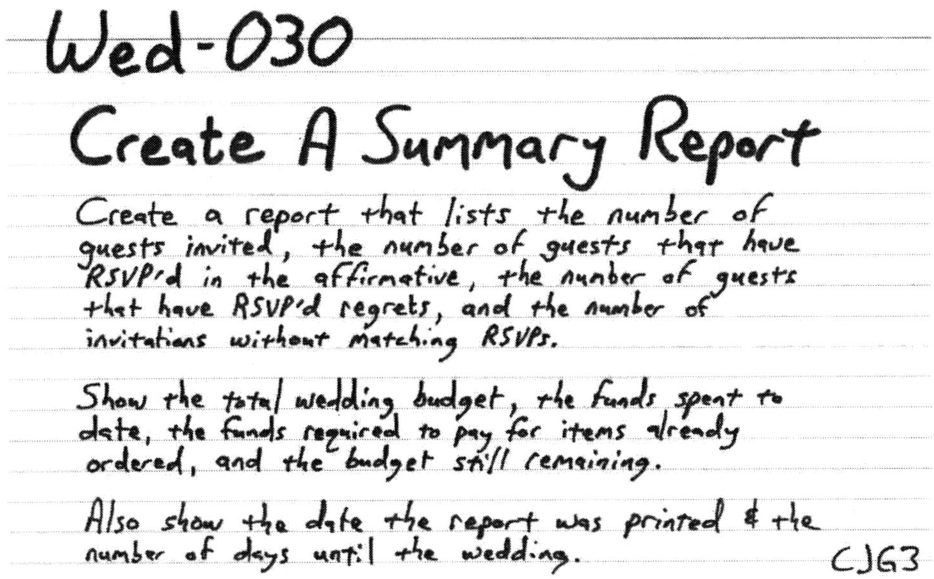
Wed-030

Create A Summary Report

Create a report that lists the number of guests invited, the number of guests that have RSVP'd in the affirmative, the number of guests that have RSVP'd regrets, and the number of invitations without matching RSVPs.

Show the total wedding budget, the funds spent to date, the funds required to pay for items already ordered, and the budget still remaining.

Also show the date the report was printed & the number of days until the wedding.

CJG3

Exhibit 2: Sample Story Card

Wed-035

Change Checkbox Styles

On the invitation tracking page, the shower gift thank you note page, and the gift registry page, change the check boxes from

☐ Chicken ☒ Fish

to

☐ Chicken ☑ Fish

CJG3

Exhibit 3: Sample Story Card

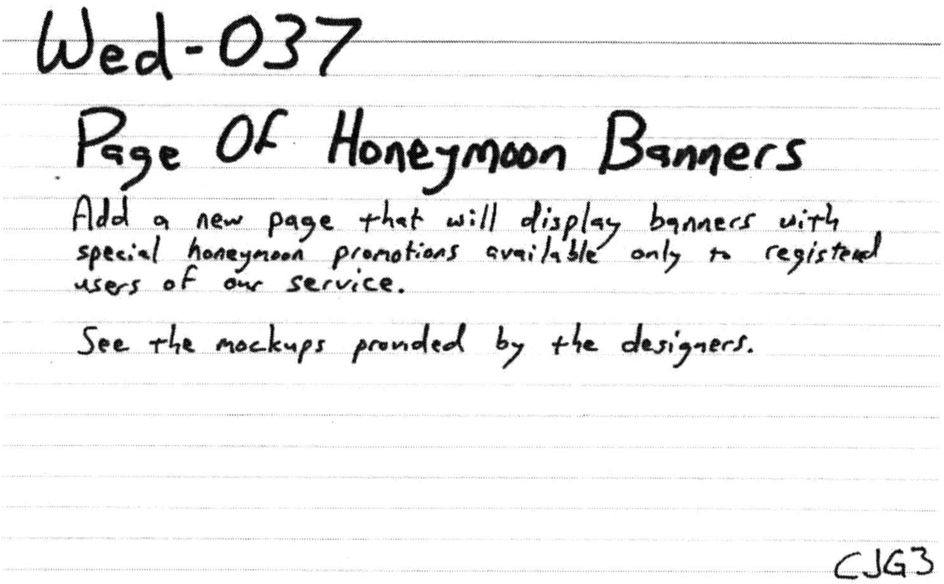

Wed-037

Page Of Honeymoon Banners

Add a new page that will display banners with special honeymoon promotions available only to registered users of our service.

See the mockups provided by the designers.

CJG3

About the Authors

Makoto Nakayama is Assistant Professor at the School of Computer Science, Telecommunications, and Information Systems at DePaul University (USA). He holds a PhD from the University of California, Los Angeles and an MBA from University of Texas at Austin. Prior to moving into academe, he served as a product marketing manager at Novell Japan. He also worked on business planning and operating system developments at Yokogawa Electric Corporation in Tokyo. His current research interests are in IT use in marketing channels and IT skills portfolio management. His papers have appeared in *Information & Management, Journal of Information Technology,* and proceedings of national conferences.

Norma Sutcliffe is Assistant Professor at the School of Computer Science, Telecommunications, and Information Systems at DePaul University (USA). She holds a PhD as well as an MBA from the University of California, Los Angeles. With extensive experience in industry, Dr. Sutcliffe has been a consultant for many Fortune 500 firms in evaluating IT needs, IT implementations, and IT strategies. She has worked as systems developer on mainframe and client/server systems as well. Her current research interests are in IT-enabled organizational change, IT leadership behavior, and IT skills portfolio management. Her papers have appeared in *Information & Management* and proceedings of national conferences.

* * * * * * *

John E. Anderson is an Assistant Professor of MIS in the Department of Decision Sciences at East Carolina University (USA). He earned his PhD at Utah State University, and his MBA and BA at the University of Utah. His research and writing interests center on organizational cognition, IS leadership, and IS innovation management. His writings have been published in the *Journal of Computer Information Systems.* Prior to joining the East Carolina University faculty, he taught information systems courses at Penn State Harrisburg, Appalachian State University, and Northeastern State University.

Kevin Barrett is a Professor of Accounting in the School of Business at Dixie State College of Utah (USA). He earned his PhD at Virginia Tech, his MBA at Indiana University, Bloomington, and his BS at Utah State University. His research and writing interests center on tax policy and tax pedagogy. His writings have been published in the *National Tax Journal, Journal of Accounting Literature, Tax Notes, Exempt Organization Tax Review,* and *Teaching & Learning at Appalachian.* Prior to joining the Dixie State faculty, he taught information systems courses at Southern Utah University and tax courses at Appalachian State University.

Susy S. Chan is an Associate Professor and directs the Center for E-Commerce Research in the School of Computer Science, Telecommunications, and Information Systems at DePaul University (USA). She is the founding director of DePaul University's pioneering master's and baccalaureate programs in e-commerce technology. As a former CIO at DePaul, she developed its six-campus IT infrastructure. Her research focuses on e-business strategies, enterprise applications and transformation, e-commerce curriculum, and mobile commerce. The Mobile Commerce Research Lab that she co-leads studies usability and development issues concerning wireless applications. She earned a PhD in Instructional Technology from Syracuse University.

Clement James Goebel, III, co-founder of Menlo Innovations in Ann Arbor, Michigan (USA), has practiced object-oriented software technology for more than a decade as a developer, architect, project manager, and mentor. His work in commercial software development has spanned several domains, including bio-informatics, medical imaging, vehicle monitoring, test generation, and online bill presentment. He led the year-long change process that dramatically improved Interface Systems' product development process. These changes included converting the programming team to extreme programming practices and establishing a human interaction design team. Mr. Goebel is currently a full-time member of an extreme programming (XP) team that is using XP developer practices within the framework of a Rational Unified Process® project. In addition to acting as a mentor and change agent for software development organizations, he is a certified Project Management Professional (PMP), a Licensed Residential Builder, and is completing his MBA at Eastern Michigan University.

Throughout her career, **Elizabeth Lahey** champions lifelong skill development for information and communication technology (ICT) professionals. In the 1980s, she directed training and skill-building activities for McDonald's Corporation's ICT staff. There she pioneered re-skilling from mainframes to PCs and Web environments. She implemented a comprehensive solution to hire, train, and retain critical ICT workers. In the 1990s, Ms. Lahey became a management consultant in the ICT human resources area. She specialized in strategic business implications of rapidly changing technology on the skill development needs of the ICT professional. In this capacity she consulted with Fortune 500 companies across the Midwest. Since 2000, her work has focused on two key projects: (1) She designed, implemented, and managed the launch of the TechCareer Compass® website at http://tcc.comptia.org which offers a comprehensive solution—directly from the ICT industry—aimed at bridging skills portfolio gaps. (2) She also manages a government-funded national effort to standardize skills portfolios for first-line ICT workers. Ms. Lahey writes for ICT industry publications, speaks at ICT skills conferences, and is widely quoted on ICT skills issues. She holds degrees from Northwestern and the University of Illinois. Her professional honors include: McDonald's Woman of the Year, McDonald's ICT Coach of the Year, and *Computerworld*'s Top 20 ICT Training Organizations.

Thomas Meloche is President of the Menlo Institute LLC (USA)and a founding member of Menlo Associates LLC. His passion is software development best practices and building successful software teams. Before founding The Menlo Institute, Mr. Meloche was the Director of Engineering at AppNet, Inc. For more than seven years, he helped lead a consulting staff that grew from 30 people to over 240 people with total revenue of over $100 million. As a result, he is intimately familiar with the real problems that befall real software development projects. He also knows how to rectify them. During his tenure, his delivery organization had a remarkable 100% successful delivery record. Mr. Meloche regularly provides training to those interested in improving their development processes. Past customers include General Motors, General Electric, 3M, Ford Motor Company, Ford Credit, DaimlerChrysler, Cummins Engine, Sun Microsystems, Edward Jones, and AAA of Michigan. He has a BCE in Computer Engineering from the University of Michigan, and especially enjoys providing training back to his alma mater. He has taught classes and provided mentoring for both the University of Michigan Law and Medical Schools.

Abdulrahman A. Mirza is the Chairman of the IS Department at King Saud University, Saudi Arabia. During the 2002/2003 academic-year, he was awarded a senior Fulbright scholarship for conducting research at DePaul University. His current research interests include e-business IT skills requirements definition, e-business transformation, and e-commerce curriculum development. Dr. Mirza has wide industry experiences in application development. He attained his PhD in Computer Science from the Illinois Institute of Technology in 1995 and his MS in Operations Research from George Mason University.

Paul H. Schwager is an Assistant Professor of MIS in the Department of Decision Sciences at East Carolina University (USA). He earned his PhD at Auburn University, his MBA at Florida Atlantic University, and his BA in Business Administration from Palm Beach Atlantic College. His research focuses on e-commerce portals and Internet-mediated relationships. His research has been published in the *Journal of Computer Information Systems* and the *Journal of Information Systems Education.* Prior to joining the East Carolina University faculty, he taught information systems courses at Appalachian State University.

As the former VP of Development at Interface Systems, **Richard Sheridan** sponsored a dramatic change to the extreme programming model as he grew his department from 14 to 36 developers. Mr. Sheridan previously worked for four years as the Vice President of Product Development at Interface Systems/ Tumbleweed Communications. Interface Systems' Extreme Programming Team and Java Factory were his creations and his latest accomplishments in a 20-year career in the software product development industry. Over the years, he has worked on and led the development of a variety of software products, including CAD/CAM, data communications, encryption, mainframe-based printing, and Web-based electronic document delivery solutions. An excellent speaker and presenter, he readily shares his knowledge of software success practices from real-world experience. Tens of thousands of products created by Mr. Sheridan's teams are still in use by customers today.

Ken Strauss has a BS in Mathematics from SUNY at Stony Brook and an MBA in Finance from New York University. Mr. Strauss has spent 20 years as an IT consultant building and designing dozens of IT applications. He has spent the last eight years in the IT skill assessment industry working for Bookman Testing Services (USA) and its premier assessment product, TeckChek. Mr. Strauss has served TeckChek as a Product Manager and most recently as the Director of Assessment Consulting, working with TeckChek's clients to help them incorporate skills testing into their overall skills management programs.

Yoko Takeda is an Associate Professor in the Graduate School of Environment and Information Sciences at the Yokohama National University (Japan). She has researched the inter-organizational and cross-functional collaboration using electronic media such as impacts of 3-D CAD on the product development process, collaboration between IT vendors and users when implementing information systems, and disclosure of technical information on open networks in order to promote innovation. Her articles have appeared in numerous journals, including the *Journal of the Japan Society of Management Information, Hitotsubashi Business Review, Keio Business Forum,* and *Organizational Science.* She was a visiting scholar at Stanford University. She holds a BA in Experimental Psychology from Kyoto University, and an MBA and a PhD from Keio Business School.

Diana J. Wong-MingJi is an Assistant Professor in the Department of Management at Eastern Michigan University (USA). She completed a PhD in Strategic Management from the University of Massachusetts, Amherst. Her research interests include strategic alliances, organization development and change, learning and technological innovations, and international management of global strategies. She has published in *Organization Development Journal* and *Organization*, as well as presented at numerous conferences such as those of the Academy of Management, Strategic Management Society, and North American Case Research Association, along with serving as a board member of two non-profit organizations. She has taught strategic management, organization development, research methods, leadership, entrepreneurship, and teams. Recently, Dr. Wong-MingJi helped launch a Master's of Science Degree in Information Systems between the College of Business at EMU and Osmania University in Heyderabad, India.

Index

A

academic and employability (A&E) skills 130
academic programs 53
Academy for Advanced Information Technology Professionals 162
adapting sub-topics 113
adaptive questioning 111
adaptive testing 112
adult learning theory 84
andragogy 89
application service providers (ASPs) 55
application-based education 223
assessment 104, 111
assessment score (AS) 40
associative phase 6
autonomous phase 6

B

B2B e-commerce 53
business intelligence (BI) 55

C

candidate pool 236
case study 84
certification 210
certification exam 111
certification tools 111
changing landscape 68
chief algorithm officer (CAO) 68
chief e-business officer (CeBO) 62, 68
chief e-commerce officer (CeCO) 62
chief knowledge officer (CKO) 68
cognitive demands 6
cognitive phase 6
collaboration 52, 233
CompTIA (Computing Technology Industry Association) 137
connective organizational capabilities 183
coordinator 151
core competencies 14
credibility of IT certification 222
critical sourcing 42
critical work functions (CWFs) 128, 140
criticality (C) 40
criticality score 40
custom training content 121
customer relationship management (CRM) 55
customized systems 151

D

database management systems (DBMSs) 63
decision support systems (DSSs) 63
deliverable descriptor 39
delivery 5
difficulty score (D) 40

E

e-business 52, 54

e-business environment 52
e-business needs 53
e-business organization 52
e-business project implementation 65
e-business transformation 54
e-business webs 52
e-procurement (EP) 55
education 210
employee benefits with certifications 211
employment 126
enterprise application integration (EAI) 55
enterprise applications 54
enterprise resource planning (ERP) 55
experience 210
extreme programming 233

G

global competition 172
global Internet network 132
government involvement 126
government policy 132
governmental skill development 127

H

high assessment score 42
hiring 104, 105, 233
hiring process 123
HR centralizing 192
HRIS 177
human capital 177
human capital portfolios 177, 180
human capital theory 9
human resource (HR) 8, 88, 211
human resource information systems (HRIS) 177
human resource management 27
human resource professional 210
human resources 4, 53

I

ICT professionals 84
ICT skill standards project 146
industrial and occupational (IO) psychologists 144
industry value chains 53
industry-wide collaboration 53
information and communications technology (ICT) 81, 126
information systems (IS) 211
information technology (IT) 53
Information Technology Association of America (ITAA) 2, 137
Internet strategies 53
interview process 233
IS vendors 151
IT 53
IT outsourcing 177
IT personnel 53
IT professionals 2, 27
IT-skill dilemma 151
IT skill gap analysis 105
IT skills 2, 27, 52, 68, 151
IT skills acquisitions 69
IT skills management 54, 103
IT skills portfolio 27
IT skills portfolio management 31, 52
IT skills requirement 53
IT-skill standards 161

J

Japanese companies 150
Japanese firms 151
Japanese IS vendors 150
job 12
job concentrations 130

K

key activities (KAs) 129, 140
knowledge, skills, and abilities (KSAs) 8, 29

L

learning management systems (LMSs) 104
local area networks (LANs) 160
local contracting 192

M

management of IT skills 14

mass validation survey 146
Moore's Law 131
multi-mission capability 27, 30
multiple correct answers 114

N

National Skill Standards Act 135
National Skill Standards Board (NSSB) 135
non-staffing vendors 194
NWCET (Northwest Center for Emerging Technologies) 137

O

occupational and technical knowledge and skills (OTKSs) 130
organization man 82
organizational benefits with certification 211
organizational capability 184
organizational improvisation 186
organizational learning 184, 186

P

people-centered organization 27, 29
performance indicators (PIs) 129, 140
portfolio 31
portfolio management 27
productivity rates 126
profession 211
project identifier 39
project staffing 104, 105
project team building 119
project's difficulty 39
proper assessment tool 111
purchasing HRIS 193

R

rational organizational capabilities 181
relational contracting 185, 186
resource needed score (RC) 40
risk level score (R) 40

S

sector skills development agency (SSDA) 2
skill 5, 6
skill analysis 106
skill classifications 7
skill "food chain" 130
skill gap 126, 136
skill mismatch 83
skill standards 127
skills issues 126
skills management 11
skills management tool 111
skills retention 63
skills search 120
Society for Human Resource Management (SHRM) 211
soft skills 233
software development 233
staffing firm 194
stars 36
strategic alliances 184
strategic business goals 37
strategic business units (SBUs) 36
strategic goals 37
strategic human resource management (SHRM) 5, 11, 28
strategic IT goals 38
sub-topic skills 106
subject matter experts (SMEs) 140
supply chain integration 54
supply chain management (SCM) 55, 177
systems integration 186

T

task performance 5, 7
task-oriented perspective 7
team participation 236
teamwork 233
teamwork skills 233
TechCareer Compass (TCC) website 146
technical skills 233
technology 131

telecommunications legislation 132
testing 106
theory-based education 223
training 104, 105
training and certification 212
transformation 52

U

Univacs 29

V

voluntary partnerships 136

W

weighted answers 115
work-based learning 27, 31
Workforce Investment Advisory Board
(WIAB) 100
writes code 129